aquapress

TECHNICAL DIVING
AN INTRODUCTION

MARK POWELL

© AquaPress Ltd and Mark Powell 2019

The right of Mark Powell to be identified as the author of this work has been asserted in accordance with the Copyright Designs and Patents Act,1988.

This book is sold subject to the condition that it shall not, by way of trade or otherwise, be lent, resold, hired out, or otherwise circulated without the publisher's prior consent in any form of binding or cover other than that in which it is published and without a similar condition including this condition being imposed on the subsequent purchaser.

Published by AquaPress Ltd
25 Farriers Way
Temple Farm Industrial Estate
Southend-on-Sea
Essex SS2 5RY
United Kingdom

First Published 2019

AquaPress and the AquaPress Logo are Trademarks of AquaPress Ltd.

A CIP catalogue record for this book is available from the British Library.

Diving is an inherently dangerous sport. The information contained in this book is supplied merely for the convenience of the reader and should not be used as the sole source of information. This book is not a substitute for proper training by a recognized diver training agency. The author and publisher have made every effort to ensure that the information in this book is correct at the time of going to press. However, they accept no liability or responsibility whatsoever for any loss, damage, accident, injury or inconvenience sustained by any person using this book or following advice presented in it, provided that this shall not limit or exclude liability for death or personal injury caused by their negligence.

For information on all other AquaPress titles visit www.aquapress.co.uk

All rights reserved. No part of this publication may be reproduced in any material form (including photocopying or storing it in any medium by electronic means and whether or not transiently or incidentally to some other use of this publication) without the written permission of the copyright owner except in accordance with the provisions of the Copyright Designs and Patents Act 1988 or under the terms of a licence issued by the Copyright Licensing Agency: Barnard's Inn, 86 Fetter Lane, London, EC4A 1EN. Applications for the copyright owner's written permission to reproduce any part of this publication should be addressed to the publisher.

ISBN: 978-1-905492-31-2

FOREWORD

Depending on how you count it, technical diving quietly turned 30-years old last year, marked by the anniversary of Dr. Bill Stone's extraordinary Wakulla Springs Project 1987, the first major mixed gas diving expedition conducted by sport divers. Once considered the radical fringe, technical or 'tech' diving has now taken its rightful place as the vanguard of sport diving and its influence has been widely felt across the recreational diving industry.

Today, nitrox is nearly ubiquitous among sport divers and helium mixes are the gas of choice for deep diving—deep air diving is no longer considered acceptable. In fact, several training agencies are even beginning to introduce helium mixes for recreational divers conducting exposures in the 30-40m range to improve diving safety.

Recreational diving equipment has also felt the influence of tech. Backplate and wings that enable divers to better maintain their trim & buoyance are gradually replacing old-style vest BCDs; recreational divers are beginning to opt for a long hose versus an "octopus" for their secondary regulator to aid gas sharing, and nitrox and mixed gas dive computers are commonplace. What's more, "tekkies" now represent the largest user group of rebreathers on the planet, surpassing the combined militaries of the world.

It's no wonder then that there is considerable interest in technical diving among avid recreational divers, which is what makes technical diving educator and shipwreck diver Mark Powell's latest book so timely and important. While there are several books that plunge into the geeky depths of technical diving, they tend to be outdated, too detailed or aimed at divers who already have their tech credentials. Instead Powell, the author of "Deco for Divers," provides interested divers with a thoughtful overview of the field including its historical and philosophical underpinnings, equipment configurations, fundamentals of mixed gas technology, the required attitude and skills, practical considerations and the issues that tekkies care about most, especially staying alive.

Powell begins by examining the origins of tech diving, what it is and what it is not. Back in the early 1990s, the difference between technical and recreational diving was stark. That's not the case anymore and Powell does a great job of describing the continuum of the activity that is now sport diving: from the holiday snorkeler lazily finning across a reef to a dedicated team of tekkies making a 150-meter jump on a newly discovered shipwreck. Along the way he explores why tech diving has become so popular, what it takes to become a tech diver, and offers practical advice on how to go about making the transition.

From the beginning, technical diving has been all about improving diving safety and performance enabling divers to conduct exposures that were beyond the limitations of early recreational diving. Accordingly, Powell discusses the increased risks of technical diving, and the mindset and requisite skills such as valve shut downs and bail out strategies that tech divers employ to mitigate these risks, including expecting the unexpected, and what to do when things go wrong.

Powell offers a detailed discussion of the diving systems or platforms used by technical divers specifically; back-mounted twinsets or doubles, sidemount systems, and rebreathers, along with the advantages and disadvantages of each. He delves into the fundamentals of mixed gas technology, which is at the heart of tech diving, along with practical considerations such as sizing cylinders and stage bottles. He also discusses decompression diving including the use of mixed gas dive computers, trending topics such as the efficacy of "deep stops," and what to do for missed decompression.

An important consideration in tech diving is whether to dive as a team or as a solo diver. Powell provides an in-depth examination of the various approaches to team diving, including diving as a team of one, and their pros and cons. He also discusses the special considerations involved in diving in cave and shipwreck environments, and in expedition diving.

Taken as a whole, Powell's "Technical Diving" provides recreational divers wanting to know more, with a working understanding of technical diving, and what is required in terms of equipment attitude, knowledge and skills to make the transition. The author has distilled his considerable depth of knowledge and experience into a highly readable and easy to understand opus that represents the latest thinking in the evolving field of technical diving.

Michael Menduno/M2

ACNOWLEDGEMENTS

Writing a book like this is done by an individual author but behind that author there are a huge range of mentors, friends, colleagues, inspirations and many other influences that have shaped that author's thoughts. I am finally sitting down to write my acknowledgements in the transfer lounge of Seoul airport on my way to dive Truk Lagoon and my layover doesn't seem long enough to go through all of the people I owe thanks to.

First of all I want to thank Chris Davey and his team at AquaPress for having the confidence to publish another of my books as well as the patience to deal with all the challenges of preparing a book in between all of my teaching and travelling and for accommodating all the last minute changes.

There are a huge number of people who have contributed in some way to the ideas I have set down in this book. In some cases these have been multiple, ongoing conversations and in other cases it might have been a single idea or thought that I have picked up from them. In no particular order a big thank you to Andy Hetherton, Phil Short, Stephen Philips, Brian Carney, Sean Harrison, Paul Montgomery, Brian Shreve, Paul Raymaekers, Travis Jung, Steve Moore, Steve Lewis, Martin Robson, Vicki Batten, Mark Culwick, Christian Massaad, Mark Rowe, Bob Scullion, Richard Walker, John Kendall, Andy Hayhurst, Eric "Spider" Webb, Finbar Taylor, Matt Jevon, Gemma Smith, Sally Cartwright, Michael Thomas, Gareth Lock, Gareth Burrows, Frank Bruce, Richard Major, Steve Cowley, Aldo Ferrucci, Greg Parker, Paul Toomer, Ian France, Steve Pavey, Adrian "Midnight" Sims, Tim Clements, Mark Caney, Tom Mount, Martin Parker, Gavin Anthony, Kevin Gurr, Bruce Partridge, Simon Mitchell, Neil Pollock, Janos Suto, Aron Arngrimsson, Roz Lunn, Martin Stanton, Tim Gort, Lauren Fanning, Randy Thornton, Paul Haynes, Bart Den Ouden, Dave Gration, Benoit Chandanson, Pim van der Horst, Vic Verlinden, Sabine Kerkau, Marco Valenti, Andrea Donati, Eduardo Pavia, Leigh Bishop, Mark Chase, John Bantin, Mark Ellyat, Mark Evans, Michael "Dr Deco" Powell, Izzy Imsett and of course everyone at MVSAC.

Even more important are all of my students who have helped me sharpen my examples, explanations and analogies. A lot of the material in this book was first presented in this way as an attempt to explain a point to a student. Whether that was a trainee diver, instructor or instructor trainer thank you for all the questions and discussions.

I want to specifically thank Michael Menduno for launching aquaCorps, coining the term "technical diving" and being a fantastic advocate for what we do. Given the title of this book I could not think of anyone better placed to write a foreword and I am incredibly grateful that he agreed to do so.

There are some people who unfortunately are no longer with us but were still hugely influential to me and on the content of this book. In particular Rob Palmer, Carl Spencer, Keith Morris and Michal Czerminski. You are gone but not forgotten.

You will notice that there are a number of manufacturers of diving equipment that are prominently featured in the photographs in this book. This is because there are a small group of manufacturers that have consistently supported technical diving and my own diving in particular. I use these brands due to the quality of the products but also for the quality of the people working for these companies. Thank you Apeks/Aqualung, Fourth Element, O'Three, Kent Tooling, AP Diving, JJ-CCR, XCCR, KISS Rebreathers, Shearwater Reseach, Suunto, Dive Rite, Light Monkey, Kubi and Halcyon for your contribution to technical diving.

I also owe a huge amount of thanks to my family. My parents, daughter, sister and nieces have had to put up with me being obsessed by diving and having to keep track of where I am through Facebook. Thank you for your support and understanding. Most of all, my wife Kate has supported me through all of my diving, teaching, writing and travelling. I could not have done it without you xxx.

CONTENTS

Part 1
Introduction 9

Chapter 1. Introduction to Technical Diving 11

Part 2
Approach 15

Chapter 2. What is Technical Diving? 17

Chapter 3. Why has it become so popular? 21

Chapter 4. Moving into Technical Diving 25

Chapter 5. What makes a Technical diver? 31

Chapter 6. Fitness for Technical Diving 37

Chapter 7. Technical Diving and the Internet 41

Chapter 8. Comfort Zone 45

Chapter 9. Expect the Unexpected 49

Chapter 10. What went wrong? 53

Chapter 11. Complacency 59

Part 3
Equipment 63

Chapter 12. Equipment Configuration 65

Chapter 13. Twinset configuration questions 67

Chapter 14. Side mount 73

Chapter 15. Backplate, Wing and Harness 77

Chapter 16. Hogarthian Equipment Configuration 83

Chapter 17. Reely important equipment 89

Chapter 18. Staying Comfortable 95

Chapter 19. How many cylinders do you need? 99

Chapter 20. Dive Computers 105

Chapter 21. What's in your Argon bottle? 111

Part 4
Skills 115

Chapter 22. Buoyancy Control 117

Chapter 23. Trim 125

Chapter 24. Finning Techniques 131

Chapter 25. Reaching Your Valves 135

Chapter 26. Shutdown Drills 141

Chapter 27. Individual or Team Diving 151

Chapter 28. Team Sizing 155

Chapter 29. Problem Solving 159

Chapter 30. Technical Skills 165

Part 5
Rebreathers 169

Chapter 31. Rebreathers 171

Chapter 32. Rebreather configurations 181

Part 6
Aspects 187

Chapter 33. Extending your diving – Longer rather than deeper 189

Chapter 34. Decompression Diving 193

Chapter 35. Nitrogen Narcosis 205

Chapter 36. Trimix 209

Chapter 37. Oxygen Toxicity 213

Chapter 38. Dive Planning 217

Chapter 39. Wreck Penetration 225

Chapter 40. Cave Diving 229

Chapter 41. Expeditions 235

Chapter 42. Missed Decompression 239

PART 1
Introduction

Chapter 1. Introduction to Technical Diving 11

Introduction to Technical Diving

"The sea, once it casts its spell, holds one in its net of wonder forever." **Jacques Yves Cousteau**

Diving is an activity which appeals to a huge selection of people and within diving there are almost as many ways to enjoy the sport as there are participants. During the 1990s scuba diving became a mass participation sport. The increase in holidays or vacations to exotic destinations, combined with a growing commercialisation of diver training agencies, meant that it was possible to do a basic open water course in a few days during the annual summer break. Whole families could do an open water diving qualification which allowed mum, dad and the kids to experience the wonders of the undersea world.

While the barriers to this underwater world were gradually broken down, a small group of experienced divers were starting to push the limits of traditional recreational scuba diving. This movement, which has been christened 'technical diving'[1], started with just a few dedicated individuals. Over the last few years, this area has seen a huge increase in interest and now a significant number of divers are moving towards technical diving. In this book we will explore what is meant by technical diving; what is involved, the risks that arise and how you can move towards this type of diving. For those who are not tempted to venture into this area of the sport, we will also discuss what lessons can be gained from technical diving in order to improve normal recreational diving. This is similar to the way in which the majority of motorists will never come close to a Formula One Grand Prix car, but make use, in their own cars, of many of the innovations that have been developed by the Formula One teams.

In order to talk about technical diving we will first try to define what is meant by the phrase 'technical diving'. This is not as easy as it might seem. There is no agreed definition of the phrase and different people use it to mean different things. One common definition is that technical diving is everything beyond recreational diving limits. This is a good starting point but does have a few problems. First of all, different organisations have different limits for what constitutes recreational diving. For example, some organisations do not allow decompression diving within the limits of recreational diving while other organisations quite happily allow recreational divers to go into decompression. A second problem in defining technical diving as everything beyond recreational diving is that the dividing line between the two is not fixed. For example in the early 1980s nitrox was considered to be firmly in the technical diving area. It was

---

1 Menduno, M. AquaCorps. Winter 1991

thought to be too risky for use by recreational divers. Yet over the last twenty years, nitrox has become much more widely accepted and today, when used correctly, is recognised as offering significant safety benefits for all divers.

Another definition is that technical diving is the type of diving that is at the leading edge of the sport or the type of diving that is carried out by the pioneers. This is another appealing definition but suffers from some of the same problems as the previous ones. Where do we draw the line between the leading edge and mainstream but adventurous diving? Therefore, we can see that a firm definition of what constitutes technical diving is difficult to pin down. Despite this, it is usually easy to recognise it when we see it. Furthermore, it is clear that there are certain aspects that we can use to identify technical rather than recreational diving.

In recreational diving we often hear the term 'no-decompression dive'. In reality, there is no such thing, as all dives require decompression to some extent. It may be that during the ascent, sufficient decompression occurs, and no decompression stop is required, but we have still been decompressing during this ascent, and will continue to decompress on the surface for a number of hours afterwards. This is why ascent rates and safety stops are essential as they allow enough time to decompress during the ascent. So rather than refer to a dive where we do not need to make mandatory decompression stops as a 'no-deco' dive, we can more accurately refer to it as a no-stop dive, that is one where no mandatory decompression stop beyond the standard safety stop is required. Once we exceed the no-stop time, we can no longer ascend directly to the surface without risking decompression illness. Decompression stops are carried out at certain depths to allow the excess nitrogen in the body to

Effective buoyancy control and the ability to hold decompression stops accurately are essential before any diver considers carrying out decompression diving.

Dives to depths greater than those found in recreational diving or involving significantly longer dive times are typical in the field of technical diving. Dives are undertaken to considerably greater depths than the recreational limit of 40m/130ft. Depths of 50m/165ft to 100m/330ft are not uncommon with many dives greater than 100m/330ft or even 200m/660ft. This inevitably means that technical diving is decompression diving. However, not all decompression diving is necessarily technical diving, as some recreational agencies do allow limited decompression.[2]

reduce to a level where it is safe to continue on to the surface. In later chapters, we will look at some of the different approaches to dealing with the decompression incurred during a technical dive.

Effective buoyancy control and the ability to hold decompression stops accurately are essential before any diver considers carrying out decompression diving and so we will look at the level of skill required in each of these areas in order to safely carry out decompression diving.

---

2 The BSAC Sports Diver grade includes decompression diving.

Figure 1: My main interest is in wrecks

With longer decompression times, it is common for technical divers to carry more than one breathing mix. In addition to 'back gas' carried in large cylinders mounted, not surprisingly, on their back they will also carry one or more 'deco gases'. These are rich nitrox mixes which will speed up the decompression. This is known as 'accelerated decompression' and can make a significant difference to the amount of decompression time involved. For example, using EAN50 as a decompression gas can cut the decompression time required for a particular dive from 53 minutes to just 25 minutes.[3]

Either air or nitrox is the gas of choice for the recreational diver. However, for technical divers neither of these choices is suitable for deep diving. The oxygen and nitrogen in both air and nitrox becomes toxic as the diver goes deeper; oxygen causes oxygen toxicity and nitrogen causes debilitating nitrogen narcosis. Nitrox reduces the amount of nitrogen in the breathing mixture but only by increasing the amount of oxygen. This additional oxygen increases the risk of oxygen toxicity at depth. For deeper dives, a breathing mixture that reduces the levels of both nitrogen and oxygen is required. The only way to do this is to introduce a third gas which will replace some of the oxygen and nitrogen. This gas must have limited side effects as we don't want to reduce two problematic gases only to introduce a third. Helium is the only real option and is the gas of choice for technical divers. This combination of oxygen, nitrogen and helium is known as trimix. How we select these gases and how we managed their use will also be covered in more detail.

There are a number of reasons why people undertake technical diving. For me the main reason is for shipwreck exploration. Wrecks hold a unique fascination and diving on a previously undiscovered wreck for the first time is a magical experience. In order to find undiscovered or rarely visited wrecks, divers often have to dive deeper than the recreational limits. Another reason for venturing deeper is that wrecks at depth tend to be better preserved than wrecks in more shallow water. The wave and storm action will quickly break up wrecks in shallow waters and so the deeper we go the more intact the wreck tends to be. So, for me, technical diving is a means to an end. If there was an endless supply of intact, undiscovered wrecks in 20m of water then I would never have become involved in technical diving.

For others there are different attractions to technical diving. In general, diving is not a competitive sport but there are some

---

3   Using V-Planner with conservatism set to +2 a 25 minute air dive to 45m/150ft gives 53 minutes of decompression. By adding in 50% as a decompression gas this is reduced to 25 minutes.

people who want to dive deeper than anyone else or to dive beyond some real or imagined depth limit. In the same way as climbers want to conquer a particular mountain peak 'because it's there', there are divers who want to dive to a specific depth for the same reason. Similarly, there are divers who want to be the best in their field and who view technical diving as the pinnacle of scuba diving and a way to perfect their diving skills.

Whatever the reason for starting down the technical diving path, it is important to recognise that any type of technical diving can potentially increase the risk of serious injury or death. Recreational diving is a relatively safe activity and if we are going to increase the risks then we should do it with our eyes open. As we go deeper and stay longer, we increase our decompression obligation. In the event of a problem, we cannot simply ascend to the surface without risking decompression illness. Many divers would never consider cave diving as the thought of not being able to ascend due to being in an overhead environment would be too much to deal with. Yet any diver who carries out a decompression dive introduces these same limitations, as the decompression obligation introduces what is known as a 'virtual overhead'. Many of the chapters that follow will focus on how we can manage and reduce these risks.

As we move further into the realm of technical diving, our assumptions about decompression illness start to become tested. If we are diving at 20m/66ft then we know that millions of other divers have successfully carried out dives in these depths. While any dive will have a risk of decompression illness, we can be confident that the risk is very small. With deeper and longer decompression dives, we are moving into an area where there is much less experience of decompression principles. We are, in effect, acting as guinea pigs for decompression research. There are so many aspects of decompression that are not fully understood, and the risks of suffering decompression illness when pushing this knowledge are correspondingly higher. In addition, nitrogen narcosis, oxygen toxicity and a variety of other risks must be considered when diving in these ranges.

The risks discussed above might lead you to think that anyone who undertakes any form of technical diving must be mad.

This may be partly true but it doesn't mean that technical divers are happy to accept all of these increased risks. In order to manage these risks, and reduce them to an acceptable level, we have to review how we carry out the dive. In many cases, the solutions are the same as those adopted by the recreational diver but the emphasis placed on effectively carrying them out is much higher than for normal recreational dives. In other cases different equipment, training, procedure and techniques are adopted in order to reduce the risks to an acceptable level. This is the reason why normal recreational diving equipment and training is not sufficient for technical diving. We will look in more detail at each of these aspects of technical diving.

In the third section of the book, we will look at some of the different equipment configurations used by technical divers. These stress the need for redundancy in essential equipment, familiarity with the use of all equipment and streamlining to ensure everything is accessible without being overly cluttered.

In Part 4 we will discuss some of the additional training and skills that must be practiced and become second nature. Part 5 will consider some of the specifics of rebreather diving. The various configurations as well as the various advantages and disadvantages.

Finally the last section of the book will look at some of the various aspects of technical diving. This section will cover the different environments in which technical diving takes place. It will also discuss some of the physiological factors that have more of an impact with this type of diving. Planning will also be covered and will look at how to plan for dives to go well as well as what to do when things go badly.

As we go through each of these areas, we will see that many of the aspects that are emphasized in technical diving can also be adopted by recreational divers to further increase the safety of their dives.

PART 2
Approach

Chapter 2.	What is Technical Diving?	17
Chapter 3.	Why has it become so popular?	21
Chapter 4.	Moving into Technical Diving	25
Chapter 5.	What makes a Technical diver?	31
Chapter 6.	Fitness for Technical Diving	37
Chapter 7.	Technical Diving and the Internet	41
Chapter 8.	Comfort Zone	45
Chapter 9.	Expect the Unexpected	49
Chapter 10.	What went wrong?	53
Chapter 11.	Complacency	59

What is Technical Diving?

"So what is it?" **The Cat from Red Dwarf**

Although technical diving is still a relatively small part of the overall world of diving it is becoming increasingly popular. Yet, despite all of this it is still almost impossible to come up with a definition of exactly what we mean by the term 'technical diving'. It was first used in 1991 by Michael Menduno who was the editor of aquaCorps, the first magazine aimed at this developing style of diving. Despite being in use for almost 30 years it's still one of those terms that everyone uses but nobody can quite agree on what they mean by it. In fact many people dislike the term and have attempted to come up with a better alternative. Adventurous diving, extended range diving and many other terms have all been suggested but have not been taken up. In the absence of a better term we are stuck with technical diving.

Technical diving is often defined by comparing it to recreational diving. It is often described as being beyond recreational diving. This is a good starting point for a definition but is complicated by the fact that different agencies have different views of recreational diving. For example PADI and SDI are very clear as to what constitutes recreational diving. They define it as no-stop diving on air (or nitrox) to less than 40m/130ft. Anything beyond this is not considered recreational diving and so can be classed as technical diving. This means that any dives that go beyond the no-stop limit and require mandatory decompression stops over and above a normal safety stop would be considered technical diving. Equally any dive beyond 40m/130ft would be beyond the recreational limits and so would be a technical dive. In fact these two often go together as it is very difficult and rather

Figure 2: aquaCorps Magazine

pointless to do a no-stop dive deeper than 40m/130ft. The no-stop time is so short that there is very little point going to the time and expenses of doing a dive deeper than 40m/130ft when you only have a few minutes of bottom time. So dives deeper than 40m/130ft are almost always decompression dives and so this qualifies as a technical dive on both accounts. Up until only a few years ago the definition of recreational diving would have specified air as the breathing gas. These days nitrox has become commonplace and has become an accepted, even an encouraged, part of recreational diving. However when we switch to breathing mixtures which include helium we are once again stepping outside the recreational world and so any dive using helium falls under the technical diving sphere. This is again related to the depth. As we go deeper than 40m/130ft narcosis becomes an increasingly bigger risk and so switching to a helium based gas becomes a much more attractive option. The helium reduces the narcosis and so gives a clearer head at depth.

This would seem like a good definition of technical diving but the picture is complicated when we look at other agencies that have a different definition of recreational diving. Although both PADI and SDI specify no-stop diving to less than 40m/130ft BSAC has a different approach. For experienced divers BSAC allows the use of air and nitrox mixes for depths up to 50m/165ft. In addition BSAC divers are allowed to conduct decompression diving. The unfortunate side effect is that divers can start to do what would generally be considered technical dives but would do this with a recreational diving mindset. This grey area means that a diver could do 50m/165ft dive on air with 20 minutes of decompression while still using a recreational diving approach and mindset. However, anything beyond 50m/165ft, using decompression cylinders or trimix would still be considered technical diving

It is clear then that the difference between recreational diving and technical diving is not necessarily black and white and there are degrees of technical diving. I tend to think of it as a continuum. At one extreme you have the single cylinder air diver in a shorty and BCD who dives a couple of times a year on holiday. While at the other extreme you have a diver using multiple cylinders and gas mixes doing 120m/400ft exploration dives and incurring many hours of decompression.

Other definitions of the term have focused on various aspects of the type of dive being the criteria for whether it is technical diving or not. Depth is usually associated with technical diving and it is true that deeper dives will definitely require technical diving techniques. However depth is certainly not the only criteria for identifying technical diving. As we have already seen a no-stop dive to 40m/130ft may be within the scope of recreational divers but the same depth for a 30 minute bottom time with decompression stops and accelerated decompression is certainly a technical dive.

One of the most common features of technical diving is some sort of overhead environment. This can be a physical environment such as a cave or wreck or can be a virtual overhead as in a decompression ceiling. In either case if the diver cannot ascend directly to the surface, either because of a physical obstruction or due to the risk of decompression, then this is a significant difference to normal recreational diving. There is a strong consensus that any form of overhead environment diving should always be carried out using a technical diving mindset.

When decompression is combined with additional gas mixes to accelerate or optimise that decompression then this is clearly in the realm of technical diving. The use of rich nitrox

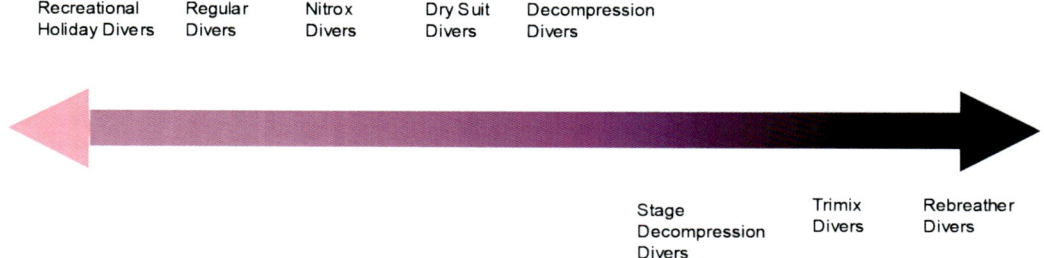

Figure 3: The continuum from recreational to technical diver

Many recreational divers may plan their dive based around leaving the bottom with 70 bar/1000 psi to be back on the boat with 50 bar/700 psi, or leaving when their computer tells them they are approaching the end of their no-stop time. There is nothing wrong with this in the world of recreational diving but this does not work with technical diving. The implications of technical diving means that it is essential that dives are planned properly. This is driven by a number of factors; diving deeper and so incurring significant amounts of decompression; the additional factors in trimix decompression; the use of rich nitrox mixes to accelerate the decompression with the associated risk of oxygen toxicity; the requirements to plan your gas so that you have enough to safely complete the dive and many other factors all mean that it is essential to fully plan your dive. All of this means that technical diving has also been described as any dive that requires specific planning.

Figure 4: A technical diver kits up for a 100m dive

mixes for decompression can reduce the amount of decompression required after a dive by allowing the nitrogen and helium to be released from the body at a faster rate without increasing the risk of decompression illness. When using a rich nitrox mix for decompression it is essential that buoyancy control on the decompression stops is very precise. If the diver drifts up above their decompression stop then they are at risk of decompression illness whereas if they drift down after switching to a rich nitrox mix they are at risk of central nervous system oxygen toxicity. This type of dive carries increased risks, requires additional planning and training and so is firmly in the realm of technical diving.

As you go deeper and narcosis becomes an increasing problem it is common to add helium into your breathing mixture to reduce the effects of narcosis. The result of mixing nitrogen, oxygen and helium is known as trimix. The only advantage to using trimix is that it reduces narcosis. Unfortunately there are also some disadvantages. When using trimix you have to deal with two inert gasses; nitrogen and helium, this makes the decompression more complicated therefore more planning needs to go into the dive. Helium is a cold gas, so a separate suit inflation system may be required in addition a decompression cylinder is essential when using trimix, all of this involves additional equipment. Buoyancy control is even more critical when using trimix than when using air or nitrox, so additional skills and training are required.

One of the common themes running through this chapter is that any description of technical diving is often framed in terms of the differences between it and recreational diving. Any dive that requires additional techniques, equipment and skills is another common definition. This covers the fact that techniques such as multiple gasses, gas switches, decompression stops are all aspects of diving that are at odds with recreational diving. This means that many of the established procedures, techniques and rules of recreational diving are no longer applicable or need to be subtly modified. In order to prepare divers for technical diving, additional specialised training is required, therefore technical diving can be described as anything that requires specialised training.

You can see that there are different aspects to any definition of technical diving. Any one of these aspects in itself is not enough to make something a technical dive. Wearing all the kit does not make you a technical diver if you don't have the right skills and training. Diving a rebreather does not automatically make you a technical diver, 40m/130ft can be a recreation or a technical dive while meticulously planning a 6m/20ft dive does not make it a technical dive. However if two or more of these factors are combined then it is fair to assume that it is a technical dive and should be treated as such. Even though it may be difficult to put a solid definition to the term it is usually easy to recognise it when you see it.

Why has it become so popular?

"Sometimes we are lucky enough to know that our lives have been changed, to discard the old, embrace the new and run headlong down an immutable course. It happened to me on that summer's day, when my eyes were opened by the sea." **Jacques-Yves Cousteau**

It can't have escaped your notice that technical diving seems to have become very popular. I am regularly asked to talk to dive clubs about the subject and the fact that one of the major UK diving magazines now contains a separate section about technical diving, as well as other regular articles about different aspects of technical diving are just further examples of how this once forbidden aspect of diving has become mainstream. We can see just how popular technical diving has become if we consider that Technical Diving International (TDI) carried out a survey in 1994 where only one person out of every 100 said that they had taken a technical diving course or were intending to take one in the following year. When a similar survey was carried out in 2008 this had changed to one person in four saying that they had taken a technical diving course or were intending to do so in the following year.

When the term technical diving was first coined in 1991 it was considered as a being completely different from recreational diving. The main technical diving agencies such as TDI and IANTD were formed as a way of providing technical diving training to those divers that were interested in the topic. However, most of the recreational diving agencies condemned technical diving to the extent that in 1991 any technical agency or manufacturer that supported the use of nitrox was banned from DEMA, the largest US diving show. The reason for this was that the recreational diving agencies considered nitrox to be too dangerous for use by recreational divers. Of course this view was driven by a lack of knowledge and a fear of anything new. Today all of the recreational agencies encourage the use of nitrox and all have introduced their own nitrox programmes

The wider availability of equipment suitable for technical diving has also helped to encourage its popularity. As I have already mentioned the equipment used for technical diving is quite different to that used in recreational diving. At the beginning it was very difficult for divers to find equipment that was suitable. Many of the early technical divers had to resort to making or modifying their own equipment. This obviously limited the number of people who had the skills and inclination to follow this route. Many of the well known technical diving equipment companies started off with the owner making a prototype for his own use in his garage and then being asked to make more for his dive buddies. Unless you had the skills to make the equipment yourself or knew someone who knew someone it was very difficult to find suitable equipment. However, these days many of the major equipment manufacturers offer a technical equipment range and specialised technical diving equipment is easily available. This means that it is now relatively easy to buy wings, backplates, regulators, canister torches, reels and sophisticated multi gas computers from your local dive shop or just order it online and have it delivered to your door.

The wider availability of information has helped to popularise technical diving. The two main developments that allowed information on technical diving onto a wider stage were the publication of the aquaCorps magazine in the 1990s and the development of the internet. The internet allowed communication between technical divers and provided a means for distributing information on the subject to the rest of the diving community. Rather than isolated pockets of technical divers each doing their own thing, the internet allowed us to develop a consensus on the best options for equipment configuration and diving procedures and to avoid re-inventing the wheel.

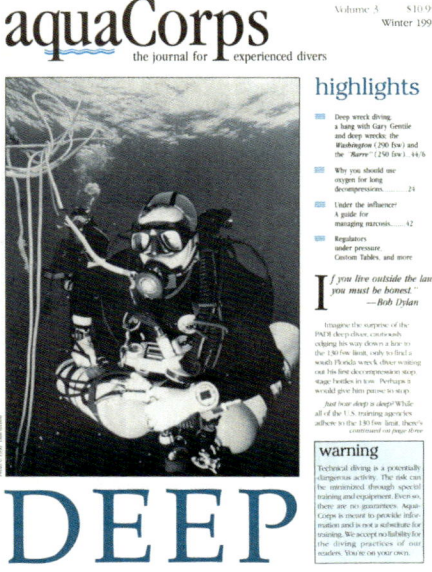

Figure 5: aquaCorps magazine did much to popularise technical diving

These days the internet is an almost essential tool for any aspiring technical diver. There is a huge amount of information available on almost every aspect of technical diving. Some of the information on the internet is true and very useful but unfortunately lots of it is neither true nor useful.

Any sport or activity will see progress over time and diving is no exception. As a result the popularity of technical diving can be seen as just the natural progression of the activity. It is human nature to want to improve, push yourself or progress your skills and abilities. Human nature also encourages a desire to do things that few other people have done or visit places that few others have seen. It is this spirit of exploration that has also contributed to the development of this aspect of the sport. Many technical divers progress their diving as a way of achieving a specific goal which is why technical diving is often associated with wreck or cave diving. In these cases the techniques used are just a tool to find unknown wrecks or explore uncharted caves.

Diving magazine stories of divers finding lost wrecks, identifying historic wrecks or piecing together parts of a historical puzzle are always fascinating to read. There are few other areas where someone carrying out their hobby can have such a big impact on identifying major pieces of history. It is no coincidence that technical diving is so popular in the UK when we have sites like the English Channel, Western Approaches, Scapa Flow and other sites that have been so important for our naval history right on our doorstep. The south coast of England contains some of the most important wrecks from the First and Second World War and while many of them are in water less than 30m/100ft there are a significant number that are in the technical diving range. These have provided a strong incentive for divers to progress into technical diving in order to explore these historic sites. Books such as *The Last Dive*[4], *Shadow Divers*[5] and *Deep Descent*[6] have further popularised technical diving and raised the profile not just within the diving world but also in general.

One of the other reasons why it has become much more common for recreational divers to undertake technical diving

---

4 Choudry, B. (2001) The Last Dive
5 Kurson, R. (2004) Shadow Divers: The True Adventure of Two Americans Who Risked Everything to Solve One of the Last Mysteries of World War II
6 McMurray, KF. (2001) Deep Descent: Adventure and Death Diving the Andrea Doria

courses is a widespread perception that these courses are a way to improve general diving skills and become a significantly safer diver whatever type of diving you do. Due to the increased potential risks; the level of buoyancy control, comfort in the water, problem solving abilities and general diving skills required to undertake technical diving is significantly higher than for recreational diving. As a result recreational divers, even many recreational diving instructors, see the skills displayed by technical divers and want to reach that same level of skill and control. "I want to be able to do that" or "I want to look like that" are common phrases I hear when I ask people about their motivation for taking technical courses. They may not want to use trimix or dive beyond 50m/165ft but they do want to be safer and more confident when diving in the 30-40m/100-130ft range or when doing some decompression. As a result the increase in technical training courses has led to an increase in the use of technical diving equipment and techniques and so many of the techniques that were once restricted to technical diving have found their way into mainstream recreational diving.

In the last ten to fifteen years technical diving has moved from being considered as heresy by the established recreational diving community to being part of the mainstream diving industry. In the past, diving deeper than 40m/130ft, decompression diving and using gas mixtures other than air were considered so revolutionary that many of these practices were considered unacceptably dangerous and banned by some agencies. This position has softened considerably with most agencies being much more welcoming of technical diving techniques. Many recreational agencies have even gone further and rather than outright banning of technical diving have even started to introduce their own technical diving courses. Clearly this is because they see there is an increasing interest in technical diving and they don't want to miss out on this business, however, this also serves to further legitimise this type of diving which can only make it more popular in the future.

Although technical diving has become mainstream and recreational agencies have started to introduce their own courses there are still important differences between recreational and technical diving. In the last few years the recreational agencies have tried to make diving as accessible as possible to the majority of people. Initial training focuses only on the essential skills that are required to get people diving and emphasise that diving is safe and fun. For the majority of diving this is absolutely true. However, technical diving introduces risks that are not present in recreational diving. The introduction of additional depth, alternative gas mixes, decompression, multiple cylinders, etc., adds risks that are not present on a typical recreational dive. Because of this technical training takes a very different form. It emphasises the risks involved and involves a much deeper understanding of some of the concepts involved. Because of this the type of approach required for good technical instruction is still subtly different to that required for good recreational instruction.

Figure 6: Technical diving allows you to explore some incredible shipwrecks

Moving into Technical Diving

4

"Attitude keeps you alive". **- Rob Palmer**

The terms recreational diving and technical diving can at times be useful to distinguish between the two aspects of the sport but at other times they can be confusing and lead to a number of misconceptions. They give the impression that recreational and technical diving are two completely different activities with a huge gulf between the two. This can be counterproductive in that it makes technical diving, and the benefits it can offer, appear beyond the reach of the majority of recreational divers. It can also create an 'us and them' situation. As we have seen the truth is that there is no firm distinction between recreational diving and technical diving. Instead it is more like a progression with pure recreational diving at one end of the scale and pure technical diving at the other end. In between there are a number of intermediate steps which can lead from one to the other. This means that there are some divers who would consider some of the intermediate steps to be technical diving while others would still consider it to be recreational diving.

The vast majority of the world's divers are recreational divers. They dive with a single cylinder, BCD, usually a wetsuit or semi-dry and wear a snorkel. For these divers this equipment setup is perfectly adequate. Their skills levels are also adequate for the type of diving they do. These divers will usually dive when on holiday or as an occasional hobby. They may choose to take further training, such as a Rescue Diver qualification or enrole in various speciality courses to enhance their skills in the recreational area but many do not. For the majority of divers this is the level they want to achieve in their diving and further equipment and training is not essential. Some of the best divers in the world are firmly in this area

In the US, UK, Europe and other temperate water locations many regular recreational divers choose to dive in a dry-suit and consider it almost a basic part of diving equipment. In other parts of the world a dry-suit is considered a specialst piece of diving equipment used only by the most experienced of divers. This is the first example of an intermediate step which in one area is considered part of normal recreational diving but in other areas is considered advanced or technical diving.

The first exposure that many recreational divers have to any of the concepts of technical diving is the level of skills and buoyancy control that are required for technical diving. Many recreational divers seek to improve their overall skills and their buoyancy control in particular. Although some of the recreational agencies offer such courses many recreational divers seek out technical diving instructors to help them improve their skills. This is usually because some technical diving instructors have reputations for high level of skills and the ability to significantly improve a diver's buoyancy. These skills and buoyancy lessons are often combined with an introduction to technical diving which allows the recreational diver to see a number of concepts used in technical diving without having to commit to going down that route.

Most divers start out on a single cylinder, as they progress a little deeper they add on a pony cylinder as a redundant air supply.

For no-stop dives up to 30m/100ft these provide a sufficient supply of air in the case of emergency. However they can also provide a false sense of security. As the diver progresses beyond 30m/100ft and especially if they have any level of decompression obligation, then a pony cylinder no longer has enough air to get the diver safely to the surface[7]. In addition, at depths beyond 30m/100ft a single cylinder starts to become a limitation as it only has a limited supply of breathing gas which can cut short the available bottom time. For this reason many divers choose to use a twinset for dives below 30m/100ft or for decompression dives. A twinset provides redundancy in the case of an emergency and also provides a greater volume of available gas for deeper dives. There are a number of different options for setting up and configuring a twinset and these will be covered in Part 3. An introduction to technical diving course or twinset familiarisation session will show you the advantages and disadvantages of the various options as well as providing advice on essential skills such as being able to perform a shutdown in the case of an emergency.

Once equipped with a twinset the diver then can look at progressing towards decompression diving. For some agencies decompression diving is considered strictly beyond the scope of recreational diving and is firmly in the technical diving camp. On the other hand there are other agencies which allow recreational divers to carry out limited amounts of decompression. It is common for decompression diving to go hand in hand with deeper diving. As we go deeper the no-stop times at depth becomes shorter. One popular set of decompression tables[8] gives a no-stop time of 51 minutes at 18m/60ft. Venture just a little deeper to 24m/80ft and the no-stop time halves to only 25 minutes. By the time we get to 36m/120ft the no-stop time is just 12 minutes and this drops further to just 7 minutes at 45m/150ft. Even using nitrox to increase bottom time will only have a limited increase in our no-stop times. We can see that in order to spend any time at these depths we inevitably have to perform a decompression dive.

It is possible to carry out decompression diving using just a twinset and do the decompression using just your back gas, i.e. the gas in the cylinders on your back. This is a common approach for divers who do not want to spend additional money on extra equipment or decompression gasses. However there are again limitations on how long we can spend on the bottom using this approach. A longer bottom time means longer decompression. This can result in using a significant volume of gas due to the extended time at depth combined with the extended time on decompression. In addition many divers do not want to spend excessive time on decompression. For these reasons many decompression divers progress onto the use of a rich nitrox mix in a stage cylinder while others combine their initial decompression procedures training with the ability to use rich nitrox in a

---

[7] A 3L Pony cylinder contains 3x200 bar assuming a reasonable fill. This gives a total of 600 litres. Assuming a normal breathing rate of 18L per minute breathing which is likely to double during an emergency then the diver will use (18 x 2) L per minute. How much gas will be required if the diver spends a minute at the bottom at 40m and then makes a direct ascent to the surface? During the 1 minute at 40m the pressure is 5 bar so they will use (18 x 2) x 1 x 5 = 180 bar. The ascent to the surface from 40m will take 4 minutes. We will assume an average depth of 20m which is 3 bar pressure and so the total usage for this ascent is (18 x 2) x 4 x 3 = 432. 180 bar at the bottom and 432 gives a total of 612 which is more than we have in our pony. Furthermore this does not allow any time for a safety stop let alone decompression stops. When doing these calculations many people use an unrealistically low breathing rate but in an emergency it is incredible how much the average diver will breathe. In addition they assume that the ascent will be immediate but even a minute delay in starting the ascent or a slow ascent from 40m to 30m can result in a much higher gas usage.

[8] This example uses Bühlmann air tables

decompression stage. The stage cylinder increases the amount of gas that is available and the use of a rich nitrox mix reduces the amount of decompression that must be carried out. In some cases this can provide a significant saving and can reduce the amount of decompression that needs to be carried out by up to half.

If a diver wants to progress to deeper dives then they will need to start considering the use of helium in their breathing mix. Air and nitrox become increasingly narcotic below 30m/100ft and in cold water diving 40-45m/130-150ft is generally considered to be the point where the level of narcosis is approaching excessive levels. Helium has virtually no narcotic effect and so it can be used to replace some of the nitrogen in our breathing gas and so reduce our levels of narcosis. The combination of oxygen, nitrogen and helium is known as trimix. By using trimix the diver can modify the level of narcosis they suffer, for example on trimix they may dive to 60m/200ft but only have the same level of narcosis that they would have at 30m/100ft on air. Trimix diving can be carried out with exactly the same equipment that is used for air or nitrox decompression diving. The only difference being the gas that is breathed. The trimix is carried in the twinset instead of air or nitrox and a decompression gas is carried in a stage cylinder.

Divers may choose to use two decompression gasses by carrying two stage cylinders. This is to allow for more effective decompression but also to provide a greater volume of gas. Trimix diving should only be considered once the diver has mastered the basics of diving with a twinset, stage and decompression diving. The training for trimix diving covers all the aspects of planning dives using trimix and multiple decompression gasses but most of the training is focused on the fact that trimix dives tend to be deeper and longer than air or nitrox dives. Deeper and longer dives give higher risk levels and the additional decompression obligation means that the time before the diver can get to the surface gets longer and longer. As a result the level of skills and problem solving required is higher than for other dives.

For depths between 40-60m/130-200ft the oxygen content of the trimix being used will be equal to or greater than the oxygen content of air. A trimix with an oxygen content greater than 18% can be breathed on the surface and is known as "Normoxic Trimix". The use of trimix and the various types of trimix that can be used is discussed in more detail in Chapter 36, page 209.

For trimix dives below 60m/200ft the oxygen content must be reduced in order to reduce the risk of oxygen toxicity. Trimix with an oxygen content of less than 18% should not be breathed on the surface and is known as "Hypoxic Trimix". In order to use a hypoxic trimix the diver has to breathe a different gas on the surface and continue to do so until they get to a depth where the trimix is safe to breathe. This additional gas is known as a "Travel Gas". The travel gas can also double up as a decompression gas during the ascent. For dives between 60-80m/200-260ft it is common for divers to use two or three stage cylinders. For dives deeper than 80m/260ft the diver will use three or more stages in addition to the main twinset on their back.

There are a number of other physiological and decompression considerations when planning dives deeper than 60m/200ft and so there are only a small fraction of divers who ever progress their training to this point. Although the difference in depth from 60m to 80m/200ft to 260ft is only 20m/60ft there is almost an order of magnitude increase in the planning and complexity of dives. The complexity of going from 80m/260ft to 100m/300ft dives is also an order of magnitude greater. At these depths the amount of gas required, length of decompression incurred, levels of oxygen exposure and simply time in the water all conspire to make dive planning and execution a significant challenge.

For some technical divers trimix diving is the point where they seriously start to consider the use of a rebreather. Trimix fills are considerably more expensive than air or nitrox and so the gas saving advantages of a rebreather start to become very relevant. The decision as to whether to switch to a rebreather or stay on open circuit is a complex one. There is no doubt that gas costs on a rebreather are much lower than open circuit. In the case of an emergency your gas supply is likely to last much longer on a rebreather than a twinset. However this must be weighed against the disadvantages of rebreathers. Cost saving on gas fills must be balanced against the considerable initial cost of the rebreather, associated training and additional equipment. Unless you are doing a significant number of trimix dives every year a rebreather will not necessarily be cheaper than open circuit. In addition rebreathers increase the risk of the dive and the complexity of preparation. The use of rebreathers is covered in more detail in Chapter 31.

We can see that technical diving is a progression through a number of steps. Firstly the switch to twinset diving followed by the introduction of decompression and accelerated decompression techniques. This is usually using a single stage cylinder. As divers progress deeper they will switch to normoxic trimix and two stage cylinders. Deeper still and they will switch to using hypoxic trimix and multiple stages.

Whether these deep dives are carried out on open circuit or a rebreather will depend on the preference of the diver but whether we are talking about open circuit or rebreather we can be sure that dives to 100m/330ft or deeper are firmly in the realm of technical diving.

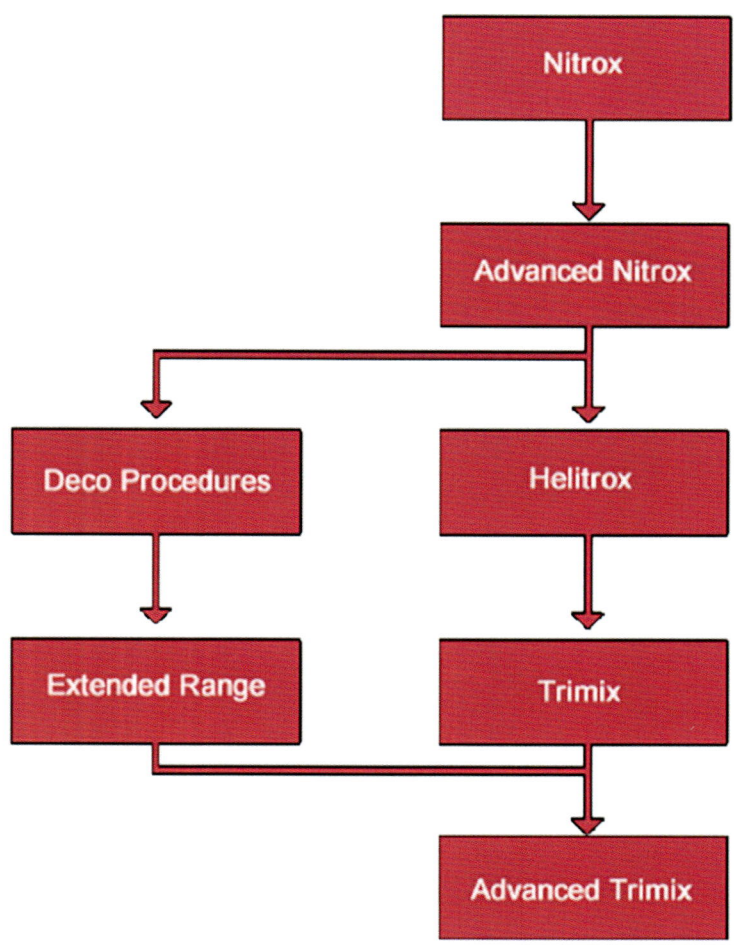

Diagram 1: TDI Flowchart

Figure 7: Using a rebreather to explore a wreck in Sardinia at 110 m

What makes a Technical diver?

5

"In wisdom gathered over time, I have found that every experience is a form of exploration." **Ansel Adams**

It's not that long ago that technical diving was considered completely outside the scope of mainstream diving and there was a huge gulf between the two. This had a significant effect on the type of person that became involved in technical diving. In most cases technical divers had significant experience of recreational diving, often with many years of diving behind them. In most cases the progression to technical diving was a gradual process involving progressing gradually deeper and slowly modifying the equipment used to deal with the new challenges being encountered. For many technical divers, including myself, this gradual change meant that there wasn't really a defining moment when we switched from being recreational divers to being technical divers. Instead it was a gradual evolution of kit and procedures. Slowly the diving involved became deeper and further away from what would be considered mainstream diving until at some point it became clear that we were no longer doing the same sort of things as the majority of divers. This led to divers seeking out like minded divers and instructors in order to dive without the stigma attached to technical diving by many recreational divers. There was almost an initiation period before you would be accepted into this group and technical instructors would often interview prospective students to ensure that they fitted in with the required mindset. This environment shaped the type of divers that were involved in technical diving. A certain level of experience, determination, focus and financial resource were required in order to break into this world. For example amongst early technical divers there was always a high proportion of firemen; their personalities, combined with shift working made them ideal for this type of diving. However there were also a significant number of people involved in the technology industry as their innovation and financial resources were also well suited to the growing technical diving area.

As technical diving has progressed and become accepted into mainstream diving, this has had a huge influence on the dynamics of, if when and how divers get involved in technical diving. Technical diving has become accepted as one of the options for extending your recreational diving experience rather than as something completely different to recreational diving. As a result a far higher proportion of recreational divers than ever before are considering technical diving. The point at which recreational divers make the transition is also changing. In the past prospective technical divers have often been recreational instructors or at least dive masters themselves before they progress to technical diving. This has meant that many of the in water skill required as well as the theoretical knowledge of diving physics have already been honed in the recreational environment. The popularity and appeal of technical diving has been boosted hugely by the internet, speakers at dive shows and by books such as this! As a result newly qualified recreational divers are seeing technical diving as a goal they want to pursue or as a way to increase their diving skills. Rather than building up significant experience within recreational diving they are increasingly looking to progress to technical diving sooner rather than later. This has a number of impacts, both positive and negative. Increased training can increase safety and technical training will increase the skills and knowledge of a diver. However, progressing into technical diving without sufficient skills or experience can be frustrating or even dangerous. As a result many agencies have launched courses specifically aimed to ease the transition from recreational to technical diving. For example TDI's Intro to Tech[9] is designed to take relatively inexperienced recreational divers with no knowledge of technical diving and give them an overview of the equipment, skills and mindset involved. This can help them to understand how to progress in technical diving as well as allowing them to see for themselves whether technical diving is for them.

The changes in the attitude to technical diving has meant that there are some clear types of people coming into technical diving and I will try and describe some of the characteristics of each of these types. See if you can recognise yourself in any of these descriptions.

First is the recreational instructor or dive master. Typically this person chooses this option for one of three reasons. Firstly they have decided that they don't want to progress any further down the instructing route but want to stretch their own diving and see technical diving as a way to achieve this.

The second group are still committed to recreational instruction or dive mastering but want to progress their own diving in another area or want to ensure that they can do some dives without always having to have their instructor hat on. They have had enough of always having to look after less experienced divers, even when they are not formally instructing, and see technical diving as something that is just for them. If a recreational instructor is deeper than 40m/130ft,

---

9   In addition IANTD Essential of Technical Diving, PADI's Tech40 and GUE Fundamentals all cover a similar syllabus. .

breathing trimix and with significant decompression stops ahead of them they can be sure that they are not considered to be instructing. The last category are instructors who don't intend to do a lot of technical diving but want to expand their own knowledge to better answer questions that their students may ask them. Increasingly students, especially at Rescue or Dive Master level, will have questions about some aspects of technical diving and many instructors feel that a depth of knowledge in all aspects of diving is an essential part of their professional development.

The next type of character who gets involved in technical diving is the adrenaline junkie. These are easily recognisable by their previous hobbies. They will already have tried bungee jumping, paragliding or some other type of adrenaline sport and are attracted by the thrill of technical diving.

The adrenaline junkie is likely to move straight from their recreational training onto technical training as they see it as part of their game plan. What they lack in experience they often make up for in enthusiasm. They will want to progress through the various levels of technical training just as they progressed through their recreational training as they see greater and greater depth as a way of fulfilling the need for an adrenaline rush. They often become committed technical divers and develop as they progress through their training, eventually gaining as much satisfaction from the experience as from the adrenaline. In some cases they can make excellent technical divers as they often have the motivation and drive to plan and arrange dives that many others wouldn't consider. Many people who appear to be foolhardy risk takers are, in fact, very good at managing the risks that occur in these adrenaline sports. This type of person is well suited to managing the risks involved in technical diving. However the pure adrenaline junkie, who is only interested in the buzz from extreme risks, is often disappointed to find that technical diving is as much about planning and preparation as it is about death defying escapes from tricky situations. This type of diver will often progress far and fast in technical diving only to wander off to the next hobby once they realise that an adrenaline rush is not the best experience to have when you are 100m/330ft underwater with several hours of decompression in front of you.

deeper wrecks. For the explorer it is the thrill of finding or identifying an unknown wreck that is the driver to go deeper rather than the depth itself. Many cave divers are cavers who have started to use diving equipment as a way to further explore submerged caves. For divers who become involved in cave diving it is the exploration of these caves that becomes the driving force to progress further with both training and exploration. Divers who are more interested in marine life are less likely to be tempted to explore the depths as the majority of marine life inhabits shallow water. There are some notable exceptions who search for marine life at depths outside the recreational diving range. Richard Pyle is one such exception;

Figure 8: Technical diving is as much about planning and preparation as it is about death defying escapes from tricky situations

The next class of potential technical diver is the explorer. This person is usually more interested in wrecks or caves than in technical diving as such but has found that some technical diving techniques are essential in order to reach many wrecks or progress further into a cave. It is common that the deeper the wreck the more intact it is. In addition there is more to discover, both from a physical and a historical point of view, on

he is an ichthyologist or fish-nerd as he calls himself, who dives in excess of 100m/330ft to identify rare or unknown fish species.

A number of divers progress into technical diving as they see diving as a competitive activity and aim to be the best that they can be. These divers see technical diving as a representation of a higher level of diving skills and their involvement in this area offers a way of proving their skill level. Again it is easy to spot these people from their previous hobbies or from their choice of careers as they tend to be what popular psychology calls "type A" personalities[10]. A background in competitive sports and a career that emphasises success when compared with others is an indication of this type of person. The majority of divers, even technical divers, do not see diving as a competitive activity and the majority may be suspicious of the motives of this group. Again it is entirely possible that someone from this group becomes a successful technical diver because of their determination and energy. Along the way they may well realise that even technical diving isn't a competitive sport and may learn to enjoy the success that this type of diving brings without having to score success over others.

The last type of technical diver is the person that simply sees technical diving as a logical progression for them. There will often be elements of the previous characteristics in this person. Progression may be measured in terms of exploration, personal development, safety or sense of achievement. These divers will often start out without expecting to progress to the highest levels of technical diving but will just want to progress one step at a time. As their diving progresses at one level and they build suitable experience and knowledge they may want to progress to further but the progression is driven by a natural development rather than an explicit goal.

Each of the groups mentioned above can become very successful and accomplished technical divers, irrespective of their initial motivations. The characteristics of successful technical divers will include many of the aspects of the personalities mentioned above. Energy and enthusiasm are important and may come from enthusiasm for exploration or from the desire to improve your own skills. A considered approach to taking risks is also a key factor.

Technical diving is more risky than recreational diving but the successful technical diver will recognise those risks and try to reduce them where possible rather than actively seeking them out.

Successful technical divers will have higher levels of skill than the majority of recreational divers but will recognise that improving their skills is a means to an end and not necessarily a goal in itself. Finally the successful technical diver will have a strong sense of teamwork and will accept that they will have to work with others, whether in a buddy team in the water or as part of a wider expedition team if they want to achieve their goals.

I asked a range of technical divers, ranging from very new tech divers all the way up to very experienced tech instructors, why they got into tech diving. The quotes on the opposite page give a flavour of the various reasons why people get involved in this type of diving. Thank you to all the divers that contributed quotes.

---

10 The Type A and Type B personality theory is a theory which describes two common contrasting personality types—the high-strung Type A and the easy-going Type B. The two types were originally described as patterns of behaviour that could either raise or lower respectively, one's chances of developing coronary heart disease. Although the link to heart disease has been dismissed the use of the terms Type A and Type B has persisted in popular psychology as a way of describing the two contrasting personality types.

> To be able to see more, spend longer at depth and challenge myself

> To go and see some amazing wrecks !

> It was never about depth for me. But it was about building my knowledge and skills and longer bottom time

> For me it was a progression as an instructor, and a need for some enhanced knowledge. It's not so much about the depth but the ability to stay longer with my camera at depth if I need to.

> 'I was ready for more of a challenge... meaning safety, use of deco bottles & helium, gas calculations & analysis, multi-tasking uw, & problem solving. I'm from Michigan, so I've had specific wrecks I've always dreamed about diving (Cornelia Windiate, Daniel Morrell, Typo, Kyle Spangler, Florida, the Detroit, etc.) which are all between 170' & 200'. I opened the door to these wrecks & can't wait for next year when I can dive more of them!

> In the early days I always saw guys walking with mass of equipment to their entry point. I used to dive with a few who seemed to have the knowledge and were safe while diving. The thrill of depth and the danger that came with that did attract me to that. It still is an escape from daily life for me just getting deep underwater, after the planning and setting up. Feels really relaxing/mind is so clear.

> The friends and instructor group I was a part of would spend the winters practicing their "tec" skills in the pool and would always happily invite us to come practice as well and challenged us to come and "play". It was fun and it was a community that was inclusive and happy to explain why they sometimes would just lie there. After that I just progressed naturally after encouragement and curiosity.

> Simply, I wanted to be a better diver, see places recreational divers couldn't go. I like being in a cave or deeper than 40m. like to expand my knowledge to more complex ways of diving. Trimix, sidemount etc. I Suppose it's also the adrenaline rush. ...?"

> I kind of grew into technical diving in the early 90s as a caver from a young age and then a cave diver in 92 it was all about learning the skills to explore the caves further. To us none of this was Technical Diving it was all just Diving to explore caves.

> After some years of diving I learned that what kept me doing it was my fascination with historic wrecks. Since these are mostly in deep waters in my area.. safest bet to enjoy them and staying alive was technical diving.

> For me when I started it was very elite and hard to do or get into, you had to want to do it and invest time money and be the right level

> For extended safety (using the tech mindset in recreational dives), to expand my knowledge - almost unlimited universe of in-deep information, exploration - do what only a limited number of divers can.

Figure 9: Quotes - Why I got into technical diving

Fitness for Technical Diving

"There is no doubt that fitness needs to be emphasised more and for divers of all levels" **Dr Bill Hamilton**

Almost all technical diving training puts some emphasis on maintaining a good level of fitness. This isn't surprising as diving is a physical activity and even entry level training emphasises the importance of a minimum level of fitness for any diving. It is clear that a certain level of fitness is required for technical diving. This will, of course, vary with the level of technical diving that is being undertaken. If we consider technical diving as a progression from moving into technical diving through to advanced exploratory dives then it is clear that the level of fitness that is required will also vary. For those thinking of moving into technical diving it is not essential to be regularly running triathlons or marathons. Instead an average level of fitness is all that is required. For the most advanced levels of technical training then a higher level of fitness is required. As a full time technical diving instructor I consider maintaining a high level of fitness to be a key part of my job and most other full time technical instructors take the same view. In this chapter I will try to look at some of the key reasons as to why fitness is important as well as put into context some of the arguments for the various aspects of fitness required.

Fitness is a very broad subject and there are a number of different aspects to fitness. General fitness training is often separated into two components; strength training and endurance training. Strength and endurance are, of course, interrelated; any exercise will have an impact on both although clearly some exercises focus on strength and some on endurance. For the technical diver a balance of the two is important as we need both types of fitness at different times.

For technical divers, strength is an important consideration. We tend to carry more equipment than recreational divers. This can range from twin 12L/80cf cylinders and a single 7L/50cf stage through to twin 18L/150cf cylinders and multiple 12L/80cf stage cylinders. Clearly a significant amount of strength is required to simply stand up and walk to the back of the boat when wearing all of that equipment. Leg and core body strength are required for these tasks. The diver needs enough strength to be able to stand but also enough strength to be able to support that weight on a moving boat. The diver who can only just stand up and is staggering barely in control to the back of the boat is putting themselves at risk as an unexpected movement of the boat can be enough to throw them off balance. It is obvious that the risks of falling over when wearing that much equipment mean that sufficient strength is a safety consideration and not just a convenience factor. Strength also comes into play when loading and unloading dive gear. If we have to load multiple cylinders and other equipment onto a boat, possibly having to carry it some way from a car, across a jetty and pass it onto the boat, then some strength is required to achieve the task. Without sufficient strength the diver is again risking strains or injury or at the very least a significant level of fatigue. In addition to the injury caused by strains and other muscle injury it can also confuse the situation with regard to decompression illness. If a diver has a sore shoulder after carrying their gear this could be a muscular injury or it could be decompression illness.

In addition to strength the technical diver also needs a good level of endurance. Early starts and three or four hour boat trips in a pitching sea can drain the energy of someone who is not as fit as they should be. Diving itself is not a strenuous activity but being in the water for long periods of time, especially during long decompression dives, can be physically draining. Unless the diver has a good level of endurance they may find themselves excessively fatigued at the end of the dives which can contribute to poor decision making. In the case of an emergency the fatigued diver may find themselves unable to provide sufficient assistance due to their level of tiredness. Endurance is closely linked to cardio-vascular fitness which also has a direct impact on decompression as we will see later.

As well as the safety aspects listed above there is also the consideration that diving is supposed to be fun. If a diver does not have the physical strength to lift their equipment; is at risk of injury due to being unsteady on a pitching boat, or is unduly tired after a dive, then this is bound to effect their enjoyment of the dive. If they are not enjoying the dive then this may put them off going through what they see as the same ordeal again. However, with an increased level of fitness these discomforts are greatly reduced, which increases your safety and your enjoyment.

There are many different types of fitness. We can see this if we look at the different types of professional athletes. Sprinters, marathon runners, rowers and boxers are all very fit but have different aspects to their fitness. Fitness for one sport doesn't necessarily mean you are fit for another sport. In diving we often use the term "dive-fit". While this term does have a component of traditional fitness it is usually meant more to mean competence and comfort in the water. Being "dive-fit" is absolutely critical for a technical diver but this doesn't remove the need for a complimentary level of physical fitness.

One of the most important impacts of fitness is in the area of decompression. Increased cardio-vascular fitness means improved function of the heart, lungs and circulation. These are also the key parts of the body involved in on-gassing and off-gassing and so increased fitness can improve performance in this area. All decompression researchers agree that fit, healthy individuals are less likely to suffer from most medical conditions (including decompression illness) than unfit individuals. As a result, exercise as part of a healthy lifestyle is recommended as a way to reduce the risks of decompression illness. Regular, moderate exercise is known to improve the level of blood circulation in muscle tissue and increases cardio-pulmonary function which should help to increase the rate of nitrogen off-gassing from the body. Some recent research in Scandinavia has studied the effects of cardio vascular exercise on the risk of decompression sickness.[11] This research found that even a single bout of cardio vascular exercise carried out approximately 20 hours before a dive significantly reduced the risk of decompression illness. This fascinating research opens up a whole range of other questions about decompression but once again the message is clear – regular exercise and a good level of fitness are good for technical divers.[12]

Dr. Bill Hamilton, one of the world's leading experts on decompression theory, summarised this view by saying; "There is no doubt that fitness needs to be emphasised more and for divers of all levels. In addition to the obvious benefits of enhanced aerobic ability and athletic performance, a good level of fitness helps in decompression. A diver who is extremely fit can decompress more aggressively than someone who isn't fit. An overweight diver may have more problems off-gassing because of less efficient circulation and because of the way fat takes up gas." [13]

---

11 Wisloff U, Brubakk AO. Aerobic endurance training reduces bubble formation and increases survival in rats exposed to hyperbaric pressure. J Physiol, 537 p607-611
12 Wisloff U, Richardson RS, Brubakk AO. Exercise and nitric oxide prevent bubble formation: A novel approach to the prevention of decompression sickness? J Physiol , 555 p825-829
13 Alert Diver, May/June 2000, pg. 42

Fitness and obesity are two issues that are closely linked even though they are still two separate issues and are worth considering as separate issues. It is possible (although not common) to be obese but still fit and it is possible (and quite common) to be average weight and unfit. There is a long history of empirical observation that obesity can increase the risk of decompression illness. Modern decompression theory can trace its roots back to an article published by Haldane, Boycott, Damant and Lister in 1908 in the Journal of Hygiene.[14] The article immediately following this was another article by Damant describing how overweight sailors had shown an increased risk of decompression illness.[15] Hyperbaric specialists from the early days of tunnel and caisson workers right through to modern scuba divers have noticed an increase in decompression cases amongst overweight, out of shape divers. Others, however, have found no correlation between obesity and decompression.

The majority of empirical observations, research and scientific papers support the view that obesity is a predisposing factor for decompression illness. However, some researchers have argued that obesity in itself is not a major contributor to decompression illness but that overweight divers tend to be unfit and out of condition and that it is these secondary factors that increase the risk of decompression illness rather than the obesity itself. This is often ignored by overweight and unfit divers who argue that their weight does not mean that they are at an increased risk of decompression illness while conveniently forgetting that their lower levels of fitness do still mean that they are at an increased risk of decompression illness.

The long-term implications of obesity are well known. Heart disease, stroke, cancer, high blood pressure, osteoarthritis, gall bladder problems, adult onset diabetes, sleep apnea and fatty deposits blocking the circulatory vessels are all likely results of obesity. Many of the conditions related to obesity such as coronary artery disease are also believed to be decompression illness risk factors and many are contra indications to diving in their own right.

> The respiratory system is one of the key links in the chain of effective decompression. As a result its obvious that any interference in the working of the lungs is going to affect the decompression process. For this reason the effects of smoking can have a considerable affect when diving.

Longer term problems associated with smoking include chronic obstructive pulmonary disease (COPD) which leads to reduced oxygen availability and an increase in carbon dioxide (CO_2) retention in the body. This has been implicated as a factor in CNS oxygen toxicity.[16] Smokers are also generally less healthy and are more prone to develop circulatory problems. Cigarette smoke contains nicotine, which acts as a vasoconstrictor and may theoretically increase the risk of decompression illness due to altered blood perfusion. Cigarette smoke also contains high levels of carbon monoxide (CO), which is a poison. This increased level reduces the ability of the red blood cells to carry oxygen. The CO combines with the haemoglobin in the red blood cells. Haemoglobin binds more closely with CO than with oxygen and so the CO reduces the capacity of the haemoglobin to carry oxygen. The effects of partial pressure on CO concentration in inhaled cigarette smoke would be the same as if the CO had come from some other source, such as from the atmosphere or from oil lubricated compressors.

We can see that it is not essential to be an Olympic athlete to start technical diving but that a reasonable level of fitness is important. An increased level of strength and endurance will make your diving safer and more enjoyable. As you progress in technical diving the required level of fitness and the importance of fitness increases. For many people the path to technical diving is the incentive they need to improve their fitness.

A slightly healthier diet and regular exercise can increase your safety, comfort and enjoyment while diving and can have long term health benefits as well. There are no obvious disadvantages to an increased level of fitness, only advantages.

---

14 Boycott, A.E., Damant, G.C.C., & Haldane, J.S. "The Prevention of Compressed Air Illness", Journal of Hygiene, Volume 8, (1908) pp. 342-443.

15 Boycott, A.E. & Damant. "Experiments on the Influence of Fatness on Susceptibility to Caisson Disease", Volume 8, (1908), pp 445-456.

16 Natoli, M; Vann, RD (1996) Factors Affecting CNS Oxygen Toxicity in Humans. Technical Report Submitted to the Office of Naval Research

Technical Diving and the Internet

"The problem with quotes on the internet; is that it's hard to verify their authenticity" **Abraham Lincoln**

Technical diving has developed in similar time frame to the development of the internet. The early development of technical diving was assisted by internet use and now technical diving still has a close association with the internet.

Technical diving is now considered a legitimate, if extreme, section of the diving world. It is easy to forget that this has far from always been the case. The pioneers of technical diving struggled with the fact that they were isolated from other technical divers and from a lack of information. They were also limited by the fact that technical diving was considered as heresy amongst the established recreational diving community. Many of the early technical divers were also instructors for recreational instructors but risked criticism from their colleagues or even cancellation of their instructor status if their technical diving activities were discovered. This inevitably led to technical diving being carried out in secret and amongst closed groups.

This isolation and secrecy meant that it was difficult to share ideas, develop standards and collaborate on improving techniques. As a result technical diving evolved independently in different areas with each group developing in isolation. These groups had no template on which to base their technical diving and so each developed their own techniques, equipment configurations and ways of working. This trial and error approach meant that early development of techniques was very slow and in some cases the cost of these lessons involved loss of life. Of course this just reinforced the mainstream view that technical diving was unacceptable, dangerous and ensured that technical divers maintained their secrecy about their activities.

The two main developments that brought technical diving onto a wider stage were the publication of a magazine called aquaCorps and the growing popularity of the internet. aquaCorps was the first magazine to address the newly emerging field of technical diving and in fact it was their publisher Michael Menduno who is usually credited with coining the term Technical Diving. The magazine was published between 1990 and 1996 and focused on providing information on all aspects of technical diving. It drew contributions from researchers such as Dr R. W. "Bill" Hamilton, Dr Richard Vann and Dr Ed Lanphier as well as the pioneers of technical diving such as Bill Stone, Richard Pyle and Billy Deans. Many of the articles from the magazine are still regularly quoted as setting the standard for technical diving information.

The second development was the increasing popularity of the internet and in particular it's expansion out of the academic world allowed various parts of the technical diving world to start to communicate and share ideas. This communication was initially by means of mailing lists. These mailing lists allowed a large number of divers to communicate easily. An email sent to a mailing list would be seen by all members of the list who could then reply and add their own views. The most popular of the technical diving internet mailing lists was the Techdiver list[17]. In addition to sharing information these mailing lists also allowed discussion of various issues. Some of these discussions were very heated to say the least as the various groups discussed which, in their view, was the best option. Many of the areas of agreement amongst all technical divers and agencies were thrashed out and agreed in this way. Equally many of the misunderstandings and biases were also developed in this way. Many of these discussions are still going on even to this day.

As consensus started to develop a small number of world wide web pages started to appear. These pulled together magazine articles, techniques and other snippets of information and began to make these available to other divers. As the internet has developed the technical diving community has continued to use it in a number of ways. These days the internet is an almost essential tool for any technical diver. There is a huge amount of information available on almost every aspect of technical diving. However, like any tool there are some positive aspects to this as well as some less positive aspects.

At the most basic level the internet is used by the majority of technical divers for arranging dives through email conversations. Dive organisers send out a list of upcoming dives to their usual diving group and then the details are also distributed by email.[18] Many dive boast skippers now send out a regular email listing spaces on upcoming trips. The use of mailing lists has continued although it is no longer the main method of sharing information. Forums have taken over from mailing lists as the preferred way of communicating with larger groups, discussing various aspects of technical diving, asking advice or just chatting about the subject.

Diving forums can provide a fantastic source of knowledge and advice. They are also used by many divers to arrange dive trips, meet like minded buddies, obtain information on instructors, dive boats and dive sites. They are without doubt the easiest and quickest way for a new technical diver to pick up a large amount of good information. Internet forums are also a good, although far from the only, way to get onto technical dive trips. It's a common theme that divers who are new to technical diving may have moved on from the type of diving that their regular buddies, dive club or local shop are interested in. As their regular buddies are not interested in technical dives and they don't yet have a network of like minded technical buddies, they can struggle to get on to technical dives. In many cases their technical diving instructor will run suitable trips that they can join in with but a dive forum gives them access to a much wider range of potential buddies and trips.[19]

Diving forums do however have their disadvantages which those interested in technical diving should be wary about. Information on a diving forum may not always be accurate. You should always treat this information with caution. There are a number of reasons why this information may not be as reliable as it seems. There are a number of diving urban myths that are continually repeated on internet forums. The fact that they are continually repeated gives weight to these stories or opinions but that doesn't stop them from being incorrect or misleading. In some cases these myths may just be misleading but in other cases they are downright dangerous.

Facebook and other forms of social media have started to take the place of some diving forums and all of the same comments about forums are likely to apply to other social media platforms in the future.

As in any discussion there will be differing points of view. Although there is agreement on many aspects of technical

---

17   The Techdiver archives are available online at
     http://www.aquanaut.com/bin/mlist/aquanaut/techdiver

18   If you would like to be added to my mailing list then just send an email
     with the word Subscribe to dive-tech@yahoogroups.com

19   The following forums are either focused on technical diving or have an
     active technical diving community. www.ccrexplorers, www.thediveforum,
     www.rebreatherworld.com; www.direxplorers.com; www.divingmatrix.com

diving there are many points of contention. Anyone asking about one of these points will almost inevitably trigger an argument about the pros and cons of each point of view. Any question of equipment configuration will turn into a debate between the supporters of different styles of configuration. Each will focus on the disadvantages of the other style while claiming that their preferred setup is perfect. For this reason advice you get from diving forums should be considered as highly biased. The same thing applies to different techniques for performing certain skills.

One of the problems with forums and other forms of social media is that it is difficult to identify people who know what they are talking about from those that are very verbose but don't actually have the experience to back up their words. Opinions are often strongly presented but can be biased or incorrect. On looking into it you find the person has previously heard those opinions and is just repeating the same thing but their conviction makes it sound more authoritative than it deserves. Misleading information, bias and inaccurate information can all be propagated in this way.

Divers looking to find out about technical diving face a completely different situation to that faced by their predecessors, rather than a lack of information on various aspects of technical diving there is now an almost overwhelming supply of information. Twenty years ago the only way to learn some of the techniques of technical diving was to discover them by trial and error or to find an experienced technical diver and learn from them. These days there are a vast range of websites dedicated to every aspect of technical diving. Within a few minutes the prospective technical diver can find out a vast array of information on subjects as diverse as decompression theory, gas blending and even the best way to tie a boltsnap onto your equipment.

The problem comes in sifting through this information and then deciding which of the often contradictory information to believe. Different schools of thought will suggest different approaches to solving each problem in technical diving. Some divers will blindly follow what they read on the internet but very often the decision as to the best option can only be made through trial and error or by learning from an experienced technical diving instructor. Ironically the vast amount of

information means that it is even more important than ever to find a good instructor who can lay out the pros and cons of the various arguments.

1.	One piece harness or break
2.	Rebreather or Open Circuit
3.	Steel or Aluminium stages
4.	Stages on the left or – lean left, rich right
5.	Agency vs Agency
6.	What depth is too deep on air
7.	Training vs experience
8.	Manifolded vs independent twinsets
9.	Sidemount vs backmount twinsets
10.	Which deco model to use

Figure 10: Top ten contentious issues in technical diving.

Comfort Zone

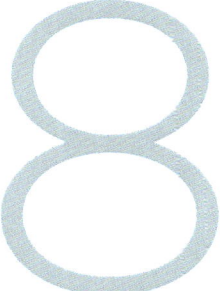

"Life begins at the end of your comfort zone" **Neale Donald Walsch**

Physical fitness is important for technical diving but mental fitness is also important but is often overlooked. In the same way that we can train the body to become fitter and better adapted for certain physical tasks we can also train the mind. This mental training becomes essential when problems start to occur. Fortunately most divers don't ever experience serious problems and so never have their mental fitness tested. After all if a problem does occur it is too late to realise that you are not mentally prepared. For this reason technical divers need to be mentally prepared as well as physically prepared.

STRESS

Many people dive to escape the stress of everyday life. When everything is going well diving is relaxing and stress free. The feeling of floating weightless in mid water is one of the most relaxing feelings you can have. However when things start to go wrong then stress can increase suddenly. Dealing with equipment failures, entanglement, getting lost or stuck inside a wreck can move you from calm and relaxed to highly stressed within a few seconds. It is at this point that your mental preparation becomes essential.

Stress can be caused by a number of factors. Being cold or uncomfortable, dealing with minor, annoying equipment problems, being in an unfamiliar environment or diving with an unfamiliar buddy can all be a source of stress but on their own each of them are easily manageable. Any one of these on their own would probably not result in a dive being aborted. Although they result in a slight increase in stress the diver is likely to still be within their comfort zone. Equipment failures can also significantly increase stress and especially when combined with any of the other factors can move the diver to the point where they are reaching the limit of their comfort zone or even just beyond.

These causes of stress can be magnified by a number of other factors. Narcosis can have an effect on the way we behave and something that we can deal with at 35m/115ft maybe much more stressful at 45m/150ft. Narcosis can affect our judgement, motor skills and the ability to think clearly. These can all compound the stress and further push the diver out of their comfort zone.

Time pressure can also be a cause of stress. Having to stick to specific timings shut down a valve before all the gas escapes or get back to a shot at a particular time can make other tasks more stressful. In rushing the diver may make mistakes, especially when combined with narcosis, which can make the time pressure even greater and so raise the stress levels further. Finally the combination of multiple factors can be a source of stress in itself. The diver may be able to handle each of the problems individually but when they are combined the total level of stress is greater than the individual parts.

As the diver gets further and further outside their comfort zone they may ultimately reach the point of panic. At this point they are no longer thinking rationally about the problem and behave erratically.

Narcosis can also come into effect here and can make a diver more prone to panic. Bolting for the surface may seem the only choice for a panicking diver but with significant decompression obligation this is no longer an option.

DEALING WITH STRESS

It is clear that being mentally fit and being able to deal with stress is an essential tool for the technical diver and indeed for any diver. In most cases the causes of stress are not, in themselves, impossible to deal with. Equipment failure can sometimes be a factor in incidents and can be very stressful but equipment failure alone will not kill you. Dealing with free flowing regulators, burst hoses, broken masks, runaway inflator hoses are all possible if the diver makes the right decisions. This means that the diver's reaction to failures is often the problem not the failure itself.

There are a number of ways that a diver can try to ensure that they react in the best possible way to any situation. The first is to practice key skills on a regular basis. Dealing with something for the first time is always difficult. We have all had the experience of doing something for the first time and making a complete mess of it. We consider what we have done and may realise there were other options for doing the task. The second time we do a little better. With repeated practice we get better and refine the technique for completing the task until we get to the point where we can do it to a high standard. From this it is obvious that trying to do a task in an emergency situation for the first time is a recipe for disaster. On the other hand if we have practiced the task in advance we have a much higher chance of doing it successfully. In addition, the very fact that we have practiced can reduce our stress as we are doing something we are familiar with and know we can achieve. On the other hand without this practice our stress levels may increase as we are doing something for the first time and may have doubts about whether we can achieve it. Clearly regular practice to ensure we can successfully complete the task will increase our physical ability to deal with the situation as well as our mental ability to deal with it.

The more we practice the more familiar and automatic our response becomes. It is these responses that will be remembered during stressful times and so we may find ourselves automatically responding to the situation. Even when suffering from narcosis this 'muscle memory' is likely to be maintained. This is one of the reasons why some people seem to be able to adapt to narcosis. They are not suffering less from narcosis but are becoming better at dealing with things automatically. With this practice our comfort zone becomes larger and there are a greater variety of situations we are comfortable dealing with before they start to cause increased stress.

Of course it is impossible to practice for every possible eventuality. The good news is that it has been shown that we don't necessarily even have to physically practice a drill to increase our ability to deal with a situation. Simply discussing the options for dealing with a situation with our buddy can increase our ability to deal with it. Rather than having to decide on a strategy for dealing with the situation as it happens we can discuss it in advance and decide on the best approach. If we discuss it in advance stress levels are very low as there is no time pressure, no narcosis and no real danger. We can then come up with a plan for dealing with a given situation. If that situation happens underwater the stress levels are very high and so we are unlikely to come up with a good solution and even if we do we have not practiced it. Therefore, as we have already mentally rehearsed the situation we know how we will deal with it and so have a lower overall level of stress.

STOP, BREATHE, THINK, ACT

There are a number of key steps in dealing with any stressful situation. I'm sure that in your open water course you were told that the first thing to do in any situation is to Stop, Breathe, Think, Act. This advice is as true at 100m as it is at 10m. Many people forget this and skip straight to Act without stopping to assess the situation or the tools they have at hand. In this case they often start solving the wrong problem, potentially making the situation worse, or attempt to solve the right problem but not in the most effective way. By stopping and thinking about the situation you can prioritise what needs to be done and the best way to do it. With multiple failures it may be impossible to do everything at once. If you try to solve all the problems you will end up failing to solve any of them. Instead work out what is critical and must be resolved straight away and what can wait. The first priority is getting something to breathe, this may involve getting to your buddy and so they are your second priority. In order to get to them and avoid going to the surface you need to control your buoyancy and so these three are your top priorities. Anything after that can be put to one side until you have resolved these points. Once they have been resolved you can then look at the other problems and again prioritise them.

In working out how to deal with a situation the more knowledge we have about our options and tools available will help to simplify the situation. This is why technical training courses place so much emphasis on dealing with various types of problems. In addition, technical training places a lot of importance on gradually building up a technical diver's comfort zone. To begin with, dealing with one problem is stressful but if you practice it then dealing with it is no longer stressful as it is now within your comfort zone. At this point, dealing with two problems becomes possible although, to begin with it will also be stressful. By building up in this way it becomes possible to deal with multiple problems, keep contact with your buddy and maintain your position and buoyancy all within your comfort zone. On many courses students are expected to deal with more and more failures. The point of this is to increase their ability to deal with multiple failures while staying within their comfort zone and not getting anywhere near the level of stress that would lead to panic. In this way the diver is much less likely to panic when a real problem occurs as their comfort zone is much wider than before and their panic threshold has been raised. The stress felt during the course may make the training seem very hard as the student is consistently at the limit of their comfort zone and is intended to make dealing with real problems much less stressful.

Thorough planning and preparation, diving within a strong team structure and a good routine of equipment maintenance can help to reduce the likelihood of an incident occurring. For many divers they will hopefully go through their entire diving careers without being involved in a serious incident. However, if a problem does occur and they get into a difficult situation then the mental fitness previously described can mean that the end result is merely a scary experience rather than something more serious. Developing this approach and practicing the necessary skills can seem like an unnecessary effort and an unpleasant way to spend your time but the mental strength gained is a bit like car insurance. You hope you will never need to use it and chances are you won't but if on the odd chance you do need to use it, you will be very grateful that you invested the time and effort.

**Stop
Breathe
Think
Act**

Expect the Unexpected

"Life is a journey to be experienced, not a problem to be solved". **Winnie the Pooh**

For many people the switch to technical diving is one of the most significant stages in their diving progression. As a result they will often research the available courses and instructors much more thoroughly than a new diver starting on an introductory course. During this research the interested diver may come across a number of course reports from the courses they are interested in. When you read technical diving course reports, either in magazines or especially on the internet, they can give the impression that these courses are some bizarre combination of military boot camp and ritual induction to an elite club. In this chapter I will try to explain why this impression is common and try to put to rest some of the misconceptions surrounding technical training.

Many divers undertake dives beyond the normal recreational range without any additional training and the overwhelming majority do not suffer any incidents. Nevertheless there is a strong indication in all accident statistics that divers without adequate training are less able to deal with problems and are less able to stop a minor problem from escalating into a major problem.

The emphasis in technical training is partly on how to plan and execute a dive to the depths covered by the course. More importantly, the emphasis is mainly on how to avoid getting into problems during these dives and how to deal with these problems should they arise. The reason why this is emphasised so heavily is that as we dive deeper and incur more of a decompression obligation the risks inevitably increase and the dangers from making a mistake also increase. A loss of buoyancy on a 20m/60ft no-stop dive is a serious matter and is not to be underestimated but the diver may well be lucky and get away with it. But a loss of buoyancy on a 45m/150ft dive with 30 minutes of decompression is a much more serious issue and the diver is much less likely to escape without serious injury. A loss of buoyancy on a 100m/330ft dive with several hours of decompression is even more serious and the diver may not even make it back on to the dive boat.

One of the most important parts of any technical diving course is looking at how divers react to problems and how they deal with stress. In order to start a technical course a certain amount of experience is required[20] and often divers will have significantly more dives than the minimum number required. This might imply that they will find the course easier but this

---

20 For example the prerequisites for TDI Advanced Nitrox and Deco Procedures are that you must be 18 or over, have a nitrox certification together with advanced diver or advanced adventure diver and have proof of 25 logged dives.

is often not the case. The vast majority of experienced divers have lots of experience of dives going well but they have little experience of dives going badly. As a result all of their experience may not help in dealing with an emergency. This is the reason why, every year, the incident reports show a number of cases of experienced divers who get into trouble and where the problem escalates into a much more serious incident.[21] In these cases the experienced divers were unable to deal with the situation and stop it developing into a more serous incident as they did not have the experience of dealing with this type of problem. One very typical example includes losing contact with your buddy once a problem occurs and the buddy separation leading to further problems. Another is divers who experience loss of buoyancy control as they are focused on the problem at hand rather than maintaining their buoyancy. This leads to a rapid ascent on top of the original problem. In each case the end result was caused as much by the diver's inability to deal with the situation as with the original situation itself. The reason why so many divers struggle to deal with an emergency is that they are unfamiliar with being in that position. This is an example of the case where we don't know what we don't know. Here the diver doesn't know how they will react in an emergency as they have never been in that situation. Once in an emergency situation, the additional problems start to increase the difficulty of resolving the original problem. This leads to an increase in stress which makes things even more difficult. Dealing with multiple activities, also known as task loading, can also cause an increase in stress.

With decompression diving we cannot ascend directly to the surface without the risk of decompression illness. As a result it is essential that anyone undertaking decompression diving is able to resolve any potential problem underwater while at the same time managing their buoyancy control in order to hold any decompression stops. This is a set of skills that will not be familiar to most recreational divers and as a result will require additional training and practice.

All of the factors above go towards determining the structure of technical courses. Great emphasis is placed on buoyancy control and in particular being able to manage your buoyancy even when dealing with other problems. Skills are practiced in mid water until problems can be managed without loss of buoyancy control. Team work is also a strong factor in most technical training. Solving a problem with the help of your buddy or team can greatly reduce the stress and risks of the situation. Good teamwork can help to defuse a problem situation before it develops into a full blown incident. The ability to solve problems is developed by providing numerous opportunities to practice this skill and by running through a number of problem situations in a relatively controlled environment. This increases the diver's ability to effectively deal with problems if they ever happen for real.

In general the first time someone attempts a task they will make a mess of it. The second time they may be slightly better and each time they practice they will have more and more chance of getting it right. You only have to think back to the first time you tried to ride a bike, drive a car, play golf, juggle or any number of other examples to see this in practice. The same thing applies to dealing with an emergency situation. If the first time you have had to deal with that kind of situation is when it happens for real then there is a huge amount of psychological pressure, not only do you have to deal with the situation but it is the first time you have ever been in that situation. By practicing for these types of situation you will still have the stress of the emergency but will have the advantage of having dealt with similar situations in the past. This can provide a key psychological advantage and can make the difference between dealing with the problem and succumbing to panic.

One of the most common techniques that technical instructors use to stretch students is to introduce a level of task loading that they are not used to. This is intended to simulate the task loading that might occur in an actual emergency. This gives the divers the chance to experience the feeling of task loading, spot the signs of it in themselves and help them learn strategies for dealing with it. To achieve this instructors aim to push the student slightly outside their comfort zone, then allow the comfort zone to catch up before pushing them slightly further. By the end of the course the student's comfort zone should be much larger than it was at the beginning. Task loading is often introduced by the use of multiple failures. This forces the diver to prioritise and helps them learn how to deal with multiple issues. In real incidents it is not uncommon to have multiple failures as one failure often leads to another

---

21 See BSAC incident reports available online at www.bsac.com/incidentreport/

which leads to another. Focusing on just one problem may result in another, more urgent, problem being ignored. Like many things in life, dealing with multiple problems becomes easier with practice. For this reason students on a technical course will deal with an increasing number of multiple failures. On the first day they may struggle with a single failure and this may easily be enough to push them outside of their comfort zone but after a few days they will be dealing with multiple failures while still inside their comfort zone. During exercises the number of failures will be unrealistically high. If you were to ever have that many real failures on a dive then you would probably give up diving straight away and take up golf! The reason for the extent of the failures is that if you know that you can deal with six simultaneous failures in a training situation then dealing with just two failures in a real situation should still be inside your comfort zone. This can provide another psychological advantage in an emergency as the diver knows that they have dealt with more multiple failures than they are currently faced with.

Task loading and dealing with multiple problems are all ways to increase the stress loading. Again, this is usually a deliberate attempt to give the student a chance to encounter stress and learn to recognise and deal with it. If left unmanaged stress can lead to panic which is the most dangerous state of mind for the technical diver. By giving the students a chance to increase their abilities to deal with stress we can try to reduce the possibilities of panic.

Repetition is also a key factor in technical training. Simply performing a task once is not enough. The goal is for many of the key skills to become instinctive through the use of continual practice. Key skills, such as shutdown drills, will be repeated many times during the course until they start to become instinctive.

Finally, technical training has a strong emphasis on objective feedback of the way in which certain tasks were carried out. The divers who enrol in a technical course are doing so to improve their skills and to achieve the level of proficiency required to dive beyond recreational limits. As such it is essential that instructors are honest and objective about the level to which students perform the skills.

This type of instruction, where candidates are allowed to make their own mistakes, repeat skills until they are mastered, receive honest and open feedback and are pushed outside their comfort zone is often mistaken for military style training. In reality nothing could be further from the truth. The old fashioned image of military training, where a drill sergeant bellows at recruits and berates their attempts in an effort to enforce adherence to the command structure and obedience to orders, is completely at odds to the aims of technical training.

When divers research technical courses and read course reports or talk to other divers they may get the wrong impression of these courses. The descriptions often make the course sound more like a trial of endurance rather than an enjoyable learning experience. Part of the reason for this is that the students are encouraged to treat each exercise as if it is completely for real. This is often carried through into the course reports so that during a dive a student may say that they ran out of air, lost their mask or missed their decompression stop. This can sound terrifying and if it had happened for real, it would have been very dangerous. It can also create the false impression of instructors ripping off masks and turning off cylinders. The reality is actually that the instructor would have given a signal to indicate that the diver should begin to simulate being out of air, or signalled the diver to remove their mask and give it to the instructor. One of the signs of a good instructor is someone who can push a student slightly outside their comfort zone and simulate an appropriate level of failures while at the same time ensuring that it is all carried out in safe and controlled environment. The other reason why course reports inevitably make technical courses sound like Special Forces selection is that once a student has passed there is a normal human desire to make their achievement sound as impressive as possible. To this end the course is described in terms which will make it sounds all the more challenging.

The truth is that technical diving courses are challenging and will significantly improve your diving ability but at the same time are certainly within the range of mere mortals and may even be fun.

# What went wrong?

10

"Experience is a dear teacher, but fools will learn at no other."
Benjamin Franklin

Technical diving, like many other adventurous activities, has a number of risks. These risks are introduced as a result of being underwater, after all none of us can breathe water. Other risks, such as decompression illness, are introduced by the physical pressures of being so far underwater while others are introduced by the gasses or equipment we select to try to reduce one of the other risks. These risks are not accepted lightly and the majority of training for technical divers is covering various techniques to try to reduce these risks to an acceptable level. One of the most useful tools is accident analysis.

Accident analysis involves looking at fatalities or other incidents that have occurred and trying to identify the causes of the incident. Once the cause is known, procedures, equipment, training or guidelines can be changed to try and prevent the same thing from happening again. From these conclusions a set of rules or best practice can be adopted.

The advantage of this type of approach is that we can try to avoid other people making the same mistakes. Diving in general and technical diving in particular has its risks but overall the number of incidents is quite low. This means that most divers will go through their whole diving career without experiencing a major incident and as a result will not have the opportunity of experiencing many of the problems that could potentially occur.

This can be seen in books like *The Last Dive, Shadow Divers* and *Deep Descent.* These books all include a series of descriptions of incidents, many of which ended in fatalities. While reading these books many of today's divers will be amazed at some of the mistakes that were made and may be critical of the choices made by the divers involved. However, it is important to remember that some of these deaths go back 20 or even 30 years. At the time, many of the procedures that we take for granted today, as well as the pitfalls to be avoided, were unknown. It was the lessons from these incidents that lead to many of the procedures we follow today. This means that it is unfair to judge too harshly the original pioneers as they were exploring what was possible. However anyone that continues to make the same mistakes, and ignores the lessons from the past, does not deserve the same consideration.

In the 1960s and 1970s there were a very high number of cave diving fatalities. This led to cave diving being dubbed 'the most dangerous sport in the world'. In order to better understand what was going wrong and to try and prevent the sport from being banned or severely regulated, cave diving pioneer Sheck Exley conducted a careful study of cave diving fatalities.[22] What he discovered was that, in virtually every instance, the same factors kept cropping up. In particular there were three causes that were involved in almost every incident. Another two factors were later added to form the five basic rules of overhead diving and as such are equally applicable to wreck penetration as much as cave diving.

The rules can be remembered using the phrase **T**he **G**ood **D**ivers **A**re **L**iving which takes the first letter of each of the key areas.

> **Training** – The majority of divers who were involved in incidents either had no training for the type of diving they were doing or were diving beyond their training.
>
> **Guideline** – Maintain a continous guideline to the cave or wreck exit
>
> **Depth** – Remain within the safest possible operating limits for your breathing media.
>
> **Air** – Keep two thirds of your gas volumes in reserve to exit the cave or wreck
>
> **Lights** – Always carry three sources of lights.

Figure 11: The Good Divers Are Living

TRAINING

The first rule focuses on appropriate Training. The majority of divers who were involved in incidents either had no training for the type of diving they were doing or were diving beyond their training. There are still many incidents today where

---

22 Exley, S. (1986) Basic Cave Diving: A Blueprint for Survival Fifth Edition. National Speleological Society and free to download from www.nsscds.org

divers get into problems when they undertake some aspect of diving for which they are not qualified or progress beyond their current level of training. In recent years there have been a number of incidents resulting from divers undertaking wreck penetration dives without any appropriate training.

GUIDELINE

The second rule relates to the use of a Guideline. Overhead environment divers should always maintain a continuous guideline to the cave or wreck exit. Without a guideline it can be impossible to locate the exit in low visibility, even if it is only a few metres away. Again there have been a number of recent incidents where divers have been found only metres from the exit but were unable to get out due to limited visibility. However, the use of a guideline can also cause problems. Without the right technique it is easy to get disoriented or caught up in the line. Many of the incidents studied by Exley were caused by divers not using a guideline but almost as many were caused by divers who became entangled in their guideline. The correct technique for line laying is essential and comes back to the first rule – appropriate training.

DEPTH

The third rule refers to the Depth and in particular remaining within the safest possible operating limits for your breathing gas. Operating limits in this case can refer to either the maximum equivalent narcotic depth for the level of nitrogen or the maximum operating depth for the level of oxygen. A significant level of narcosis can reduce your awareness, reasoning and problem solving skills and can increase the likelihood of panic or incorrect responses to a problem. Breathing a gas with an excessive partial pressure of oxygen can lead to convulsions and unconsciousness.

AIR

We always need a supply of air to breathe and so it is essential that our gas planning ensures we have enough breathing gas to complete the dive, even in the case of an emergency. When in an overhead environment, always keep two thirds of your gas volumes in reserve to exit the cave or wreck. This is enough for you and your buddy or enough for you in the case of any problems or increases in breathing rate. A suitable reserve of decompression gasses should also be carried.

LIGHTS

Finally, for any overhead environment it is essential you have enough Light. Always carry three sources of lights. Although it is possible to exit an overhead environment in total darkness if you are using a guideline the ability to see gives a psychological advantage, is faster and allows for more cooperation between you and your buddy or team.

Although these rules were drawn up for overhead environment diving many of them apply equally to all types of technical dives. In particular Training, Depth and Air are key for any form of technical diving. In the 1990s, as technical diving developed and in particular as the focus for technical diving development moved from cave diving to wreck diving, a similar analysis was done and a new set of factors determined[23]. These factors are:-

ATTITUDE:

A proper attitude is essential to conducting technical dives safely. There is no room for recklessness or carelessness. Good technical divers are careful, thorough and know when to call a dive if something doesn't feel right.

KNOWLEDGE:

Without the proper knowledge it is easy to make mistakes. Without knowledge there are no options when problems occur.

TRAINING:

It doesn't matter what level of technical diving is undertaken it is essential to have suitable training. Skills must become second nature and a part of muscle memory. In an emergency skills should be proficient and instinctive, this is only possible with extensive experience.

EXPERIENCE:

Experience is exposure and environmental specific and takes time to build. A training course can give you knowledge but you also need experience. Experience also needs to be relevant. Extensive wreck diving experience does not qualify a diver for cave diving and visa versa. In the past technical diving was restricted to a small set of divers who already had significant experience of recreational diving. With the growing popularity of technical diving it is becoming more and more common for divers to move on to some type of technical diving with comparatively few dives. It is especially important for these divers to build up their experience slowly to ensure they do not get into a situation for which they are not prepared.

EQUIPMENT:

Every dive requires an appropriate set of tools. Equipment should be suitable for the dive, suitable for the diver, streamlined and safe. Equipment maintenance is also critical. Diving equipment is your life support system while you are underwater and should be cared for as such.

Training courses from the main technical diving organisations are all built upon these fundamental principles. In many cases the exercises carried out in the classes are designed to provide tools to avoid the incidents that have occurred in the past.

The introduction of new technology into technical diving is, on one level, changing the way we dive but at the same time is highlighting the importance of the basic rules. Rebreathers are significantly more complicated than open circuit diving equipment and there are more opportunities for equipment problems. It is essential that rebreathers are maintained properly and sufficient care is taken when setting up the equipment. Experienced open circuit technical divers are moving onto rebreathers but forgetting that experience must be relevant. Significant open circuit experience does not mean that you can dive to the same level on a rebreather without building up a suitable amount of rebreather experience. In a similar way the introduction of mixed gas PC planning programs or wrist computers means that divers can plan and execute dives without necessarily understanding how all the planning factors such as gas reserves, narcotic

---

23   Menduno, M & Deans, B. (1993) Blueprint for survival 2.0 aquaCorps June 1993 and widely available online.

depth and oxygen toxicity fit together, how one can influence another and the implications in the case of an emergency. Both PC planning tools and wrist computers can be a very useful tool but only if the diver has the appropriate training and knowledge to use them safely. Finally the internet has had a big influence on technical diving. There is a huge amount of knowledge available on the internet but it is often difficult to tell good advice from bad or downright dangerous advice. Reading about a skill or technique on the internet (or in a magazine or even a book) is not the same as practicing it repeatedly in open water

Another common factor that occurs time and time again in accident analysis is the combination of stress and multiple failures. In many cases there is no single factor that can be definitively identified as the cause of the incident. However in many cases it is a combination of the factors already described that causes the problem. Any one of these factors on its own is unlikely to cause an accident but when there is a combination of several then overall it is possible that they may collectively cause an incident. The impact of multiple factors can raise the stress level, reducing your ability to deal effectively with any problems and ultimately leading to panic.

Diagram 2: The Incident Pit

This is sometimes described using a concept known as 'the incident pit' which is shown in Diagram 2 above. The sides of the incident pit become steeper as more and more problems occur. A single problem can easily be resolved using the standard response to that problem. The sides of the pit are still shallow at this point and as a result it is relatively easy to step back out of the incident pit. Nevertheless as more problems occur the sides get steeper and steeper and it becomes increasingly difficult to get back out. This is because of the stress of dealing with multiple problems, having to prioritise which problem to solve first as well as the fact that one problem may make it harder to solve another problem. Eventually a point is reached where it is impossible to escape the pit.

Another way of looking at the issue of dealing with multiple problems was proposed by safety researcher James Reason. He created what is known as the Swiss cheese model of accident causation. In this model the layers of cheese are the barriers that stop an accident occurring. A hazard will not cause an accident if the barrier is in place and effective. Be that as it may, the barriers are like Swiss cheese in that they have holes in them. The holes appear and disappear, change in size and move around based on the effectiveness of the barrier. If a hazard occurs and there is a hole in the barrier then that hazard will not be blocked by that barrier. There are a number of layers of cheese and even if the hazard is not blocked by the first barrier then hopefully it will be blocked by a subsequent layer. A hazard will only cause an accident if the holes in each layer of cheese happen to line up so that the hazard can go straight through each of the barriers.

In the diagram opposite I have labelled each of the barriers to illustrate how this might work in a diving related context. The first barrier is the training that the diver has received. This should have equipped the diver to avoid or deal with any hazards that may occur. If the diver received poor training this results in a hole in the barrier as they are not able to avoid or deal with that hazard. Even so a diver deciding to ignore their training can also result in a hole in this layer. The next layer is equipment. The correct equipment, properly maintained and used by a knowledgeable diver can be used to block a hazard. Getting caught up in line (a hazard) is easily resolved (blocked) if the diver has a suitable and accessible cutting device (no accident). If the diver does not have a suitable cutting device then that will not necessarily cause a problem unless they are caught up in the line, i.e. unless the hazard occurs. The third level is preparation/skills. It is all very well to learn how to deal with problems or to know how to plan a dive but that does not help unless the diver puts these ideas into practice. If the diver has planned their dive thoroughly and practiced their skills regularly then this barrier will be effective and they will be able to deal with most hazards and will be able to avoid an accident. If the dive has not been planned and the diver has not practiced the skills required to deal with an emergency then there will be a hole in this layer. The last level is teamwork. Problems that the diver not trained, equipped or prepared to deal with, can be resolved by their buddy or team and so this last layer can still be effective in stopping the hazard becoming an accident. For all that, a poor buddy or weak team can introduce a hole in this layer which means that the barrier will not stop the hazard from becoming an accident.

As you can see there are numerous opportunities to prevent a hazard becoming an accident. This is why divers often get away with making huge mistakes. Even though they are introducing a huge hole into one of the layers there may be no hazard present or, even if the hazard is present, it may be blocked by another barrier. As you go through this book you will see that many of the sections are specifically aimed at blocking up some of the holes in the layers of cheese. The knowledge contained in each chapter has often been gained through accident analysis and is aimed at ensuring that despite the presence of hazards we can use that knowledge to avoid accidents.

Despite all the effort that has gone into identifying the causes of accidents and looking at procedures to reduce the likelihood of them happening, it is all too common to see people breaking the established procedures. This is all the more frustrating when incidents occur which result in fatalities that could have been avoided. There are two reasons why divers tend to ignore the results of accident analysis. The first is that, as previously mentioned, most divers will go through their diving careers without experiencing any major incidents and as a result they become complacent about the risks. They have taken short cuts and ignored the procedures in the past and nothing has gone wrong and so they assume that they can ignore the procedures each time and get away with it or that the procedures are overly conservative. They may even have had some problems and been able to deal with them. As a result they assume that the problem is manageable, however, when that problem occurs in conjunction with another problem it may not seem quite so manageable. If they are lucky they will continue to get away with their shortcuts but every so often a more serious problem occurs or a combination of problems occur and they don't get away with it. The second reason is that for technical diving the implications of getting things wrong can be fatal and so you don't always get a chance to learn from your mistakes.

This is why accident analysis is so important. We don't have to experience every possible failure ourselves in order to learn from it.

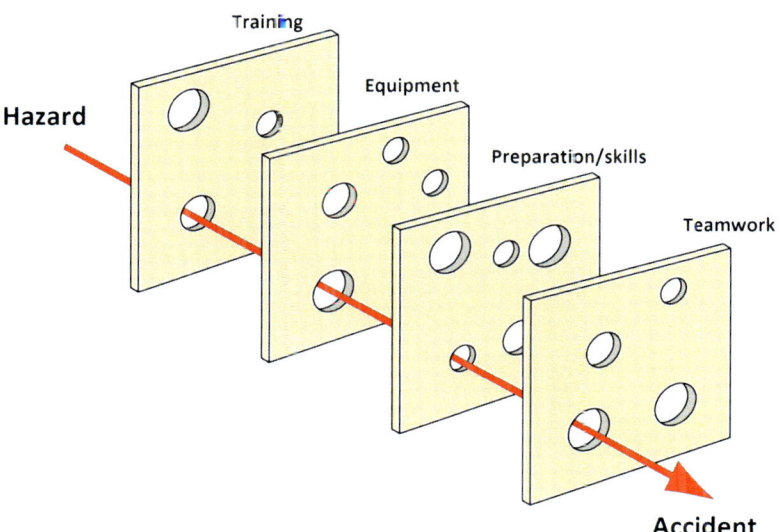

Diagram 3: Swiss Cheese Model

Complacency

11

Complacency (com·pla·cen·cy)
A feeling of contentment or self-satisfaction, especially when coupled with an unawareness of danger, trouble, or controversy.

There are many risks that have to be considered when technical diving; decompression illness, oxygen toxicity, narcosis, cold, equipment failure and many other aspects all need to be considered. However, these risks are not the biggest danger we face. They may cause problems, incidents and even fatalities but there is an even more dangerous risk we have to face. A risk which can lead to any of the problems listed above. The biggest risk to any technical diver, indeed to most divers, is complacency.

The single most effective thing that divers can do to reduce the number of incidents and fatalities is to stick to the procedures they were taught in their training courses. It doesn't matter if it was a PADI Open Water course or a TDI Advanced trimix course the procedures taught in these courses are there for a reason. They have been shown to be the things that prevent accidents. For technical diving in particular accident analysis is a key part of designing training courses. We look at incidents and fatalities and put together a set of rules and procedures designed to avoid those situations happening again. Despite this we see, time and time again, that accidents occur because divers break the key rules they were taught during their training. This is usually down to complacency.

The single most effective thing that divers can do to reduce the number of incidents and fatalities is to stick to the procedures they were taught in their training courses.

There are numerous examples of complacency causing incidents and even fatalities. Many technical divers have incorrectly switched to the wrong decompression gas after failing to check the cylinder they were switching to or failing to mark up the cylinder correctly Many rebreather divers have jumped in knowing that they have a warning showing on their rebreather, a known fault; insufficient diluent gas or limited time left on their scrubber. Very experienced divers and instructors have died in just a couple of meters of water despite having successfully achieved hundreds of deeper dives. In each case complacency was a major part of the problem.

Complacency affects a number of aspects of our diving. The first and probably the most important is in the procedures we follow. We are taught right from our first course that buddy checks are essential; as we progress they are reinforced. In technical diving courses they are again reinforced as a way of catching problems or omissions. Despite all this it is very unusual to see certain groups of divers, either recreational or technical, routinely performing buddy checks. Every single technical diving agency insists that divers analyse their gas and mark up their cylinders before every dive. Especially when multiple cylinders are used it is easy to forget about this unless it is a standard routine. Despite this many technical divers get lazy when it comes to analysing and marking up their cylinders. The same applies to gas switches. Switching to the wrong gas or at the wrong depth can easily lead to oxygen toxicity and yet many divers neglect the gas switching procedures that they are taught on courses. All the technical agencies also teach that divers should keep sufficient reserve gas or carry sufficient bailout in the case of a rebreather. However it is common to see people pushing well past their reserve limits or carrying bailout that is insufficient for the dives that they are doing.

Many divers also get complacent about equipment maintenance. We cannot breathe water and so our dive equipment, whether it is a twinset or rebreather, is the only thing that is going to allow us to breathe underwater. For this reason it is essential that it is in working order. However, it is common to see divers neglecting equipment maintenance or diving with clearly inadequate kit. One of the areas where a significant amount of complacency can build up is narcosis. Trimix allows you to control the level of narcosis experienced irrespective of the depth you are actually at. Many divers push the limits by using air at depths beyond a sensible depth or by using minimal levels of helium resulting in a higher level of narcosis than is sensible.

Divers also become complacent about performing build up dives. It is important to build up your experience by using build up dives before attempting any type of deep dive. This is especially true after a long layoff such as a long winter break. It does not make sense to jump in and start doing the depth you were diving at the end of the previous year without some level of build up dives. Despite this many divers completely ignore build up dives and jump straight back in for a major dive. This tends to be done more by experienced divers. It is the reason why there is always such a spike in incidents at Easter as this is often the time during which people carry out their first dives of the year. Finally many divers get complacent about the level of physical health and fitness required for technical diving. Carrying large numbers of cylinders, maintaining stability on a rocking boat, spending a long time in the water and rescuing a casualty all require a level of health and fitness. While it is possible to get away without this level when things are going well, any complacency in this area, will be shown in an emergency situation

Of course this raises a number of questions, why is complacency such a problem? And if it really is such a problem then why don't we see more incidents? The answers to both these questions are interrelated. The first reason is that despite the various risks that can occur in technical diving or in any type of recreational diving, it is in fact a very safe activity. There are not that many incidents and although divers know the potential risks, they do not really believe that it will happen to them or anyone they know. This is combined with the fact that many divers break the rules day in and day out and yet they get away with it. Many of the signs of complacency listed above on their own will not cause a problem but when other factors come into play it is only then that they become important. Of course this means that the diver can break the rules time and time again and get away with it and therefore they believe that the rules are overly conservative or don't apply to them. In fact they will continue to get away with breaking the rules right up to the point where they don't get away with it. We can see this every year in the incident reports. In almost every case there is a significant exception to one of the key safety rules. Often the diver will have broken this rule many times in the past but in this particular case some other factor combined to create an incident and another statistic.

Equipment can also lead to complacency. Modern equipment is extremely reliable and in many cases divers assume that it is so reliable that it will not go wrong. As a result they become complacent and take more risks than if they had been more worried about equipment failure. If, on the odd occasion, an equipment failure does occur they are then in a worse position and have a greater problem to deal with.

Trainees or newly qualified divers rarely suffer from complacency. They are often nervous and worried about what they are doing. This can be a good thing as that nervousness stops them from being complacent. They know their limits and are wary of the underwater environment. This is the reason that, if properly trained, newly qualified divers rarely get involved in fatal accidents. Ironically it is more experienced divers that are more likely to suffer from complacency and the more experienced they are the more likely it is that they will get complacent. Experience can be represented by length of time diving, number of dives or by qualification level.

Each of these different aspects of experience brings it's own problems. Some divers who have been diving for many years believe that simply through time they will gain experience. They may also be seen as more experienced by friends and other club members. However, they may have been diving for a long time but they may not have done that much diving. Someone who has been diving for 10 years but who only does 20 or 30 dives per year will only have a total of 200-300 dives. In addition by spreading the dives out they may not get the chance to build on their experience and hence their skills may stagnate after the first couple of years. These divers are particularly at risk after a period of non-diving, for example after a long winter break. This is another one of the reasons why there are often so many incidents around Easter. Divers who have had a long break, are rusty and yet consider themselves to be experienced, get into problems due to their lack of recent diving activity.

Divers who have built up a significant amount of dives can also become complacent. Divers who build up hundreds of dives (or hours on a rebreather) but do this in a single location are not extending their experience. If you have done 100 dives at a single site then have you really done 100 dives or have you done a single dive 100 times? Finally qualification levels can be a source of complacency. Once a diver gets to a particular level of diving or instructing qualification then they may feel that this gives them a level of experience that allows them to take risks that would otherwise not be safe. A qualification in itself does not guarantee experience.

Just before performing your deepest dive you are likely to be nervous, more than a little anxious and will probably double or triple check everything. All of this is the very opposite of complacency and shows someone who appreciates the risks of what they are doing. For this reason it is comparatively unusual for technical divers to suffer any of the problems of complacency on one of these 'peak' dives. Nevertheless many experienced technical divers and even instructors have died on dives that are much more shallow than they are capable of. It is when we are doing 'just a shallow dive' that we are at risk of becoming complacent. Of course the definition of deep and shallow will vary from person to person. If a technical diver is capable of doing dives of 130m/430ft then 60m/200ft or even 80m/260ft may be considered shallow. Of course these depths are still significant depths at the limits of what recreational technical divers where doing less than 20 years ago. Even 30m/100ft or 10m/33ft is still deep enough to get a problem and so experienced technical divers need to be very wary of becoming complacent on 'shallow' dives.

All training agencies agree that complacency is a bad thing. Despite this, in some aspects, agencies and instructors may unwittingly be making the situation worse. Some cold water based instructors promote the idea that cold water diving is the only 'real' diving and that if you learn to dive in cold water, such as in the UK, you can dive anywhere. While it is true that cold water conditions do develop strong skills this can then lead to complacency when diving abroad. I have seen numerous UK divers ending up much deeper than anticipated in the Red Sea due to being deceived by the clarity of the water. Equally agencies that teach that their approach is the only correct approach and build up a myth that their skills are far superior to any other agency, are also building complacency in their members.

As technical divers, complacency is the biggest risk we take and we need to be aware when this insidious condition is overtaking us. If you are nervous about a dive then that's a good thing as it will help to prevent complacency. However, if you find that you feel very comfortable about an upcoming technical dive; feel that this dive is easily within your capabilities, feel that it doesn't require all the precautions and considerations of a peak dive', then beware. You are detecting the first signs of complacency.

> If you are nervous about a dive then that's a good thing as it will help to prevent complacency

PART 3
Equipment

Chapter 12. Equipment Configuration 65
Chapter 13. Twinset configuration questions 67
Chapter 14. Side mount 73
Chapter 15. Backplate, Wing and Harness 77
Chapter 16. Hogarthian Equipment Configuration 83
Chapter 17. Reely important equipment 89
Chapter 18. Staying Comfortable 95
Chapter 19. How many cylinders do you need? 99
Chapter 20. Dive Computers 105
Chapter 21. What's in your Argon bottle? 111

Equipment Configuration

12

"The farther one goes, the less one knows" **Tao Te Ching**

One of the most visible differences between recreational and technical diving is in the equipment that is used.

The majority of recreational divers worldwide use a single cylinder, BCD and wetsuit. There are local variations, for example, many UK based recreational divers wear a drysuit and pony cylinder due to the local conditions, whereas for many divers in warm water locations, these would be sophisticated and advanced types of equipment. Nevertheless, on the whole recreational diving kit is very similar. Technical diving however, uses very different equipment. Twinsets are the standard for open circuit diving rather than a single cylinder. Wing, backplate and harness is much more common than a BCD and decompression gas is worn in an additional stage cylinder that may be as big as the main cylinder used by many recreational divers. Technical diving equipment is based on two main principles; redundancy and streamlining. If the equipment is essential for the dive then we want redundancy. So an additional regulator, method of telling depth and time, DSMB and mask are all items of backup equipment carried by a technical diver. This then has to be balanced by the requirement to be streamlined and only take what is really necessary. Technical divers aim to be as streamlined as possible in the water. This is to reduce the drag when swimming through the water but more importantly so that they can get to every piece of essential kit without having to wade through lots of unnecessary other equipment. Of course just having the right kit or the latest configuration does not make you a technical diver but it is an essential part of getting started.

As an alternative to twinsets technical divers also use rebreathers. A rebreather is a much more sophisticated setup than open circuit and requires additional training and preparation but it also offers significant benefits in terms of gas supplies for the technical diver. There are many divers who choose to dive with a rebreather within recreational diving depths and there are a number of new rebreathers being launched that are aimed at recreational divers. So using a rebreather does not necessarily make you a technical diver and a number of manufacturers have introduced "recreational rebreathers" but on the whole the majority of rebreathers are still used for more technical diving. Rebreathers are discussed in more detail in Chapter 31.

Twinset configuration questions

13

"On the occasion of every accident that befalls you, remember to turn to yourself and inquire what power you have for turning it to use" **Epictetus**

In the previous section I mentioned the fact that many internet forums and mailing lists have been the site of a number of contentious discussions on various aspects of technical diving. No aspect of technical diving generates as many arguments as equipment configuration. In this section I will look at some of these contentious arguments and try to lay out both sides of the various arguments. The idea is to provide an objective view of these topics, something that is not always easy to come by. For non divers or even for standard recreational divers the strength of feeling on some of these issues can seem baffling. Some of the arguments take on an almost religious fervour.

Anyone looking to start technical diving will need to invest in specific equipment and making a choice here can affect all future decisions. One aspect that is often overlooked is that many of the points that we will look at are often argued in isolation. So people will argue the merits of bungied wings against those of unbungied wings, steel stage cylinder versus aluminium, stages on the left versus stages on the right. However what few people realise is that many of these discussions affect each other, a decision in one place will have an effect on subsequent decisions. By choosing a specific set of equipment a new technical diver may be constraining their future options. For this reason we will start off by looking at the different issues surrounding what for most people is their first step on the road to technical diving: a twinset.

The first issue to be decided when buying a twinset is what size do I go for? It is common to see twinsets made up of cylinders ranging from 7L/50cf cylinders through to 10L/72cf, 12L/85cf and 15L/108cf. Larger sizes such as 18L/120cf, 20L/130cf and even larger are possible but not very common now. A twinset made up of twin 7L/50cf cylinders is a nice light setup but does not really have the volume of gas required for technical diving; after all it has less gas than a single 15L/108cft cylinder. As such it is not really suitable for decompression diving. These tend to be used by divers who want additional redundancy on relatively shallow dives without having to use a pony cylinder or by technical divers who want to use a similar configuration for recreational dives. Twin

10L/72cf cylinders are the smallest conceivable size suitable for any type of decompressions diving. They have the advantage of still being quite light, they are similar in weight to a single 15L/108cf cylinder and a pony. There are a number of disadvantages though. Gas volumes can still be a limiting factor with these cylinders, especially for deeper dives or if you want to do a second dive. The other disadvantage of twin 10L/72cf cylinders is that they are very short cylinders. When wearing the cylinders we want the valves to be at the same height irrespective of the height of the cylinder in order to be able to reach the valves. This results in the cylinders sitting very high up the divers back, which means that the bottom of the cylinders are quite a way above the bench that the diver is sitting on and they cannot rest the cylinders on the bench without leaning back at an uncomfortable angle. This can put a strain on the diver's back and shoulders if he is waiting for some time before jumping in. A further disadvantage is that because they sit high up on the diver's back they tend to cause the diver to be head heavy. This makes it more difficult to maintain a horizontal position in the water.

Twin 12L/85cf cylinders are longer than 10L/72cf cylinders and hence avoid two of these disadvantages. When sitting down the average height diver will find that the bottom of the 12L/85cf cylinders will rest comfortably on the bench. As they are longer the weight is also distributed along the diver's body and so they are less head heavy which makes it easier to maintain a horizontal position in the water. The larger size also provides additional gas volume. For many divers moving from recreational diving to technical diving they will often have 12L/85cf cylinders available which can be re-used in a twinset and even if they have to be bought from new, the easy availability of 12L/85cf cylinders makes it straightforward to obtain suitable cylinders. Of course the larger size also has the disadvantage that twin 12L/85cf cylinders are heavier than twin 10L/72cf cylinders. This is considered a fair trade off by the majority of technical divers and twin 12L/85cf cylinders are by far the most common configuration for technical divers.

Twin 15L/108cf cylinders provide even more gas and are used by divers wanting to go even deeper, typically beyond 60m(200ft), further into caves, or by those with very high breathing rates. However, they are heavier and this weight can create additional problems. The excessive size makes them impractical for many dives and the extra weight can result in the diver having to work harder and breathe more which ends up defeating the point of having larger cylinders in the first place. Twinsets comprising cylinders of 18L, 20L or more are occasionally used for very deep dives but this is no longer very common as rebreathers are often used for dives that previously would have required cylinders of these sizes.

	Advantages	Disadvantages
2 x 7	Light	Very limited gas volumes
2 x 10	Fairly light	Limited gas volumes Horizontal trim affected Unable to support weight
2 x 12	Good gas volumes Horizontal trim easier Easier to support bottom of cylinder Easily available	Can be heavy for lightly built divers
2 x 15	Additional gas volume	Heavy

Table 1: Advantages and disadvantages of a variety of twinset sizes

Once the diver has decided on the size of cylinders the next decision is whether they use them as independent cylinders or manifold them together. Independent cylinders involve having two completely separate cylinders with no connection between the two whereas a manifolded system has a manifold which connects the two cylinders together. This manifold usually has an isolating valve in the middle which allows the two cylinders to be isolated in the case of a free flow or other problem.

Independents have the advantage of complete redundancy. It doesn't matter what happens to one cylinder, you will always have a second, completely separate backup. They are also fairly easy to set up. For a typical diver who has a single 12L/85cf cylinder plus a second as a spare they can just use the two together. This can be done using twinning bands on some existing BCDs. For this reason it's very easy to get started using this route. The disadvantages of independents are that you must manage the usage of gas between the two cylinders. It is no good breathing one cylinder all the way down then switching to the other because if there was a problem with the second you have no redundancy. Therefore, it is common to switch from one cylinder to the other every 50 bar/700 psi or after breathing one down a third. This is no problem on a normal dive but in an emergency it's possible that the diver will forget to switch.

If the diver experiences a freeflow then one potential advantage of independents is that they do not need to switch off the free flowing regulator as they still have the gas available in the other cylinder and therefore could leave the freeflowing regulator to bleed down. This appears to remove the requirement to be able to reach their valves. However, this is not such an advantage as it first appears because the diver may still wish to shut off the valve as the bubbles will be very distracting and may cause buoyancy problems. This reintroduces the need to be able to reach your valves. This may not be easy for a number of reasons. Divers often adopt independents so that they do not have to reach their valves or because they know they cannot reach them. Divers who use independents are less likely to practice reaching their valves than those using a manifold due to their perception that they are less likely to need to be able to reach them. Finally, many independent twinsets are set up using standard cylinder and standard valves. This has the disadvantage that the right hand valve will be pointing out but the left hand valve will be pointing in and will be all but impossible to reach. It is possible to buy "handed" valves so that both point out but these are not common and for divers who are using existing standard cylinders it is usual to keep the standard valves.

Once shut off, the gas left in the cylinder is now inaccessible and the diver must complete his ascent on the other cylinder. The only way to access the gas within the cylinder is to 'feather' the valve. This involves opening the valve, taking a breath and then shutting it again. Although possible this is not easy and again, can only be done if the diver can easily reach and manipulate their valves. The biggest disadvantage of independents arises if the diver is using a long hose because it can be confusing in the case of his buddy being out of air.

As the diver on independents is switching from one regulator to the other then at times he will have the long hose in his mouth and at other times he will have the short hose. When it comes to donating this can cause confusion as, ideally, he will want to donate the long hose. In order to do this the diver has a number of options. They can think about whether they are breathing the long or short hose and then donate the long one, either from their mouth or from the restraining device. Of course this introduces a delay and the potential for confusion into the process just at the point where delay and confusion are least welcome. The other option is to donate a set regulator each time, either the one in the mouth or the one in a restraining device. This removes the delay but introduces the possibility that around half of the time the diver will donate the short hose and then will have to try and swap them over. This may well be difficult as an out of gas diver may not want to give back a working regulator and you may be forced to do an ascent on the short hose even when a long hose is available. Finally, the other option is to have two long hoses, one on each regulator. This removes the dilemma of which regulator to donate but introduces a further problem of how to safely and cleanly store two long hoses.

The problem of which regulator to donate is, of course, only relevant if you are diving with a buddy. If you do not have a buddy this is not an issue and for this reason independent cylinders with two short hoses are popular with solo divers.

A manifolded twinset has the opposite set of advantages and disadvantages. The major issue with this configuration is that it is essential the diver can do a shutdown. If they are unable to at least close the manifold isolator then in the case of a free flow both cylinders will be drained. In effect the diver is diving on one large single cylinder rather than a twinset. It's frightening the number of divers who dive a manifolded twinset but don't know whether they could shutdown in an emergency or even worse those that know that they cannot reach their valves but insist on diving a manifolded twinset because it is the fashionable setup. The ability to do an effective shutdown is essential, as all the time they are struggling to complete the shutdown, gas is leaking from both cylinders. One big advantage of a manifolded setup is that once a valve is shutdown the gas in that cylinder can still be accessed, via the manifold, by the regulator on the other post. In addition during normal dives no gas switching is required. The diver breathes from the one regulator, usually on the right hand post, but because the manifold is open, they use the gas evenly from both cylinders. In addition, if the diver is breathing the long hose then he always knows to donate the long hose from his mouth. This is an advantage as the drill for donating in an out of air situation is more straightforward and can be practiced in order to become second nature.

	Advantages	**Disadvantages**
Independent	Complete redundancy Easy to set up	Requires gas switching Unable to access gas in case of shutting off the valve Confusion when using long hose
Manifolded	No gas switching required Can access gas in cylinder even after post is shut down Donating long hose is easier	Essential that the diver can do a shutdown Loss of gas while doing shutdown

Table 2: Advantages and disadvantages of independent and manifolded twinsets

Figure 12: An inverted twinset

The next choice that the twinset diver faces is whether to have the cylinders upright, i.e. with the valves at the top, or inverted, with the valves at the bottom. There are three reasons why divers look to invert their twinsets. The first is to make it easier to reach the valves to do a shutdown. The second is to protect the valves from damage when in an overhead environment such as a wreck or a cave. The third and last reason is because that's the way Navy divers have it. The first of these is undoubtedly true, it is much easier to reach your valves and do a shutdown when the cylinders are inverted. This is the real advantage of an inverted twinset and for anyone that cannot reach their valves it is an option worth considering. The other two reasons are less valid in my opinion. Any argument that starts with "if you are in an overhead environment and you bang your valves" is a slightly tenuous argument. I do a lot of wreck penetration diving and whenever I'm in an overhead environment my head is slightly in front of my valves. If I was going to bang my valves hard enough to damage them then it's likely that I would also be banging my head hard enough to damage it as well. Realistically, in this type of restricted overhead environment I would be manoeuvring so carefully that there wouldn't be the momentum to do any sort of damage. Inverting, with all the associated disadvantages seems an over the top solution for such an unlikely problem.

The last of the reasons, that it's the way the Navy dives, is really just a fashion argument. Navy divers use a completely different style of diving to recreational or technical diving and this type of setup suits their operations. It doesn't mean it is necessarily the best for technical diving. Finally Navy divers have moved on and these days you are more likely to see a Navy diver wearing a single and pony with a BCD as an inverted twinset.

Inverting also has a number of disadvantages. The first is that most diving equipment is designed to be used in conjunction with upright cylinders. This means that the invert diver always has to adjust equipment and buy non-standard equipment. For example, hose lengths are designed on the assumption that they come from just behind the head to around the head and chest area. For an invert dive they need custom length hoses for almost everything. The wing hose, for example, must come from the lower back area, up the back, over the shoulder and back down the front to the wing inflator. This makes the configuration expensive to set up and difficult to find spare hoses. In order for an inverted twinset to stand up when not being worn a stand or other valve protector is required. Without this the twinset would be standing on the valves which would be unstable and almost certainly damage the valves. Even with a valve guard it is easier to store an inverted twinset with the cylinders upright and so the invert owner will be continually having to turn the twinset around to kit up or stow the equipment.

With an upright twinset it is more difficult to reach the valves in order to perform a shutdown. While some divers will never be able to reach their valves, either due to injury, stature or some other reason, the vast majority of divers, with the right training and some practice should be able to reach their valves.

	Advantages	**Disadvantages**
Upright	Standard hose lengths No need for valve guard/stands Easier to manage	Training/practice required to reach valves
Inverted	Easier to reach valves Protection in an overhead environment	Non-standard hose lengths Valve guard/stand required Continually turning over the twinset

Table 3: Advantages and disadvantages of upright and inverted twinsets

With the arguments on each side of these issues there is clearly scope for many differences of opinion. Despite this there is a growing consensus in the technical diving world. If you look around most technical diving boats then you will see that for dives in the 30-60m(100-200ft) range the majority of twinset divers in the UK and much of Europe have adopted twin 12L/85cf cylinders, manifolded with an isolator and mounted upright. In other parts of the world the divers may use twin 11L/80cf aluminum cylinders but other than that the basic configuration is unchanged. Although there are other valid options this combination of equipment selection provides a solid basis for a technical diving configuration.

Side mount 14

"You need a little bit of insanity to do great things." **Henry Rollins**

In addition to the various options for configuring a twinset there is another option for using twin cylinders. The side mount approach to configuration mounts the cylinders on the diver's side rather than on their back.

The concept of side mount diving originated from cave diving in the UK, during the 1960s. During explorations of Wookey Hole, Swildon's Hole and other underground systems, divers occasionally encountered submerged passages that blocked further exploration. These cavers began using scuba equipment specifically to progress beyond underwater areas. However, because they operated in very confined spaces, and most exploration remained primarily 'dry', they began experimenting and improvising with extremely minimalist configurations, minimising bulk, allowing cylinders to be easily removed and replaced, and retaining the capacity to squeeze through the tightest restrictions.

During the 1970s the 'English system', as it was initially known, began to be incorporated by Florida cave divers[24]. These cave systems are predominantly 'wet' and involved much longer in water time rather than 'dry' caving; thus more emphasis was paid towards developing the diving performance of the system, in particular buoyancy and trim. Divers required buoyancy control devices for extended finning and began shifting the location of the cylinders from against the thigh, up to the armpit and against the torso. Some of these American developments were then incorporated back into UK cave diving.[25]

In recent years side mount has seen an increase in popularity and has been adopted in a range of other areas. Some divers now use side mount configurations for open ocean technical diving and even for recreational diving. A number of major diving manufacturers now produce dedicated side mount equipment systems.

Side mount offers a number of advantages over conventional back mount configurations. The first advantage is flexibility. Unlike back-mounted configurations, acquiring and transporting side mount suitable cylinders is often much more convenient and accessible. Side mount diving configuration allows the travelling diver to conduct technical and/or overhead environment dives without having to source traditional back-mounted twinsets. When diving in remote locations, the transportation of diving cylinders, especially by hand, is considerably easier.

Unlike back-mounted cylinders, the side mount diver has immediate access to and a clear view of, the regulators and

---

24 Kakuk, Brian; Heinerth, Jill (2010). Side Mount Profiles. Heinerth Productions.

25 Price, Duncan. (2015 . Underwater Potholer. Whittles Publishing

tank valves of their cylinders. This enables immediate problem identification and allows swifter resolution, without having to adopt the traditional shutdown drills which require a certain level of flexibility.

Side mount diving configuration places the cylinders under the diver's armpits, in line with their body. This decreases water resistance which results in improved air consumption and reduced fatigue while also allowing the diver to pass through smaller restrictions than would otherwise be possible with back-mounted cylinders. The flexibility to remove tanks, and propel them in front, allows the diver to pass through very small passages and holes when penetration diving — being limited only by the size of the diver and their other equipment. In addition, mounting the cylinders next to the diver's body and beneath their armpits, serves to protect vulnerable valves and regulator first-stages from impact or accidental shut-down through contact with a ceiling. It also significantly reduces the risk of entanglement behind the diver.

Many side mount divers will testify that side mount diving configuration offers greater stability in the water and can make it easier to achieve good trim. The ability to attach, remove and replace cylinders while in the water allows the diver to avoid ever having to carry heavy back-mounted cylinders. This is combined with reduced physical exertion when conducting regulator shut-down procedures, which is a major benefit to technical divers who suffer from shoulder or back discomfort or reduced mobility from old injuries.

A side mount system is in many ways the same as an independent twinset. It has all the same advantages as independents for gas management but has the added advantage of making it much easier to reach the valves in the case of a problem. This means that it is easier to shut down a leaking valve or even to feather the valve in the case of a free-flow.

Despite all of these advantages there are also a number of disadvantages of side mount systems. The first is that, like independent twinsets, the diver will need to switch from one cylinder to another in order to maintain sufficient gas reserves in both. This also means that donation to an OOG (out of gas) diver can be more complicated as the side mount diver will sometimes be breathing from the long hose and sometimes from the short hose.

The other complication with side mount diving is that although with two cylinders the system is extremely clean, simple and streamlined, this starts to break down once additional decompression gas cylinders are added. The additional decompression gasses are also worn under the arms and so we start to get multiple stages on each side. This reduces the streamlining but also introduces significant gas switching issues. The side mount diver will regularly switch from one cylinder to the other. However, when switching from the left hand cylinder to the right hand cylinder, the diver will need to put in place gas switch procedures to ensure that they are in fact switching to the bottom gas cylinder under their right arm rather than the rich deco mix which is also mounted under their right arm. When carrying out dives with three or more decompression gasses, the streamlining benefit of side mount is completely lost and the configuration become much less advantageous.

Finally kitting up with side mount is much easier in the water than with back mount but kitting up on a dive boat can be considerably more of an issue. Side mount divers tend to take up more room than back mount divers on a bench seat and this may be an issue when space is tight. In addition, with some side mount systems the diver will only clip on their cylinder once they are on the water or will need to adjust the cylinders when they are in the water. This is fine for cave diving where they may be kitting up in a sheltered entrance pool but is impractical when jumping off a dive boat with a current running.

It is clear that side mount is a very effective tool with some major benefits for some dive applications but it is not necessarily the right tool for all applications.

Backplate, Wing and Harness

15

"The man who has no imagination has no wings." **Muhammad Ali**

Twinset diving doesn't necessarily have to mean using a backplate, wing and harness. There are plenty of divers who use a twinset with a standard jacket style BCD. The Buddy Commando, that standard of the UK club diving scene for many years, can easily be used for twinset diving. However the majority of twinset divers eventually migrate to a backplate and wing configuration, especially if they then progress further into technical diving and start using stage cylinders.

This type of setup has a number of advantages. A wing provides buoyancy in the same location as the twinset and so is more effective at counteracting the weight of the twinset. Having the buoyancy behind the diver but next to the twinset helps to support the weight of the twinset and lifts the twinset off the divers back. All of this means that a wing is usually considered a more comfortable way to provide the buoyancy required for a twinset.

When it comes to the style of wing to choose the longest running discussion is whether to go for a bungied or unbungied wing. This is probably one of the most controversial decisions in technical diving and one that prompts the most disagreement. A bungied wing uses bungie cord, surgical tubing or some other method to squeeze the material in the wing into a smaller shape. On the other hand an unbungied wing leaves the wing to adopt it's natural shape.

The main advantage of a bungied wing is that it means a single wing can be used for all diving configurations. A very large wing with 100 pounds[26] of lift provides more lift than the majority of technical divers will ever need. However, with bungies this will be squeezed down to a manageable size and only expand as it is inflated when that lift is required. This means that the wing can still be worn with a single 12L/85cf cylinder, twin 12L/85cf cylinders or even a twin 18L/120cf twinset with multiple stages. Of course this gives the advantage that a single wing can be used with any configuration. This contrasts with the situation where an unbungied wing cannot be constrained down to a manageable size when only part of the lift is required. The wing will stay the same size at all times. This leads to the situation where wings must be matched to the size of cylinder they will be used with. Wings that are two large for the cylinder(s) in use will wrap up around the side of the cylinder and can cause problems when trying to dump air. As a result you will need different wings for different cylinder configurations. You can get a 30 pound single cylinder wing which provides the right amount of lift

---

[26] I have used pounds when referring to the buoyancy characteristics as they are usually described in this way. To convert this to kg simply divide by 2.2.

and the right shape for a single cylinder setup. Alternatively you can get a 45-50 pound wing that provides the right amount of lift for twin 12L/85cf cylinders and stages or larger wings that provide the right lift and size for larger cylinders and additional stage cylinders. If you always dive the same cylinder configuration this is not a problem but if you switch configurations then this will be a disadvantage.

Bungied wings have a number of disadvantages but this is where the discussion gets interesting. Many of the disadvantages claimed by critics of bungied wings are discounted by the supporters of these wings as fanciful or even imaginary. The first disadvantage is that the external bungies are likely to get caught up on any protruding piece of wreckage or other sharp area. This is undoubtedly a real risk and this is enough to discourage many people from adopting this style of wing. To be fair the bungy or tubing used can often be snapped with only a reasonable level of force but this is still a major disadvantage. Critics of bungied wings also claim that in the event of a punctured wing the bungy would squeeze out the air in the wing and cause a loss of buoyancy. Supporters counter that this argument ignores the fact that the water pressure will provide more squeeze than the bungy would and so while the bungy may result in slightly more pressure than if it were absent it is not the most significant factor. In fact, the position of the puncture and the position of the diver are much more important. If the hole is in the top of the wing and the diver is upright then all of the air will escape through the puncture whether the wing is bungied or not. Equally if the hole is in the bottom of the wing and the diver is again upright then most of the air will stay in the wing irrespective of whether it is bungied or not. Critics also point out that bungied wings can increase drag because of the turbulence caused by the uneven surface. The supporters would counter that the reduced surface area of the bungied wing would reduce drag and counteract any turbulence. They also argue that the turbulence is only significant when travelling at speed such as when using a Diver Propulsion Vehicle (DPV) or scooter and as such for the majority of divers, who will never use a DPV, it is not an issue. Another supposed disadvantage of a bungied wing is that I have heard it said that it is impossible to orally inflate a bungied wing. This is simply not true. I have seen bungied wings orally inflated on several occasions and in the interest of research have done it myself. In my experience one of the most common disadvantages of bungied wings occurs when the tension on the bungy varies from one side to the other. If one side is more loose then more air will migrate to that side causing the bungy to stretch further which can ultimately lead to a significant imbalance in the distribution of the air and can leave the diver in the uncomfortable position of having all the air in one side of their wing. Ultimately the choice of a bungied or unbungied wing will come down to personal choice and, to a large extent, current fashions.

	Advantages	**Disadvantages**
Bungied wing	One size suitable for multiple cylinder configurations Reduces size when not inflated	Could become caught on wreckage Faster deflation when punctured Increased drag due to turbulence? More difficult to orally inflate? Can result in uneven distribution of air
Unbungied wing	More streamlined	Requires wing to be matched to cylinder configuration

Table 4: Advantages and disadvantages bungied versus unbungied wings

The arguments for having a dual bladder in your wing versus a single bladder are more straightforward. The dual bladder is intended to provide backup buoyancy in the case of having a puncture in the wing. A great deal of technical diving, especially in cold water locations, is performed in a drysuit and so this can act as our redundant buoyancy. This means that dual bladders are unnecessary for dry suit diving and in fact can introduce additional issues. An additional inflator hose is required which can complicate equipment configuration and hose routing. Divers with dual bladder wings can inadvertently inflate the second wing and then have buoyancy issues as they forget to also vent this bladder. For this reason divers with dual bladder wings tend to dive with the inflator for the second bladder disconnected. For warm water diving in a wetsuit or semi dry then a dual bladder system may be more relevant, however, some technical divers choose to use a dry suit, even when they could use a wetsuit, because even in warmer waters you can still get cold on long decompression stops. Alternatively some divers use a lift bag or DSMB as an additional buoyancy source. For rebreather divers the counter lungs can also provide a source of redundant buoyancy.

A harness configuration is popular with many twinset divers as it removes much of the clutter from the diver's chest. If the diver is looking to progress to technical diving then they will be adding additional equipment and so streamlining the basic equipment provides a good platform for additional equipment. Unlike a traditional jacket style BCD, which surrounds the diver and provides bulk under the arms and across the chest, a harness has very little at the side or the front of the diver. Despite the additional weight, equipment and complication of a twinset, the use of a harness can provide a sense of freedom and a sense of being un-encumbered that can increase the enjoyment of being in the water. Even single cylinder divers who do not want to progress down the technical route often find the streamlining and freedom of a harness to be a welcome change.

Harnesses come in different styles, from the minimalist single piece harness to the highly complex harness 'systems'. A simplistic webbing harness has a number of advantages in that it reduces the clutter on the diver's chest and can easily be adjusted to fit any size. A more complex harness means that the sizing and the configuration of clips buckles and D-rings is also more complex. Ironically a single piece webbing harness is usually more adjustable than a custom made harness with multiple adjusters. This is because the single piece harness can easily be adjusted by adding more length to the shoulder straps and can be expanded up to the length of the webbing. This means that a very small or a very large diver can both use the same harness by taking in or letting out the amount of webbing in the shoulder straps. An adjustable harness system, on the other hand, is limited in the amount of adjustment that can be made by the placement of buckles, D-rings and other equipment that are often sown into place and so immovable. Harness systems are also considerably more expensive than a simplistic harness.

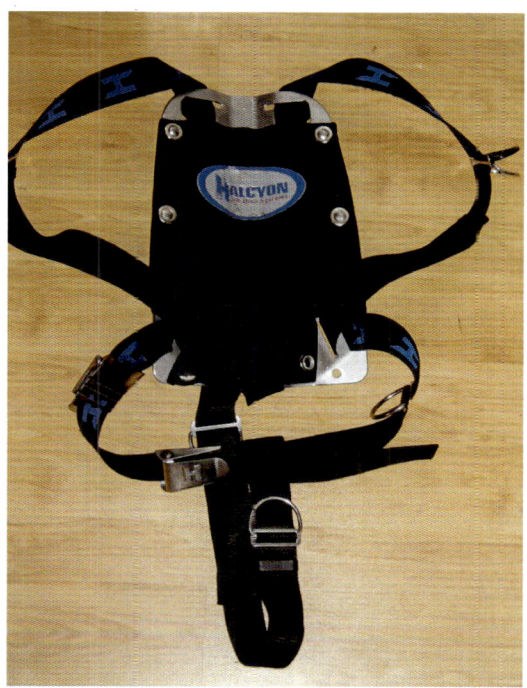

Figure 13: One piece harness

There are many discussions about the merits of single piece harnesses versus a harness with a break. On one side there are arguments that a single piece harness is very difficult to get out of, while on the other side there are arguments that any break in a harness is a potential failure point. Both arguments have their pros and cons. Despite arguments to the contrary a single piece harness can be used quite successfully for RIB diving provided that you have the harness fitted correctly and have the right technique for getting out of it. Correctly fitting a harness means that the webbing is neither too tight nor too loose. If it is too tight then it will be difficult to get in and out of the harness and it might restrict your movement when doing shutdowns. If the harness is too loose then the twinset is likely to move around on your back which can make the whole setup unstable as well as making it more difficult to reach your valves during a shutdown. There are a number of steps required in order to ensure that a one piece harness is correctly fitted. The first is that when just wearing the harness over your undersuit the shoulder straps should be tight enough that you can only just get your fists under the harness. Secondly when you reach back you should just about be able to reach the top of the backplate. In order to ensure the D-rings are in the right place you should hold your arms out to the side level with the shoulders and then bend your elbows and bring your thumbs in to touch your shoulder. The level that your thumb touches your shoulder is the level that the D-ring should be on the harness. This is because this is the natural position that your arm will reach, any higher or lower and you are straining to reach. Finally, you should check that the hip D-ring sits directly on your hip. Again, this is because this is a natural position to reach, any further forward or back on the waist strap will make it less convenient to reach.

Figure 14: A correctly fitted one piece harness

a complete break in the harness. The ideal solution will depend very much on the type of diving you do. RIB or shore dives have one set of considerations while technical dives using a hardboat will have a different set of considerations.

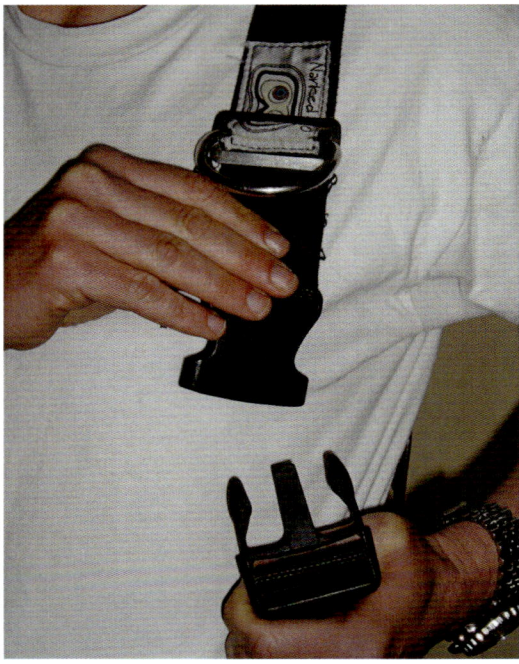

Figure 15: One piece harness with a break

Despite the fact that a correctly fitted harness can be removed fairly easily, for many people the advantage of a break added to the minimal risk of a failure of the break point makes it a preferable option for some types of diving. Getting out of a harness is easier if it has a break in it than getting out of a one piece harness. Even if the break does fail then it is not a major problem, especially if a stage is also worn on that side as the stage will act to hold the two parts of the harness together anyway. In an emergency situation there is no doubt that it is easier to remove a casualties harness if it has a break than if it is a one piece harness. Correct technique and a Z knife or a pair of shears, rather than a knife, can make it easier to remove a one piece harness but a break will be quicker. For other divers even the very small risk of the break point failing is too high to justify the flexibility it might provide in getting out of the equipment and a one piece harness is considered preferable. A compromise is to have a harness which has a continuous piece of webbing where the webbing is looped around behind the break so that it will open up a certain amount but never come apart completely. This allows the diver to get out of the harness more easily but without risking

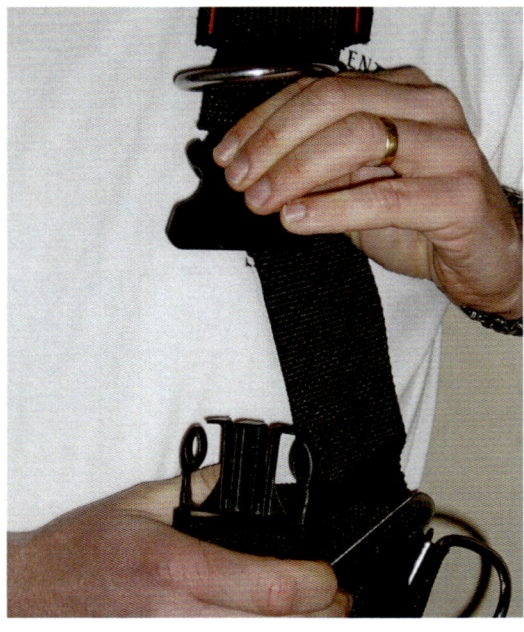

Figure 16: One piece harness with a break and safety loop

	Advantages	**Disadvantages**
One piece harness	Simplicity Low cost Easy to adjust	Can be difficult to get out of
Break in harness	Easy to get out of Easier in an emergency situation	Breakpoint could fail

Table 5: Advantages and disadvantages of one piece harness versus harness with a break

Despite the increased comfort and freedom of a harness, one of the main disadvantages is the lack of storage space. Unlike a traditional BCD, with its convenient storage pockets, most harnesses do not have any storage pockets. This can lead to the situation where the diver adds additional clutter by clipping on various pieces of equipment as they do not have any storage space. With harnesses it is possible to add on pouches and pockets while other divers will prefer large thigh pockets on their dry suits. Another option is to store soft items such as lifting bags and DSMBs behind a pad on the backplate. This also has the advantage of providing additional padding but it can sometimes be difficult to quickly deploy the lift bag or DSMB when needed.

In the same way that a twinset does not automatically mean a wing and harness the opposite is also true. A wing and harness can just as easily be used on a single cylinder as on a twinset. Rather than switching from a wing and harness when using a twinset to a jacket style BCD when using a single, many divers will have a single cylinder wing and harness. This allows the same kit configuration irrespective of the cylinders being used.

As with many equipment configuration choices the best choice for an individual diver will depend on the importance they place on the relative advantages and disadvantages of each option. For one diver a single disadvantage in one configuration may be enough to outweigh all of the advantages of that configuration. This means that some decisions are made on the basis of the advantages of the chosen option while others are based on the disadvantages of the other option.

No one configuration is perfect and each choice is a trade off between the advantages and disadvantages of the various options. Each diver will put a different level of importance on each of these points and that is why there will always be discussion amongst divers as to what constitutes the 'best' equipment configuration.

Hogarthian Equipment Configuration

16

"Keep it Simple Stupid" **Kelly Johnson**

Despite the fact that there are so many opinions on kit configuration it is interesting that if you are on a boat with a group of technical divers you are likely to notice a great deal of similarity in the way their equipment is set up. Over the last few years it has become increasingly true that it doesn't matter if the diver was trained by one of the major technical training agencies or any of the other smaller agencies, there is likely to be a lot of similarity. In many cases their equipment might not just be similar but identical. The reason for this is many technical divers adopt an overall approach to their equipment philosophy. This can be summed up by the phrase KISSSS which in addition to it's traditional meaning of Keep It Simple Stupid can also be interpreted as the more politically correct Keep It Simple, Streamlined, Safe and Suitable. A more detailed approach to equipment configuration is known as the Hogarthian approach and increasingly many technical divers are using this approach when setting up their equipment.

The Hogarthian equipment configuration developed out of the North Florida Caving community. The very formal sounding name of "Hogarthian" is in honour of Bill "Hogarth" Main who is credited with bringing together the major parts of the system. Bill Main tried to develop a safer and more efficient system of diving than the confusion of styles that was present at the time. He adopted the technique of breathing from a long hose from cave diving legend Sheck Exley and from this basis Main began applying the "safer and more efficient" philosophy to every component of dive gear. He reduced the amount of gear taken underwater, he removed unnecessary D-rings and clips and he rearranged his gear to promote efficiency and safety to the extreme. He examined every assumption and convention and if they were found to be inadequate he changed them. He was one of the first to propose a standardised system where each diver wore the same configuration. This gives the advantage of greatly simplifying repair and allows for swapping of equipment. In addition if your buddy is using the same equipment as you then you instantly know where everything is and how it works. Nevertheless, Main did not intend his system to be permanently fixed with no allowance for flexibility. Rather he developed his philosophy to be dynamic so that new developments could be incorporated into the system. He also recognised that there is no single configuration that will work in all situations and that the proper configuration for a warm water cave dive, for example, is different to that used for a cold water wreck dive in the English Channel.

The Hogarthian style was quickly adopted by most of the Florida cave diving community and now most cave divers in this area dive in this style. It also began to spread beyond this starting point. Many other cave divers around the world started to adopt the same system. Other areas of technical diving including wreck diving also started to adopt some or all of the Hogarthian system. Wreck penetration diving has many features in common with cave diving and wreck divers also started to adopt this style of diving. There were some exceptions. On the North East coast of the United States a different configuration style had been developed and there were a number of discussions of the merits of a "cave style" versus "NE wreck style". However, the advantages of the Hogarthian style gradually won round a large number of divers and it is now considered the norm in many US diving communities. The UK was also a different story. UK cave diving is very different from US cave diving and the equipment requirements are also very different. For this reason UK cave diving could never adopt the same style of diving which meant that there wasn't the same foothold for Hogarthian diving to break into the country. As a result UK technical diving equipment initially developed along quite a different route with more similarities to the NE Wreck diving style. A small number of UK divers started using the Hogarthian system, primarily as a result of learning the system while undertaking technical training in Florida. Notwithstanding, it wasn't until communications within the technical diving community improved, through dedicated newsletters and in particular the internet, that awareness of the Hogarthian system began to be more widely noticed. The promotion of the Hogarthian system by the Do It Right (DIR) movement under the banner of the Global Underwater Explorers (GUE) training agency raised the profile of the Hogarthian system and generated increased awareness. The DIR/GUE group are the most rigid followers of the Hogarthian system and this has led to the incorrect assumption in the UK and much of Europe that the Hogarthian style was invented by the DIR/GUE group. In fact most of the leading technical diving agencies advocate some form of the Hogarthian system. The Hogarthian style is focused on simplicity and efficiency. It focuses on carrying sufficient safety equipment without carrying unnecessary clutter and as such is more a philosophy than a recipe book. However, there are some key components that make up a Hogarthian configuration.

Rather than a traditional BCD the Hogarthian configuration uses a backplate, wing and harness. This type of setup has a number of advantages. A suitably sized, unbungied wing provides buoyancy in the same location as the twinset and so is more effective at counteracting the weight of the twinset. Having the buoyancy behind the diver but next to the twinset helps to support the weight of the twinset and lifts the twinset off the diver's back. All of this means that a wing is usually considered a more comfortable way to provide the buoyancy required for a twinset. A simple one-piece harness made from a continuous length of webbing is used. This reduces the clutter around the front of the diver when compared to a standard BCD and increases their streamlining in the water. The harness should be properly fitted and adjusted so that the diver can easily reach their manifold in order to be able to carry out a shutdown if needed.

> Single cylinders can be used for shallow recreational dives with a Hogarthian configuration. Single cylinder wings are available and the backplate and harness configuration will be unchanged. However for deeper dives and any decompression dives a manifolded twinset is preferred. Manifolded twinsets are preferred to independents due to the complexity of air sharing rules when using independents. The use of inverted cylinders is also discouraged due to the complexity of configuring the hose routings.

One of the most distinctive aspects of a Hogarthian configuration is the use of a long hose on the primary regulator. A typical recreational diver will have their main regulator and then an 'octopus' regulator which can be donated to their buddy in case of emergency. This octopus regulator is often, but not always, on a slightly longer hose than the main regulator. The Hogarthian configuration uses a much longer hose, from 1.5m to 2m /5ft to 7ft in length and it is placed on the primary regulator rather than the octopus. There are a number of reasons for this. In an out of air situation in a wreck, cave or even during an ascent on a decompression dive, the use of a long hose enables you to be slightly further away from your buddy. If you try to ascend while breathing off your buddy's short hose, you will need to be very close together. Sending up a delayed SMB, controlling the ascent and holding a safety stop are much more difficult when you are very close together and 'in each others faces'. Combined with the stress of the initial out of air event this can be enough to turn a difficult situation into a full blown incident. A long hose gives you the space to perform all of these tasks with enough room to remain comfortable and composed. Once you have passed over your regulator and deployed your long hose you can maintain your normal in-water position and the ascent is then no more difficult than if your buddy was breathing their own regulator.

The long hose could go on the octopus but the Hogarthian configuration puts the long hose on the primary regulator. This is because in the case of an out of air situation the diver would plan to donate the regulator in their mouth. This is not what the majority of divers were taught on their entry level course so why should this method be adopted? The first reason for donating the regulator in your mouth is that you know this regulator is working. The out of air diver will be under stress and putting a working regulator in their mouth is the quickest way to calm them down. Another reason is that many people believe that an out of air diver is more likely to take the regulator from your mouth rather than hunting around for an octopus.

The last reason is that technical divers frequently carry multiple cylinders. These cylinders carry gasses which are only breathable at certain points of the dive. If you breathe the gas at the wrong depth then oxygen toxicity could be a very real risk. We know that the regulator in our mouth always contains breathable gas and so by donating this regulator we are ensuring that the out of air diver is getting a safe source of gas.

Of course if we donate our regulator then that leaves us with no regulator in our mouth. This is not a situation that we want to be in for very long. If we now need to start hunting around for our backup, ensuring that we don't take a deco gas regulator by mistake, then we are just moving the problem along from the out of air diver to ourselves. For this reason a diver using the Hogarthian configuration does not store his backup in his pocket, dangling by his hip or clipped somewhere on his chest but instead he stores it on a bungee around his neck. This means that once they have donated their primary it is just a question of ducking the head and putting the bungeed backup into their mouth.

The excess length of the long hose is stored by "wrapping" it around the body. The hose passes down behind the wing on the right hand side, around the right hip, across the chest from right to left and behind the head. There is a common misconception that it goes around the neck. This is not true because it would be dangerous to have the hose fully around the neck. By having the hose on the back of the neck it is held in position but can be released by ducking the head and/or flicking the hose off the head. This method of storing the hose is known as a Hogarthian loop or it is often shortened to "Hog Loop".

The use of a long hose is closely associated with technical diving and is often seen in conjunction with a twinset. All of the major technical diving agencies support the use of a long hose and a number promote it as the preferred system. GUE go further and mandate this system as the only permissible configuration. However a long hose is not restricted to a twinset and it is possible to use this configuration even on a recreational single cylinder set-up.

The use of a Hogarthian or technical configuration is often compared to a traditional or recreational configuration. Before going into the arguments around this it is worth clarifying the terminology. I think it is confusing to talk about a technical or recreational configuration as the Hogarthian configuration can be used for both recreational and technical diving. So instead of referring to technical versus recreational configurations it is more productive to discuss Hogarthian versus traditional configurations. A single cylinder Hogarthian setup can quite easily be used for recreational diving and in fact has a number of advantages. It is a more streamlined setup and can help divers achieve good trim more easily than with a traditional BCD configuration. The use of a primary and backup regulator works for both technical and recreational diving whereas the traditional primary and octopus works in a recreational setting but not in a technical setting.

Many divers criticize the Hogarthian configuration and believe that new divers should not be taught in this configuration because it is not 'standard'. The problem with this argument is that the definition of 'standard' changes over time. It used to be 'standard' to dive without any form of buoyancy control but then Adjustable Buoyancy Life Jackets (ABLJ) were introduced and became the new 'standard'. Over time these were improved and jacket style Buoyancy Control Devices (BCD) started appearing even though they were not 'standard'. Eventually BCD's became 'standard' but that does not mean that equipment is not moving on and in a few years wing style BCD's may well be the 'standard'. Diver training needs to move forward and evolve as equipment evolves.

Many recreational agencies already embrace the use of a Hogarthian style setup for recreational diving and with the increased popularity of this setup it is becoming increasingly likely that you may be buddied up with a diver equipped in this fashion at some point. In order to deal with this it is important that all recreational diving agencies at least discuss the existence of this configuration with new divers.

Other equipment and accessories should be firmly attached to the body or stored in pockets. This is to avoid any dangling equipment that could get snagged or damaged. Dangling consoles, regulators, DSMBs, reels or any other equipment are to be avoided. A single pressure gauge, as opposed to gauge consoles is used and this is attached to the left hand hip D-ring by a boltsnap.

Hogarthian divers use torches for signalling and so require a powerful primary torch. A canister torch is preferred as this allows a small light head to be carried easily. A Goodman handle is used so that the diver can hold the torch in his hand without losing the ability to use that hand for other tasks. The canister torch is mounted on the waist strap on the right hand side of the body. This allows the long hose to be hooked under the canister in order to hold it in place. Backup lights are also carried and should be streamlined by attaching to the shoulder D-rings with a boltsnap and are then held in position along the harness by surgical tubing or inner tube. The idea behind the Hogarthian configuration is to try to be equipped to deal with realistic emergencies rather than prepare for every possible emergency. This is based on the view that most accidents don't happen as a result of equipment failure. Instead most accidents are due to the diver failing to adequately prepare. This can be as a result of not properly cleaning and servicing their equipment, or by overweighting themselves with too much equipment, or by configuring their equipment in a manner that is confusing, or by failing to practice basic skills. This means that the Hogarthian configuration is not just about the equipment configuration but the attitude that goes with it. Being properly trained for the type of diving you are carrying out, strong buddy or team diving skills, good buoyancy control, regular practice of basic skills and maintaining a good level of fitness are as much a part of the Hogarthian approach as simply adopting the equipment configuration. As a result the equipment configuration must be seen as part of the overall diving system in the same way that this equipment section is only part of the overall view of technical diving covered in the rest of the book.

Figure 16A: The author in a single cylinder hogarthian configuration

Traditional	Hogarthian
Jacket style BCD	Backplate, harness and wing
Multiple breaks and clips	One piece harness
Adjustable harness	Harness must be set up in advance
Primary and octopus	Primary and backup
Donate the octopus	Donate the primary
Multi instrument console gauges	Single pressure gauge
Only suitable for recreational diving	Works for recreational or technical diving
Can lead to clutter	Reduces clutter

Table 6: Hogarthian vs. Traditional Equipment Configuration

17

Reely important equipment

"Let us drop these bread crumbs so that together we can find our way home. Because losing our way would be the most cruel of things." **Hansel and Gretel**

There are many different opinions about kit configuration when it comes to technical diving. So it should come as no surprise to find that when it comes to accessories for technical diving there are just as many discussions.

The ability to send up a Delayed Surface Marker Buoy (DSMB) is one of the key skills for any technical diver. There are a number of styles of marker buoy, each with their own strengths and weaknesses. The traditional marker buoy with an opening at the bottom that is inflated by purging the regulator or exhaled gas is still very common and the simplicity of the design has many supporters. However, there are a number of alternatives. The most common is a buoy with a small gas cylinder attached. The cylinder is used to inflate the buoy which is intended to simplify the overall process. The diver just 'cracks' the bottle and the buoy inflates. This saves the effort of having to fill it manually and when it works correctly is definitely easier. For rebreather divers these are very popular as filling a conventional open circuit DSMB is much more complicated on a rebreather. There is no exhaled gas to fill the cylinder and the smaller size of the diluent cylinders makes purging a regulator to fill the DSMB a much less attractive solution. Nevertheless, many technical divers are of the opinion that if you struggle to fill a DSMB without a crack bottle, especially on open circuit where there is no reason not to be able to do it, then it is better to practice your technique a bit more. It is also amusing to watch technical divers trying to fill a DSMB at the end of a dive after they realise that they forgot to fill the crack bottle. There is also a safety concern with these bottles. They are rarely tested in the same way as regular cylinders as they are filled from another cylinder and there is no dive shop to enforce testing. They are usually very corroded due to the fact that they often get water contamination in them. Combined with the fact that many divers purge the connector on them by hitting it with a lump of lead, you can see that care should be taken with them.

Most technical divers carry at least two DSMBs, a primary and a secondary. It is common for divers to have a crack bottle type as their primary but then have a standard design as their backup. This is less than ideal because if there is a problem with the primary they are then left trying to send up the less familiar manual version. At this point they may be rushing in order to begin their ascent within their planned time or sending it up from one of their decompression stops. For this reason the secondary should either be of a similar type as the primary or the diver should be just as familiar with the secondary as the primary. For divers using the crack bottle type this can cause a problem as the bottle with the DSMB is quite large and storing one of them, let alone two, can be a challenge. If the secondary is a standard type then the diver should make sure that they practice with it regularly to ensure they are just as familiar with it as their primary.

Another option is to have a low pressure inflator on the DSMB, similar to the inflator on your drysuit or wing. To use this system the diver disconnects their dry suit inflator and uses it to inflate the DSMB. At first most divers are wary of this idea as they think that there is a risk of the inflator becoming jammed onto the DSMB and pulling them up to the surface. In reality this isn't a problem as the inflator, unlike the one on the suit, has no locking groove and therefore the DSMB just pulls off when full. Like many things it is a case of practice. After a few practice attempts the whole process is very easy. This style of DSMB is ideal for rebreather divers because it doesn't involve removing or purging a regulator or the use of exhaled gas.

Figure 17: DSMB with low pressure inflator

When it comes to DSMBs, size really does matter. Smaller ones are fine for practice or as a backup but, for long decompression stops in the open sea a boat skipper is not going to appreciate having to keep an eye on one of these small DSMBs. A larger one will be much easier for a skipper to spot and keep an eye on.

As well as the DSMB there are different options for the reel. The main choice is between a reel and a spool.

Within general recreational diving reels are used almost exclusively. In technical diving reels are still very common but there are some technical divers who will use spools in place of reels for some specific uses. A spool is just a drum of steel, plastic or Delrin onto which line can be wrapped. They evolved from overhead environment diving such as cave diving or wreck penetration where they are used to 'jump' from one guide line to another or in the case of losing the guideline. As such they are much simpler than a reel, there is no handle, frame or ratchet and therefore they are also much smaller. Their small size is an advantage as they do not take up much room and can be stored in pockets. Reels on the other hand tend to be considerably bigger. There are some reels which are designed to be more compact and can fit in a pocket but many are too big, especially if you are also carrying a backup reel. The other differences between different types of reels and spools are the length of line that they contain. This is particularly relevant for technical divers because if the reel or spool contains less line than the depth at which you are diving then it will be impossible to send it up from the bottom. Many recreational reels have 40-50m/130-165ft of line on them and if you are diving beyond this depth you will have to ascend part of the way before you can send up your DSMB. This is one of the reasons why mid water DSMB deployment is stressed so much in technical courses.

There are some reels, specifically designed for technical divers, with 80-150m of line on them.

In many cases sending a DSMB up from the bottom is not necessary or desirable. The time taken to send it up and the time for the buoy to reach the surface from 100m/330ft can significantly add to your decompression obligation. So it is common for technical divers to send up their DSMB from one of their decompression stops. Of course, this still needs to be fairly early in their overall ascent so that they will not have drifted too far from the dive site and the boat skipper can keep track of them. Spools tend to have considerably less line on them than reels, therfefore for any type of technical dive there is no chance of sending it up off the bottom or, for many deeper dives, even from some of the early decompression stops.

Figure 18: A selection of reels and spools

The techniques for using reels or spools are quite different. In any case where technique differs there will inevitably be differences of opinion as to which is best. Supporters of reels claim that spools are fiddly, difficult to use, prone to error and likely to case problems. On the other hand supporters of spools claim that reels are fiddly, difficult to use, prone to error and likely to cause problems! Much of this disagreement stems from familiarity with one approach and the typically human reaction to change.

If you have spent years using a reel and have perfected the technique then trying to use a spool is going to cause problems.

The technique you are used to is no longer applicable, you experience problems you never had before and struggle to perform what would otherwise have been an easy operation with your familiar equipment. It is no wonder that long time reel users when using a spool for the first time will struggle and many will simply give up and return to what they know. The reverse situation can also occur although is less common. Most divers first learn to use a reel and then later come across the idea of a spool. However, there are divers that primarily use a spool and have little or no experience of reels. For them trying to use a reel results in the same situation, they are unfamiliar with it, do not know the right technique and are likely to make mistakes. If they have poor technique with a reel then they are likely to prefer to revert to using the more familiar spool. It is a shame that there is this split between reels and spools because each has its own advantages. My own preference is to use a reliable reel with 65m/215ft of line and a a large DSMB as my primary and then use a spool with 30m/100ft of line and a smaller DSMB as my backup. The simplicity and reliability of my primary reel removes one potential source of stress during the ascent and the size of the DSMB makes it easy for the boat skipper to keep track of me. Then the compactness and simplicity of the spool is ideal as a backup, the small DSMB is already attached to the reel and can be quickly sent up if required. This is an ideal setup for me and is becoming more common. However, it is interesting to see how many people adopt this approach

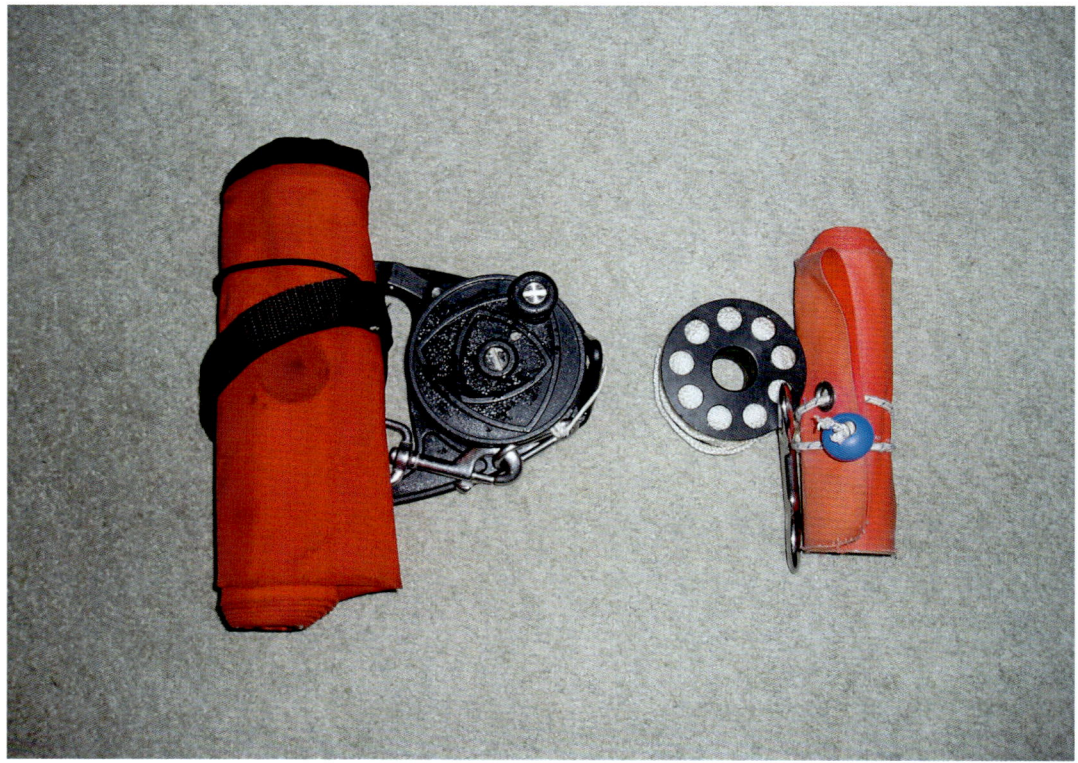

Figure 19: A reel as a primary and spool as a backup is a common choice

but have never practiced sending up the backup DSMB using the spool. As we have seen spools are great, as long as you have practiced with them. The worst time to practice the correct technique for using a spool is just after your primary reel has jammed and shot to the surface. So my advice would be that if you have a spool as a backup use it occasionally instead of your primary so that when you need to use it for real you are just as familiar with the spool as with your reel.

In addition to a primary DSMB and a backup many technical divers also carry a third, emergency DSMB. While the primary and backup are orange the emergency DSMB is yellow. This is used to indicate that there is a problem or that the divers may need more gas. The use of a yellow DSMB as an emergency signal is becoming more common with some inland sites treating any yellow DSMB as an emergency signal. The British Diving Safety Group (BDSG) recommends that recreational divers use an orange DSMB rather than a yellow one to avoid confusion[27]. The yellow emergency DSMB is usually just clipped onto the same line as the already deployed main DSMB, inflated and sent up the same line. In this case the skipper will see a normal orange blob as well as the yellow blob on the same line. It is also common to attach a slate or waterproof notebook to the top of the DSMB in order

---

27 The BDSG Recommendations Concerning the Use of Surface Marker Buoys are shown below. These are available at www.bdsg.org.uk
Divers using surface marker buoys should clearly label buoys with the full name of their owners. Avoid nicknames as these may not be known to the dive marshal. If using the delayed surface marker buoy for decompression the buoy should be clearly marked with the words "Decompression" in addition to the diver's name. To avoid confusion it is recommended that the colour of a single DSMB should be orange or red but not yellow.
When carrying two DSMBs on a dive, the general European consensus is that an orange or red buoy is deployed under normal diving conditions. In an emergency, or when assistance is required, a yellow buoy should be deployed.
When using a yellow buoy clearly mark on the buoy the word "Emergency" together with the diver's name. Once a yellow buoy is seen the support team and or boat can then initiate the standard emergency protocols depending on the situation

to tell the skipper what the problem is. A yellow DSMB is only of use if you have agreed the protocol with the skipper and have suitable gas available rigged up ready to be dropped down to a diver. It should not be considered as a 'get out of jail free card'.

It should be noted that in the US the convention is the other way around with yellow being used as the normal DSMB colour and orange being used for emergencies.

Figure 20: Emergency DSMB in use

Staying Comfortable

18

"Any fool can be uncomfortable" **Unknown**

The image that many technical divers try to promote is that they are rufty, tufty macho divers. The shaved heads and stubble combined with equipment that would make the SBS or Delta Force look inadequate all add to this image. The message is that they can leap tall buildings in a single bound and endure conditions that no mere mortal could withstand. However, the truth is a little different to this image. In fact, many technical divers spend as much time thinking about how to stay comfortable during their dives as they do planning the dive itself. The reason for this is that technical dives are more challenging than many recreational dives. They are typically deeper, longer, colder and more uncomfortable. The intelligent technical diver recognises this and tries to reduce this discomfort wherever possible.

One of the main concerns of any technical diver is warmth, both from a comfort and a safety point of view. In general the deeper we go the colder it gets. A few years ago I was teaching an Advanced Trimix course in Turkey and between the surface and 80m/260ft there was a difference in temperature of 10ºC/50ºF. This meant that while we might have been comfortable on the surface you would get very cold at depth. Gloves which were essential for keeping my hands warm at depth were uncomfortably warm during the decompression. A more common problem is that technical dives generally are much longer than recreational dives and will usually involve long decompression stops. Even if there is no difference in temperature during the ascent it is common to get colder during the decompression. I don't normally get too cold during the main part of the dive due to choosing the right undersuit, swimming around and the fact that my mind is occupied but during decompression it is much more common for me to feel the cold. During long decompression stops you are not swimming around or moving to any great extent and your mind is not as occupied. It is during these long periods of mental and physical inactivity that I often feel the cold.

In addition to the comfort aspect of getting cold there are a number of very real safety issues involved. The cold can slow down your reaction speed and thought process which, when combined with narcosis can affect how quickly and effectively you react to problems. Cold hands can also quickly lose dexterity which can make it difficult to effectively handle equipment, operate computers, switch to decompression gas, etc. Finally there is growing evidence that there is a strong link between getting cold towards the end of a dive and decompression illness[28]. During the early parts of the dive the

---

[28] Leffler CT. Effect of ambient temperature on the risk of decompression sickness in surface decompression divers. Aviat Space Environ Med (United States), May 2001, 72(5) p477-83

diver is fairly warm and blood flows to all parts of the body. Nitrogen is carried by the blood flow to the whole body and the level of nitrogen dissolved in the body increases. Towards the end of the dive, during the ascent and decompression stops the nitrogen is normally carried by the blood back from all parts of the body to the lungs. However if you get cold then one of the bodies reactions is to restrict blood flow to the extremities and concentrate it in the main core of the body in an effort to conserve heat. This has the effect of reducing the level of blood flowing to the heavily nitrogen laden tissues in the extremities which in turn reduces the level at which nitrogen off-gasses from these extremities. In effect being cold has slowed down the release of nitrogen from these tissues. As a result the speed of off-gassing is slower than predicted and the excess nitrogen in these tissues can cause decompression illness. Recent research has shown that this can cause a significant increase in the risk of decompression illness.

Due to the risk of decompression illness suit floods and leaks are much more important to a technical diver. I know many recreational divers whose suits regularly leak and for them it is merely an inconvenience; however, for a technical diver it can be a much more serious problem. Similarly a flooded suit can be cold, uncomfortable, inconvenient and irritating on a recreational dive but on a long decompression dive it can also be very dangerous. As the diver gets cold their decompression become less efficient. This means that the very time that they want to get out of the water, is the time when they need to stay longer to make up for the inefficient decompression. Here it is a balancing act between the dangers of hypothermia and decompression sickness.

It is a combination of the comfort and the safety that makes technical divers so concerned about the particular design of undersuit they use. There are a range of undersuits that use different materials to keep the diver warm. Thinsulate Type B has been the material of choice for most divers as it maintains most of it's thermal properties even when wet or compressed.

In addition to keeping the body warm it is vital to keep your hands warm. As we have seen cold hands can cause problems with dexterity making it much more difficult to carry out certain tasks. For this reason a technical diver will also think long and hard about their choice of gloves for long cold dives.

One option is to simply wear thicker gloves. 5mm or 7mm gloves are available. The extra thickness helps provide better insulation for the fingers although the thickness of the gloves also results in reduced dexterity. The same problems apply with three finger mitts. These mitts have one compartment for the thumb, one for the index finger and a third compartment which contains the remaining three fingers. Having the three fingers together helps to keep them warm although the thumb and index finger get just as cold as in standard gloves. In addition having the three fingers together significantly reduces dexterity for some tasks and can make some standard hand signals difficult if not impossible. Again there is a trade off between warmth and dexterity. By getting cold we can lose dexterity but many of the gloves designed to keep our hands warm have the side effect of reducing our dexterity anyway!

Another option is dry gloves. These are gloves that are fully sealed against the drysuit and allow no water into the glove. In some designs the glove is linked directly to the airspace of the drysuit. This removes any problems with equalising the two air spaces but has the risk that a punctured glove can cause a complete suit flood. Other designs have a standard seal on the dry suit so that the dry gloves are a separate air space. In this case some mechanism is required to allow equalisation of the air space in the gloves so that the diver doesn't get uncomfortable squeeze on their hands on the way down or excessive expansion of air in the gloves on the ascent.

One of the golden rules of diving has always been to ensure you are properly hydrated. Dehydration has long been considered as a significant factor in decompression sickness. When carrying out long decompression dives with significantly more decompression obligation than usual it is obvious that hydration is even more important. We want to try to reduce or eliminate as many of the potential causes of decompression sickness as possible in order to reduce our chance of suffering a bend. As a result technical divers try to stay well hydrated, not just by drinking some water just before the dive, but by starting up to 24 hours before the dive to ensure they are at the correct hydration level.

Despite the almost universal acceptance of dehydration being a major risk factor in DCI there has been very little research into this area and it is only in recent years that any link between

DCI and dehydration has been discovered. There is even some evidence that overly aggressive hydration just before a dive coupled with rapid onset of heavy swimming exercise on the surface can cause problems with immersionary pulmonary edema (IPE)[29]. Despite these concerns the general consensus is that correct hydration, i.e. gradual hydration starting at least 24 hours before a dive is still a positive thing.

Unfortunately being correctly hydrated has one unfortunate side effect. Much of the water that goes in will also need to come back out again at some point. A correctly hydrated person will need to urinate regularly. In addition, being in the water increases the frequency with which we need to urinate. This is because on dry land the force of gravity means that much of our available blood is pooled in our legs. When we enter the water and the force of gravity is reduced this blood redistributes itself around the rest of the body. Our body's reaction to this is to try and reduce the volume of blood in circulation by removing some of the water and transferring it to the bladder[30]. This is one of the reasons why you often get that urge to go just after you have entered the water. The cold has the same effect as it causes peripheral vasoconstriction which drives fluid back into the core increasing the blood pressure and further stimulating the removal of water from the circulation and into the bladder.

With decompression dives lasting potentially several hours the size of your bladder can become an important planning consideration. For any dive over two hours some method of dealing with this problem becomes essential. There are two potential ways of dealing with this problem, neither of which make for very appealing accompanying photographs. The first is to use an overboard discharge valve, more commonly known as a P-valve. A P-valve consists of a valve fitted to the suit in the inner thigh area. The valve is connected to a tube which is in turn "plumbed in" to the diver. For male divers plumbing-in involves a condom catheter. For ladies it is possible to use a P-valve by using what is known as a she-pee. Using a P-valve allows the diver to urinate during the dive, the urine travels down the tube and is discharged out through the valve in the drysuit. This allows the diver to urinate freely and as often as they need. Unfortunately using a P-valve can be fraught with problems, for male divers the problems start with ordering the condom catheter. If you order a size that is too large then it will not fit well enough and you will end up with significant leakage into your dry suit. Needless to say this is not desirable as you will end up cold, uncomfortable and smelling very unpleasant. Similarly if you order a size that is too small it will be very difficult to fit, not to mention the impossibility of any male ordering a small catheter. Many catheters also have a layer of glue which has the advantage of increasing the effectiveness of the seal Unfortunately it also has the disadvantage of being painful to remove from sensitive areas and there is a very real risk of losing skin and especially any stray hairs from that area. It's no surprise that many technical divers resort to shaving or creams to remove stray hairs from these areas. Even when the catheter is fitted there are still a number of pitfalls to catch the unwary. If the tube has a kink in it as it is routed out of the undersuit and to the valve then the flow can be obstructed and a build up can occur. This can build up pressure in the tube or can have a balloon effect on the catheter. Finally, with an unbalanced P-valve, the valve on the drysuit can also introduce problems, open it too early and you get a rush of cold water, leave it too late and you can get a build up of pressure which may lead to that damp feeling. A balanced P-valve with a non-return valve prevents the risk of cold water coming back up the tube.

For those that feel that P-valves are too much risk or embarrassment the alternative is to wear adult nappies. These are a much more straightforward technology with less to go wrong. The main disadvantages of nappies are the embarrassment of buying them and putting them on while onboard a busy dive boat. The other disadvantage is their limited capacity. This capacity makes them suitable for intermediate length dives but for very long dives they simply do not have the capacity to absorb enough liquid.

The typical image of a technical diver is some macho tough guy, however in truth the reality is that technical divers are more concerned about comfort than most other divers. They may have shaved heads but that's not all that may be shaved and beneath that rugged looking equipment may be a very large nappy!

---

[29] Harper, B. (2011). Immersion Pulmonary Edema, Alert Diver, DAN, Fall 2011
[30] This is known as immersion diuresis

How many cylinders do you need?

"Winning is the most important thing in my life, after breathing. Breathing first, winning next." **George Steinbrenner**

One of the things that distinguish technical divers from recreational divers is the amount of equipment and in particular the number of cylinders that are carried. A recreational diver might carry a single cylinder and for some dives may add on a pony cylinder for redundancy. Technical divers will use either a twinset or a rebreather but in addition they will carry a number of stage cylinders. They can easily be identified as they are usually clipped onto the diver's side.

The term "stage cylinder" is used as a generic term to describe these cylinders but in fact there are a number of different uses for which we use these cylinders and their names reflect the purpose that the cylinder is serving at the time. Another term that is used, is "side-slung" or just "sling" cylinder. This comes from the fact that the cylinder is usually mounted or slung on the side of the diver. The term "stage" cylinder comes from cave diving where divers would "stage" or drop cylinders at various points in the cave for use on the way out. So for example a cave diver might swim in breathing from his stage cylinder and when he has breathed a third of it he would remove it and clip it to the guideline. He would then continue using his twinset until that was also a third used. At this point he would turn around and start swimming back out. Using this method he should get back to his stage cylinder with a third still left in his twinset. At this point he would pick up his stage cylinder, which still has two thirds left and breathe that for the rest of the exit. Using this approach he will exit the cave with a third reserve in his twinset and a third reserve in his stage. This approach works as the cave diver knows that he will be exiting along the same line that he entered and so will always be returning to his stage cylinders.

This approach is normal in cave diving but is much less common with wreck penetration diving. The two reasons for this are that firstly the penetration distances in wreck divers are not usually as long as with cave dives. Secondly the number of exits may mean that you exit the wreck at a different point to the one you entered and so you may not always get back to the stages. As a result it is much less common to stage gas on wreck penetration dives. The exception to this is that some divers remove their stages before entering a narrow restriction or hole. This allows them to get into more restricted areas but should be used with caution, because if they cannot get back out or have to exit in another area, then they cannot easily get back to their staged gas. For this reason it is recommended that wreck penetration divers do not stage their cylinders.

The most common use of stage cylinders for wreck dives or any other open sea dives is to carry a decompression gas. When used in this way stage cylinders are usually referred to as deco cylinders. In this case they will contain a rich nitrox mix which is used to accelerate or reduce the diver's decompression obligation. For deeper dives multiple decompression gasses might be used requiring multiple decompression cylinders.

Figure 21: Decompression cylinders

Wreck divers may also carry a stage cylinder containing the same gas as in their twinset. This is known as bottom gas as it is breathed on the bottom rather than deco gas which is breathed on the ascent and decompression stops. A bottom gas stage might be used to extend the bottom time of the dive if the twinset doesn't contain sufficient gas to allow a safe reserve. It can also be used on expedition diving or in remote locations where getting subsequent fills may be difficult. In this case the diver may plan to use their bottom gas stage and a proportion of their twinset on one day and then use an additional pre-prepared bottom gas stage and the rest of their twinset for the next day. In this way they can get two dives from a single twinset and two stages of bottom gas.

The last use of stage cylinders is as a bailout stage for rebreather divers. A rebreather diver would normally plan to use their rebreather for the duration of the dive. However, if there is a problem with the rebreather then the diver would "bailout" to the stage cylinders he is carrying. In this case the diver would need a bailout cylinder that they could start using at the maximum depth and would then need sufficient bailout to get to the surface completing all their decompression. Unlike the open circuit diver the rebreather diver will not use their stages unless there is an emergency but will still need to carry them.

Figure 22: Bailout stages being used with a rebreather on a deep wall dive in Grand Cayman

One of the biggest dangers facing the technical diver is breathing from the wrong cylinder and in particular breathing a rich nitrox mix at depth which will almost certainly lead to oxygen toxicity. For this reason it is essential that all stage cylinders are analysed before use and labelled accordingly. The maximum depth at which the gas can be breathed, known as the maximum operating depth or MOD, should be clearly marked on the cylinder in a position where the diver's buddy can clearly see it. The contents and date analysed should also be marked on the analysis label but this can be smaller and less obvious. It can cause significant confusion if the diver or the team combine depth and MOD markings on cylinders. For example if a cylinder is marked up as 50 then does this cylinder contain 50% and can be breathed at 21m/69ft or does it contain a mixture with 26% oxygen that can be breathed at an MOD of 50m? Similarly a cylinder marked 21 could also be 50% that can be breathed at

Figure 23: Picture of a gas analysis tape

21m/69ft or it could be air[31]. In order to avoid confusion it is essential that the cylinder is primarily marked with the maximum operating depth (MOD). This means that we can instantly tell that a cylinder marked 21 is breathable at 21m/69ft. To be even more explicit it can also help to write 21m rather than just 21. Just in case users of imperial measurements were starting to feel smug the same problem can be found with 70. Is that 70% or breathe-able at 70ft? Where the contents are marked, usually on the neck, this should be smaller and include a percent sign to confirm that it is an analysed contents reading. In addition it is common practice to write down the analysed value including one decimal place. This is not because we are really interested in the reading to this level of accuracy but instead it is to distinguish between a requested value which would not have a decimal place and an analysed value. For example 50.2%.

There is occasionally reluctance amongst some divers to use the MOD as the primary marking and they will sometimes mark up the cylinder using the percentage. This doesn't really make sense. They claim that it is important to always know what you are breathing. This is only partly the case, what we really want to know is the partial pressure of the gas we are breathing, or rather that we are not exceeding a partial pressure of 1.6. Without doing a partial pressure calculation[32] in our head the only way to be sure of this is to know the depth at which we hit the 1.6 maximum partial pressure, in other words the MOD. If knowing the MOD is the ultimate goal then why not just write it on the cylinder!

Every time that the diver switches to a stage cylinder he must get his buddy to check that the gas is safe to breathe at that depth. This is to ensure that the diver has not made a mistake and is switching at the wrong depth or in the case of multiple cylinders is not switching to the wrong cylinder. This is why the depth is marked rather than the percentage of oxygen in the mixture. As we have seen it is much easier to check your depth rather than look at a percentage and work out the maximum safe depth in your head. The key point here is that the buddy must actually look at the MOD label and check this against their depth. It is easy to get complacent about gas switches and OK a switch without actually reading the MOD and comparing it against the current depth. Gas switches are

---

31 It is believed that confusion similar to this was a contributory factor in the tragic death of Carl Spencer during a dive on the Britannic in 2010

32 Partial Pressure = Fraction of gas x Absolute Pressure. Therefore partial pressure of 70% at 12m is 0.7 x 2.2 = 1.54. You can see why we don't want to have to do this in our head underwater.

usually very straightforward and for the vast majority of times no mistakes are made. Be that as it may, when using multiple stages, using unfamiliar mixes, outside your comfort zone or when already in an emergency situation it is all too easy to make a mistake. These are the times that divers are tempted to skimp on following the correct procedures but these are exactly the times when following the correct procedures are vital.

There are a number of slightly different procedures in use by different agencies. However, each procedure has the same goal; to ensure the correct mix is breathed at the correct depth. TDI use the acronym MODS to describe this process;[33]

M

Stands for **MIX**. The diver will identify the bottle containing the correct mix using the contents tape or MOD stickers and show it to the team. Team members will validate and confirm that the correct mix has been selected and is appropriate for use at the current depth.

O

Stands for **OPEN**. The diver will now open the valve of the decompression cylinder and deploy the hose and second stage.

D

Stands for **DEPTH**. The diver will reference his depth and confirm that he is at or above the mix's MOD.

S

Stands for **SWITCH**. The team member will double check the depth and mix and OK the switch. The diver may now switch second stages and begin breathing from the decompression cylinder.

The key point here is that the diver checks the bottle before switching to it and at least one other member of his team will also check before he switches. This provides a double check and ensures that a single mistake cannot lead to a diver breathing the wrong gas. In order for this process to work the team member must actually check that the mix is safe to breathe rather than just going through the motions. In fact the team member's role is not to OK the switch but to stop the switch. Their approach should be that their job is to stop the diver from switching and that they will stop them unless the diver can absolutely convince them that it is, in fact, safe to do so. If there is any doubt the team member will stop the switch, if the markings are missing or not clear then the team member will stop the switch. Only if everything is correct will they eventually give the signal to switch. This approach will make it much more likely to spot any potential mistakes as the team member is conditioned to look for mistakes rather than looking for the correct situation.

The main choices when using a stage cylinder are the composition of the cylinder and the size. It is common to see both steel and aluminium stage cylinders. On the surface steel cylinders are smaller and lighter than the equivalent capacity aluminium cylinder. Nonetheless in the water they are considerably more negatively buoyant than aluminium cylinders. The buoyancy characteristics of each different size of cylinder will vary but in general steel cylinder will always be negatively buoyant, even when almost empty, whereas aluminium cylinders will be almost neutral or even slightly positively buoyant when almost empty. The second choice is the size of cylinder required. Stages can vary from 5L/40cf all the way up to 12L/85cf. The right choice of size will depend on a number of factors. The larger the capacity the larger the physical dimension and weight of the cylinder and so the diver needs to consider what size cylinder they are happy to carry, both on the surface and on the bottom. The choice of decompression gas will also have an impact on the size of cylinder required. For example if a diver uses 50% for their decompression gas then they will switch to it at 21m/70ft and breathe from this cylinder for the majority of their decompression, as a result they will need a large volume of decompression gas and will need a larger cylinder to carry all of that gas. Yet if the same diver uses 100% oxygen as their decompression gas they will not switch until they get to 6m/20ft and as a result will use much less decompression gas and so can carry a smaller decompression cylinder. Seven litre stages are the most common but in recent years

---

33 TDI Decompression Procedures Manual: A Complete Guide to Decompression Diving. (2011)

with the increasing popularity of using 50% as a decompression gas it has become more common to see larger decompression stages. Although most European cylinders are measured in terms of litres some cylinders are now measured in cubic foot. 40 cubic foot and 80 cubic foot cylinders are becoming more common. 40cf is approximately equal to a 5.5L cylinder with 80cf cylinders containing approximately 11L. For divers using 50% as a deco gas and requiring more volume of decompression gas an 80cf cylinder is an attractive option.

With a single stage cylinder it is common to wear this on the left hand side. Typically the top of the stage cylinder is clipped to the D-ring on the left hand shoulder with the bottom clipped to a waist D-ring on the left hand hip.

However, when using multiple stages, either because of using multiple decompression gases, using a bottom gas stage together with a decompression stage or with multiple bailout cylinders while diving a rebreather, you need to consider where you will carry the cylinder. One option is to carry two or more cylinders all on the left hand side. The other option is to clip one cylinder on the left and one on the right. In this case the leanest mix, the one with the lowest percentage of oxygen, is worn on the left hand side and the richest mix, with the highest percentage of oxygen, is worn on the right hand side. For this reason this approach is known as lean left – rich right. The decision as to which is the best option, all stages left or lean left - rich right, will depend on a number of factors. For example, if the diver is using steel stages then the fact that they will be very negatively buoyant will make wearing them both on the left very uncomfortable as they will pull the diver over to that side. In this case wearing them lean left – rich right will be much more balanced. Nevertheless, if the diver is using aluminium stages then having them on the same side is

perfectly feasible and can be more comfortable in the water. In addition the other equipment the diver wears will drive them to one option or another. Using a hip mounted canister torch on the right hand hip will make wearing a stage on the right less feasible and so will push the diver towards using both on the left hand side. Similarly a Hogarthian configuration with the long hose coming around the right hand side of the body will also push the diver towards having both on the left.

As the number of stages increases, the decisions get more complicated. With three stages it is still possible to wear them all on the left hand side whereas with lean left – rich right you will need to have two stages on one side and one on the other. With four stages it is no longer feasible to have them all on the same side although it is possible to have two on the left and two on the right. Beyond this additional solutions have to be used, either stages staged on the shot line, support divers carrying additional stages for use on the later parts of the decompression or the use of a leash to attach additional cylinders behind the diver. Neither of these options are particularly desirable for open water diving. Using stages on the shot line or support divers mean that the diver is no longer self sufficient and adds significantly to the complexity and organisation required for the dive. In addition there is always the risk that the diver will have to ascend away from the shotline. Multiple cylinders can be carried by the diver if they use a leash; this is a loop of rope with a boltsnap attached. Multiple stages can be attached to the leash and then the leash clipped on to the hip D-ring so that the stages trail behind the diver. This approach will only work with aluminum stages as steel stages will be negative and will not sit comfortably on the leash. Only certain types of aluminum cylinder and even then only at certain pressures, will sit comfortably. The use of a leash is better suited to cave diving but adds an additional level of complexity and risk to open water wreck dives. Jumping off a boat with multiple stages clipped to a leash runs the risk of losing one or more of the bottles whereas passing the leash and bottles down to a diver in the water may not be feasible. For these reasons it is quite unusual to find open water divers using more than three or fours cylinders without additional support.

Dive Computers

20

"To err is human - and to blame it on a computer is even more so."
Robert Orben

In the recreational world the bias against dive computers has almost completely disappeared. Some agencies now even insist on trainees having a dive computer[34] and almost all include the safe use of personal dive computers in entry level training. This is a natural development within the sport because if divers are going to be using computers almost as soon as they finish their training then it makes sense to include computers in their training so that they can be taught how to use them safely.

The use of tables is still taught at both recreational and technical levels but this is more as a teaching aid or as a method of ensuring that the trainees understand the principles behind the use of the computer rather than with any expectation that they will solely be using tables for their diving.

It is clear that in the recreational world the use of dive computers has become widespread and accepted. Diving using a computer is perfectly safe if it is used safely. In technical diving a similar evolution of ideas can be seen. Initially computers were not considered to be as safe or reliable as planning a dive using tables. This was partly due to the fact that many computers were not designed for technical diving. With the development of more sophisticated dive computers and procedures for using them, computers have become an accepted part of technical diving.

The resistance to using computers to plan and execute technical dives originally developed from a number of criticisms. The first criticism often aimed at computer users is that they have a lack of discipline. As you will see shortly, a dive computer can provide a lot of flexibility in planning the dive. This flexibility can be taken to the extreme where the diver just jumps in and follows whatever the computer tells them. In this case there is no planning and hence the diver is correctly criticised for their lack of planning. For recreational dives this might be considered bad practice but can be much more serious for a technical dive. For deeper dives using trimix and multiple decompression gasses it is essential to make sure the diver has enough gas, plus reserve, to safely complete the dive and the required decompression. Rebreather divers must ensure that they have sufficient bailout gas to complete their decompression in the case, however unlikely, of a problem with their rebreather. In addition for longer dives, especially when pure oxygen is used for decompression, there is a risk of oxygen toxicity. In order

---

34 Scuba Diving International (SDI) teach their trainees to use a dive computer right from the initial confined water lessons.

to prevent this, the diver may choose to use a different decompression gas or insert 'air breaks', where they breathe a lower pressure of oxygen, into the decompression. These issues should always be taken into consideration and should be planned in advance. With no advance planning the dive computer will tell the diver exactly how much decompression they have to do but won't tell them if they have enough decompression gas to complete the decompression. The computer will track the exposure to oxygen toxicity but won't indicate in advance that there is going to be a problem. It will only inform the diver once the preset limit is reached.

One of the other criticisms that is often aimed at computer users is that they have poor ascent rate skills. Divers that use prepared tables with fixed run times know that they must ascend at the correct rate in order to hit their first stop on time. Failure to follow the correct ascent rate results in more time at depth which can increase the overall decompression required. With a computer it is possible to come up at any ascent rate. If the diver comes up too slowly this can have a significant effect on the total amount of decompression. Taking three minutes to come up from 25m/82ft to 20m/66ft is not a problem but taking three minutes to come up from 60m/200ft to 55m/180ft will significantly increase the overall amount of decompression required. This has a number of knock on effects. The diver will need additional decompression gas; they will be in the water longer and so will get colder. Finally they are likely to be over their planned total dive time and therefore the boat skipper will be starting to wonder if there is a more serious problem. For all these reasons it is important that divers using dive computers still maintain the correct ascent rate.

The last criticism of the use of dive computers is that divers who use them do not understand the basics of decompression diving or dive planning. This may be true for some divers in the technical area in the same way as in the recreational area. There are indeed many divers in both areas that blindly follow their computer without understanding the principles on which it is basing it's output. However, there are also many other divers who have a good understanding of decompression, the particular algorithm that their computer uses and the effects of changing the details of their dives. This is a criticism of the diver's knowledge rather than of their use of a dive computer.

It is equally possible for a diver to dive on tables or any other method of dive planning and blindly follow their plan without understanding the principles behind it. A dive computer, like a set of dive tables, a PC planning program or any other method of dive planning is just a tool to be used in the appropriate way.

Using a dive computer for technical dives can provide a number of advantages. For recreational dives we almost always know the depth and structure of the wreck. This makes it easy to plan a dive profile that is suitable for the particular site. For technical dives, on the other hand, it is common to be diving on wrecks that are not very well known or in some cases have never previously been dived. The wrecks are also often more intact than those in shallow waters. All of this introduces a great deal of uncertainty into the dive planning. You could plan for the maximum depth only to find that the wreck stands 20m/66ft proud of the seabed. Using tables you would have to plan a number of different options depending on whether you ended up on the top of the wreck or the bottom. In addition, a large wreck may involve a significant difference in depth during the course of the dive. Although many of the PC based dive planning packages can plan multi level dives this doesn't help as you don't always know in advance what your profile will be. Using a dive computer for this type of dive removes many of these problems. Although you will still need to carry a backup plan and take into account gas planning and oxygen toxicity you can use the computer to calculate your actual decompression.

In the case of an emergency a computer can simplify things. If there is a problem and you go significantly over your planned run time then a dive computer will just recalculate your decompression. Rather than having to manually recalculate or switch tables there can be an advantage in having the computer take care of it for you with minimal effort. Similarly with multiple deco gas dives it can be cumbersome to calculate lost gas plans for all combinations of problems with deco gasses. If using a suitable dive computer you can simply tell the computer that there is a problem with any deco gas and let it recalculate your decompression.

Prepared tables and plans work well when you know in advance what gas mixes you will be using. There are times however, especially with expedition diving, when it is not always so easy to get the mixes you want. Fills may be inaccurate or may have to be topped off resulting in unusual mixes. If you have pre-prepared tables then the mixes may no longer match the tables. With a suitable dive computer you can just adjust the gas mixtures programmed into the computer.

If a computer is to be used for technical diving then it is important that you use a suitable computer. Many recreational diving computers are not designed for use with technical diving. At the very least you must have a computer that will handle decompression diving although there are few these days that do not. In addition it should handle multiple gas mixtures. There are a range of nitrox computers that can use two or three gas mixtures. This allows the use of air or nitrox as a back gas and one or two rich nitrox mixtures for use as decompression gasses. For air or nitrox diving it is common to only use one decompression gas and therefore a two mix computer is perfectly adequate. There are a number of computers aimed at the recreational market which can easily be used for this type of decompression diving.

For trimix diving the choice becomes more limited. The vast majority of dive computers do not support trimix diving. This means that trimix dive computers are more specialised and more expensive pieces of equipment. The Delta P VR3 was responsible for popularising the use of trimix compatible computers. It allowed the use of up to 10 different gasses including any combination of trimix and rich nitrox mixtures. In addition to the VR3, which is no longer produced, there are a number of other trimix computers, notably the Shearwater, OSTC and Ratio range of computers. Interestingly, Suunto have also introduced a trimix computer, the HelO2 which was the first such computer by a mainstream diving company and followed this by the DX, Eon Steel and Core.[35]

Most of these trimix computers can also be used in closed circuit rebreather mode so that the decompression calculations are based on the fixed partial pressure being maintained by the rebreather[36]. Other companies, such as Ambient Pressure Diving with their Evolution and Inspiration Vision rebreathers, provide a full trimix enabled computer already included in the handsets of the rebreather.

One of the main considerations behind the choice of a computer for technical diving is the particular decompression algorithm used by each of the computers. Most recreational dive computers use some variant of Bühlmann's algorithm. Although this has been used successfully for many years by a large number of technical divers, the current preference is for a model which has a more gradual ascent during the middle part of the ascent. This is sometimes referred to as the "deep stop" approach but, as we shall see in Part 6, the term deep stops is not always a useful term. Some of the recreational dive computers, such as the Apeks Quantum, are sympathetic to the use of deep stops. Suunto have also started to introduce a range of computers such as the Vytec-DS and Vyper-2 which have the option of including deep stops whereas the HelO2 always includes deep stops.

The more sophisticated trimix computers use one of a number of more modern algorithms. The Shearwater Petrel, OSTC MkII, Liquivision Xeo as well as the Vision decompression computer included with AP Diving's Evolution and Inspiration Vision rebreathers, use the gradient factor extension to the Bühlmann algorithm. Some computers such as the Shearwater Petrel and OSTC can also also run the VPM-B model. Clearly the technical divers preferred option of algorithm will have a large impact on their choice of decompression computer.[37]

No matter what computer is chosen for technical diving the focus should be on the safe use of that computer in order to gain the advantages and flexibility provided by the computer without increasing the risks.

---

35 One of the disadvantages of including this type of information in a book such as this is that it is almost certainly out of date almost immediately. By the time this is published I am sure there will be several other options available.

36 The exception is the Suunto HelO2 which is open circuit only.

37 For more information on all these models and many other aspects of decompression theory I would recommend "Deco For Divers" by Mark Powell and published by AquaPress.

Don't forget to still plan the dive in advance; using a computer doesn't remove the need for dive planning.

Make sure it is set up correctly and all the gases are programmed in.

Always carry a backup, either a second computer or backup tables.

Don't forget your gas planning calculations.

Make sure you computer is compatible with the computer or plans of the rest of your team. Ideally you should all have the same computer with the same settings.

Stick to the correct ascent rates.

Make sure you know how to operate it and understand what it is telling you.

Make sure you understand the decompression model used by the computer and the implications for your diving

Table 7: Guidelines for technical diving using a computer

Figure 23A: A selection of technical dive computers

What's in your Argon bottle?

21

"Build a man a fire, and he'll be warm for a day. Set a man on fire, and he'll be warm for the rest of his life." **Terry Pratchett**

Technical diving is sometimes referred to as mixed gas diving. This refers to the fact that technical divers use gasses other than air. The term is not used as much as it used to be as recreational divers are increasingly using mixtures other than air. These days nitrox is recognised as providing significant safety advantages when used correctly and is regularly taught to entry level recreational dives. Even helium, in the form of trimix, is becoming more mainstream. For many years trimix was considered as "Voodoo Gas" and anyone who used it was considered to be recklessly exceeding safe diving limits. These days trimix is recognised as a good tool to reduce narcosis at depth and divers are regularly using it in the 40-60m (130-200ft) depth range. The one gas that still has an image of mystery to it and for which there are still many misconceptions is argon.

You can't go far in the technical diving world without coming across the terms "Argon bottle", "Argon inflation system" or something similar. Equally most pictures of technical divers will show a small cylinder tucked under the diver's arm or attached to the twinset or rebreather. Unlike the main cylinders or stage cylinder these "Argon bottles" are not designed to be breathed but are simply for suit inflation.

The first reason for using a separate suit inflation system is related to keeping warm. Keeping warm is important for comfort on long dives but also for safety reasons. Getting cold on a dive, especially towards the end during the decompression stops can increase the risk of decompression illness. On a typical recreational configuration and even on many twinset configurations, the drysuit is fed from the main cylinder(s) When using trimix as a breathing gas, especially in cold water it is advisable to avoid using this gas for suit inflation. The reason for this is that helium is a very light gas. The physicists can argue over the details of the exact mechanisms but it has two practical effects. The first is that it provides much less insulation than air and therefore heat is conducted away from the body much faster if you use your trimix for suit inflation The second is that it enters the dry suit much faster than air and when you inflate the suit the incoming gas can feel extremely cold, so much so that some divers have been convinced that cold water is being squirted into their drysuit rather than gas. When using a trimix with only a small percentage of helium these effects might be barely noticeable but with increasingly higher levels of helium, as used for deeper dives, both effects become more and more noticeable. The combination of these two effects can result in the diver becoming extremely cold during the dive.

The best way of avoiding this is to not use trimix for suit inflation. One option is to have a separate inflation cylinder filled with argon. Argon was the first of the noble gases to be discovered and its name derives from the Greek word 'argos' or 'lazy' because of its chemical inertness. In other words it doesn't react chemically with very much. Argon is a much more dense gas than helium and is also more dense than oxygen or nitrogen. This means that it is a much better insulator and is more effective at reducing heat loss. However, before we all go off and start looking for argon fills it's worth considering that the vast majority of suit inflation "Argon" bottles don't get filled with argon and are in fact usually filled with air. The reason for this is that although argon is much more dense than helium it is only slightly more dense than air. As a result, air is almost as effective as argon for suit inflation. It's also a lot cheaper and much more readily available. Using either argon or air for suit inflation will give a significant difference when compared to using helium but the difference between argon and air is considered by many divers to be negligible. As a result the vast majority of technical divers will have air in their argon bottles and so many technical divers jokingly refer to their suit inflation bottles as 'Airgon' cylinders.

The second reason for using a separate suit inflation bottle is specific to rebreather divers. Whether they are using trimix or air, most rebreathers have much smaller cylinders than a twinset. The gas a rebreather diver breathes out is re-circulated rather than being wasted as it is when using open circuit. As a result rebreather divers don't need anywhere near as big a cylinder as an open circuit diver and the cylinders used in rebreathers are often only 2-3L/14-21cf in capacity. This is plenty of gas for breathing purposes but using these smaller cylinders for suit inflation can use up a significant amount of gas. By using a separate suit inflation bottle they can reduce the amount of gas used from the rebreather cylinder and provide an additional level of redundancy.

The final reason for using a separate suit inflation system applies to technical divers who sometimes use trimix and then at other times use air or nitrox. One option is to use a separate suit inflation system when diving trimix but then to switch back to using the twinset for suit inflation when using air or nitrox. This involves removing the suit inflation system and potentially reconnecting a dry suit inflation hose to the twinset regulator. It may also require the diver to change their weighting to account for the removal of the inflation system cylinder. Alternatively some divers will just continue to use a suit inflation system even if they are breathing air or nitrox to avoid the hassle and configuration change from one setup to another.

There are a number of options to consider when setting up a separate suit inflation system. The first is the cylinder size to use. It is common to see anything from 0.85L to 2L (7-16cf) capacity cylinders in use. Obviously the larger the cylinder you have, the longer it will last and less regularly you will have to fill it. If you make extensive use of the drysuit for buoyancy and are regularly injecting and dumping then you will need a greater volume. If you primarily use the wing for buoyancy then you will use much less out of the suit inflation bottle. However, even an 0.85L/7cf cylinder should easily give you a good days diving provided you are not using the suit excessively. In addition to the size of the cylinder there is the material to consider. Both steel and aluminium cylinders are available. Steel cylinders tend to be smaller than aluminium which can be an important consideration depending on where you mount the cylinder. On the other hand steel cylinders are more negative and will need a weight adjustment if you remove them when for example diving on air or nitrox. Aluminium cylinders are larger for the same internal capacity but are more neutral in terms of weighting. Historically argon cylinders have been peacock blue although colour coding of cylinders is largely ignored amongst many recreational divers. Although you will still see peacock blue cylinders it is common to see suit inflation cylinders that are green, black, white or even bare aluminium.

The most important decision with any suit inflation system is where to mount the cylinder. The two main options are under the arm on the side of the backplate or attached to the main cylinder or body of the rebreather. If the cylinder is attached to the backplate then there are usually one or two mounting straps around the body of the cylinder which attach it to the holes on the side of the backplate. A loop of bungy is often added at the bottom of the backplate which goes around the neck of the bottle to hold it in place. Even quite large inflation cylinders can be mounted this way as they sit quite comfortably under the diver's arm. The alternative is to mount the inflation cylinder on the side of one of the main cylinders on a twinset or on the side of the body of a rebreather. This keeps it out of the way but has it more exposed to damage and reduces streamlining.

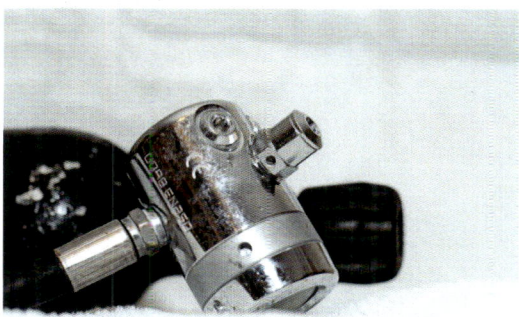

Figure 25: A suit inflation regulator with inflation hose and OPV

As there is no second stage on the regulator it is essential that an Over Pressure Valve (OPV) is fitted. Normally if there is a problem with the first stage the excess pressure will cause a free flow in the second stage. Because there is no second stage this excess pressure has nowhere to go except into the inflation hose. The result is likely to be a ruptured hose or a runway inflation of the dry suit. Fitting an OPV allows the excess pressure to escape by blowing off through the valve in case of a failure. An OPV is a thimble shaped turret that screws into one of the medium pressure ports on the first stage. It's not necessary to add a pressure gauge to a suit inflation system. Most divers simply check it with a different regulator after the dive or just refill the bottle after each day's diving.

Figure 24: Suit inflation system mounted on the backplate

The first stage attached to the suit inflation bottle doesn't need to be a sophisticated regulator, in fact the more straightforward the better. Some manufacturers produce a first stage specifically for this purpose which has just two ports and is much smaller than a standard first stage. These are popular with many divers while others will use the same style of regulator that they use on their twinset or stage cylinder to allow switching around. If the suit inflation system is to be used with argon then no second stage should be attached to the first stage and the cylinder should be marked as argon or non breathing gas. Although argon is inert and as such is not poisonous it contains no oxygen and anyone that inadvertently breathed it would suffocate.

PART 4
Skills

Chapter 22. Buoyancy Control 117

Chapter 23. Trim 125

Chapter 24. Finning Techniques 131

Chapter 25. Reaching Your Valves 135

Chapter 26. Shutdown Drills 141

Chapter 27. Individual or Team Diving 151

Chapter 28. Team Sizing 155

Chapter 29. Problem Solving 159

Chapter 30. Technical Skills 165

Buoyancy Control

22

"Gravity is a habit that's hard to shake off." **Terry Pratchett**

Buoyancy control is the most fundamental of all the basic diving skills. The feeling of weightlessness, which is the reason why many people want to dive, is dependent on having good buoyancy control. With good buoyancy control a diver uses less air, will feel more comfortable in the water and is less likely to suffer an uncontrolled buoyant ascent. Despite being such a key skill, many of the diver training agencies have noticed a reduction in general buoyancy skills. This reduction in skills is not restricted to novices; many experienced divers have poor buoyancy control

The level of control that divers have in managing their buoyancy can be split into four levels. The first is where the diver has very little idea about how to control their buoyancy and they are often unable to maintain any level of control. Someone learning to dive for the first time would usually start off like this but they usually move past this by the end of their initial training. The second level is where the diver understands the principles of buoyancy control and can manage their own buoyancy to a large extent. They may still have to work very hard at it and divers at this level are easily identified by the fact that they keep a constant hold on their BC inflator hose. Some divers never progress past this level, especially if they only dive very occasionally. The third level is where the diver is growing in confidence and can hold their buoyancy without constantly thinking about it. They will appear to be fully in control and be able to maintain position at the depth required. The majority of divers will get to this third level but then do not progress any further. They may seem to have mastered buoyancy control although, when they become distracted, by sending up a DSMB or dealing with some type of problem then their buoyancy is affected and they may start to drop or rise in the water. They may not realise that a higher level of control is desirable, or even possible, as they may get into the habit of sending up a DSMB from the bottom and unless they get into trouble, will not realise that a problem will interfere with their ability to control their buoyancy. The fourth level of buoyancy control is where the diver can control their buoyancy precisely, even when they are focusing on other tasks or dealing with a problem.

For technical diving it is essential that we aim to reach the fourth level of buoyancy control. There are a number of reasons why we must aim for this level and not be content to remain at the third level. Technical diving inevitably means decompression diving and a decompression ceiling puts restrictions on how far we can ascend without risking DCI. If a problem at depth results in a loss of buoyancy control then a rapid ascent may result. Technical divers must be able to deal with any problem at depth without risking a rapid ascent and so must be able to deal with any problem while still maintaining their buoyancy control. Obviously this level of control is also very useful for recreational divers who will then also be able to deal with problems without a subsequent loss of buoyancy. In addition to the risk of an uncontrolled ascent there is also the risk of sinking further. A diver who becomes fixated on dealing with a task and is unaware of their buoyancy may sink deeper. This can make the original problem much more serious. By sinking deeper the diver is using up their breathing gas faster, they will experience a higher level of narcosis and ultimately they will be incurring an even greater decompression penalty.

Finally, decompression dives will involve significant periods of decompression stops. These stops may be longer than the bottom part of the dive. These are often done in mid water with very little visual reference. In order to follow the decompression schedule the diver will need to accurately control their ascent rate and then be able to hold their position at the required depth in order to complete their decompression stop. Unless your buoyancy control is good enough to hold a safety stop, without moving up or down more than half a metre (1-2ft) then you should not even think about doing decompression diving. If you are unable to hold a safety stop then it is likely that you will be unable to hold a decompression stop and missing a decompression stop is likely to result in a decompression incident. For this reason it is good practice to do at least a three minute safety stop on every dive in order to perfect this skill. Once you can reliably hold the safety stop for at least three minutes without exceeding half a metre (1-2ft) variation from the target depth, then you can start to think about decompression dives. Ideally you should be aiming for a variation of +/- 0.3m/1ft or less from the stop depth. For cave divers or wreck penetration divers, buoyancy control becomes even more important. Dropping down onto the bottom or floating up into the ceiling can produce a blinding cloud of silt that can reduce the visibility to zero. When swimming through an overhead environment it is vital that you can hold your position in the water without excessive use of the hands or fins to maintain position. Excessive use of the hands or fins can also kick up significant amounts of silt and further reduce the visibility. In order to navigate through a wreck or cave without touching the bottom, ceiling or either of the sides, you need to have full control over your buoyancy.

The first step to good buoyancy control is correct weighting. The majority of divers carry more weight then they need, this ranges from a couple of kilos to tens of kilos. Again this is not just restricted to new divers. Experienced divers are often over weighted, some to a remarkable extent. They set up their weight belt when they first start and then never change it. In the meantime, with experience, they need less weight; their equipment may change, they may add pony cylinders, switch to a twinset, add deco cylinders, torches, etc. As a result they may be significantly overweight without realizing it. They have come to think that it is normal and change their diving technique to compensate for being over weighted.

If you dive over weighted then you must put more air into your wing/BCD or dry suit in order to achieve neutral buoyancy. This additional air significantly increases the risk of an uncontrolled buoyant ascent because as you ascend there is more air in the suit or wing/BCD to expand. This leads to the surprising situation where, by adding weight, you can make yourself more buoyant on your ascent rather than less. I have lost count of the times I have heard divers saying that they struggled with their buoyancy on their ascent and so are going to add on more weight. They are just making the problem worse.

The reality is that by reducing the amount of over weighting you reduce the chances of an uncontrolled buoyant ascent.

It is good practice for all divers, no matter how experienced, to do a buoyancy check at the start of each diving season, mid way through the diving season and whenever they dive with a new or different kit configuration.

Once you are correctly weighted that isn't the end of the story. Anytime you change your equipment you will need to re-check your weight. If you switch between cylinders then you will need to adjust your weight and even two similar cylinders with the same capacity can vary in weight by 2 or 3 kg (5-7lbs). A new dry suit can vary considerably in buoyancy characteristics and even wearing an extra layer under your dry suit can make a significant difference to your buoyancy

– remember layers keep you warm by trapping air and that air is going to change your buoyancy. There is a definite link between divers suffering uncontrolled ascents and the use of new or different equipment. If you are using any new equipment – even a new set of fleecy underwear – then do a buoyancy check before diving.

In open water you should try to keep your buoyancy under control at all times. This starts with the descent. Do not just dump all your air and sink to the bottom like a stone; instead you should be doing a controlled descent where you can stop the descent at any point. I once dived with a buddy who used to descend so fast that even with no air in my BCD and suffering with suit squeeze in my dry suit, I couldn't keep up with him on the descent. After struggling to keep up with him for a few dives I convinced him to do a weight check - we managed to remove 6 kilos (13lbs) from his weight belt while still allowing him to descend easily.

A controlled descent will help in a number of areas; it will help in avoiding narcosis, as rapid descents are a predisposing factor to nitrogen narcosis; it will help if you have trouble clearing your ears as you have time to clear them or to stop and ascend slightly. A controlled descent is especially important if the dive site is deeper than you expected. There are numerous examples of experienced divers jumping into the water after being told that the site is 30m/100ft, doing an express descent to the bottom without checking their gauges and getting to the bottom only to find that they are at 40m/130ft rather than 30m/100ft. This will ruin even the best planned dive plan and if diving on nitrox could be fatal!

Once on the bottom it is important to maintain neutral buoyancy rather than just bump along the bottom. In many countries British divers have a bad reputation for buoyancy control due to their habit of crawling over the bottom rather than swimming over it. This is due to their tendency to be negatively buoyant as a result of not putting enough air into their wing/BCD or dry suit. Once you reach the bottom, take a few seconds to adjust your buoyancy so that you are neutrally buoyant. This will make the rest of the dive much more comfortable and is likely to reduce your overall air consumption. Struggling with incorrect buoyancy during the dive will cause you to breathe harder or more irregularly than if you are neutrally buoyant. Being neutrally buoyant also gives a much more enjoyable feel to the dive as you really do feel weightless and can move effortlessly in three dimensions. If, on the other hand you are negatively buoyant on the bottom then you do not get the feeling of weightlessness and can only move in the same two dimensions as on land.

One of the biggest steps a diver can take in improving their buoyancy is to move from the situation of reacting to changes in their buoyancy to a position of anticipating these changes and taking corrective action before any major change takes place. Divers who react to changes after they have happened can be recognised by their yo-yo movements. They start to drift up and as they do so the gas in their suit and wing starts to expand this means they start to drift up further, by the time they have reacted the air has expanded even more and they have drifted up yet further. As they are now moving up quite quickly they need to dump air quickly to avoid drifting up any further. They start dumping air but end up overcompensating and dumping too much. As a result they now start sinking. To counteract this they start putting more air in and the cycle starts over again. A diver with this type of buoyancy control spends the majority of the dive fighting to maintain buoyancy control and is continually one step behind their buoyancy. This means they are working harder and of course their breathing rate goes up.

If the diver in question is over weighted then the situation is even more exaggerated. Because they are over weighted they have more air in their wing to compensate. As they drift up, the excess volume of air expands more than if they had less air in the wing. As it expands it makes them more positively buoyant and so they start to drift up even faster – which causes the air to expand even more. In order to regain buoyancy they need to dump air quickly, but of course this increases the risk that they will dump too much air and become negatively buoyant and start to sink........

To picture this situation we can imagine the 'swingometer' as popularised by so many election night broadcasts. The presenter will stand in front of the swingometer and show the swing from one political party to the other. If we imagine the swingometer as indicating our level of buoyancy then in the middle we have neutral buoyancy. This is the point that we are

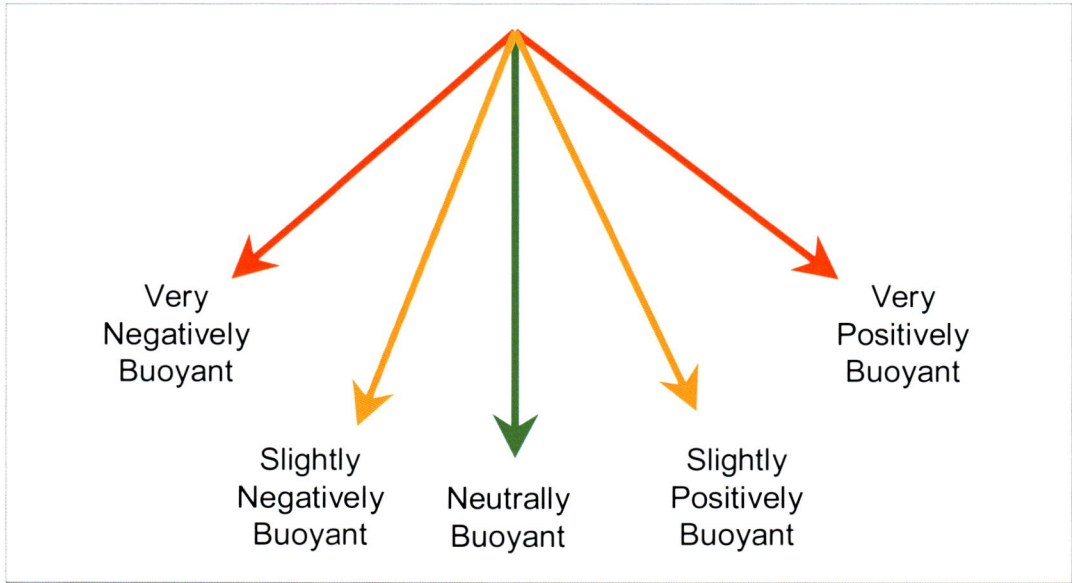

Figure 26: The buoyancy swingometer

always aiming for. As we move further to the right we become more and more positively buoyant. As we move to the left we become more and more negatively buoyant. Ideally we want to stay in the middle at all times. If we are in the middle then we are perfectly neutrally buoyant and can hang in mid water without drifting up or down.

If we have this picture in or mind we can start to anticipate what will happen to our buoyancy as we move through the water column. If we ascend slightly, to swim over a reef or a piece of wreckage, then the air in our lungs, suit and wing will expand and we will move to the right of the swingometer and become more positively buoyant. If we don't take any action then by becoming more positively buoyant we will drift up further and so the air will expand further and we will become even more positively buoyant. This shouldn't be a surprise to us and so we should be able to anticipate this change. As we can anticipate this change then we can anticipate what action we need to control the change. In this case as we swim up over the piece of wreckage we know that we will become positively buoyant and so we can dump some air to avoid becoming too buoyant. As a result by the time we get to the top of the wreckage we will have already have dumped some air and will have already have ensured we are back at neutral buoyancy. In this case the swingometer moved briefly to the right but before it could go too far we anticipated it and

ensured it moved back to the centre neutral point.

As we swim deeper we can anticipate that the gas in our lungs, suit and wing will contract, this will make us less buoyant and we will start to sink. If we don't do anything then this will result in the gas becoming more compressed which will result in us becoming more negative. In terms of the swingometer we will move further and further to the left. Again we can anticipate this. As we move deeper we know that we will become more negative and move to the left on our swingometer. In order to counteract this we can start to put more air into our suit or wing to offset this effect.

Once we are aware of the swingometer we can start to anticipate what effect each movement will have on our buoyancy. Will we move to the right and become more buoyant or will we move to the left and become less buoyant? Once we can anticipate what will happen to our buoyancy we can anticipate what action we will need to maintain neutral buoyancy.

The result of this anticipation is that we always stay at or near the neutral point. As we move up we are only slightly positive and so to regain neutral buoyancy it is only a small change to move from slightly positive to neutral. Similarly as we move down it is only a small change to move from slightly negative back to neutral. In this way, by anticipating what changes to our buoyancy we are going to experience we can anticipate what changes we need to make in order to maintain control over our buoyancy. This removes the yo-yo tendency as well as removing the stress and effort required to maintain our buoyancy.

The final technique required to master buoyancy control is breathing. Now you might think that you already know how to breathe but it is important to realise how breathing affects our buoyancy and how we can use our breathing to fine tune it.

The important part here is that although we can use our breathing to fine tune our buoyancy, we should not be using it as our primary buoyancy control method.

If we take the biggest possible breath then our lungs can contain a total lung capacity (TLC) of approximately 6L/0.21cf of air. If we breathe out all the air possible from our lungs we will still be left with some air in the lungs, this is known as the residual volume (RV) and is around 1.2L of air. This means that we can change our lung volume by 4.8L of air. This is a significant volume of air and will have a major impact on our buoyancy. However it is very unusual to completely fill or empty our lungs and when breathing normally the change in volume, known as the tidal volume (TV) is a much more modest 0.5L. This means that in addition to a normal breath we can breathe out an additional 1.2 L, this is known as the Expiratory Reserve volume or ERV. We can also breathe in an additional 3.1L which is known as the Inspiratory Reserve Volume or IRV.

If all these names and numbers are confusing then the diagram below should make it all clearer. The point is that we can breathe in much more than the normal tidal volume if we need to and can also breathe out much more. This is to allow us to increase our breathing at times of exercise when we need to increase the amount of oxygen being carried to the lungs and remove the carbon dioxide being generated in the muscles. It just so happens that we can temporarily use this ability to fine tune our buoyancy.

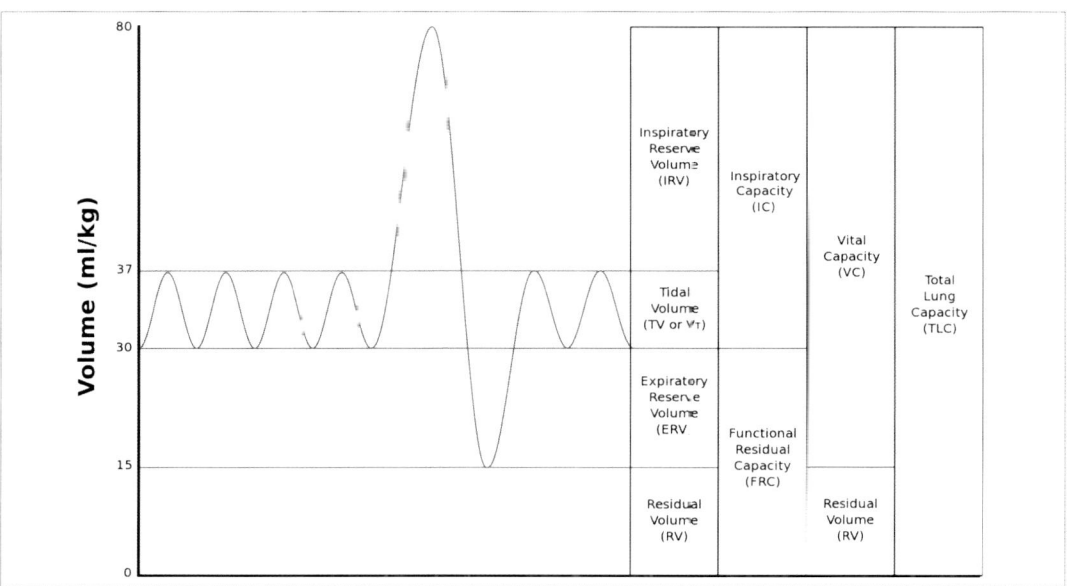

Figure 27: Lung Volumes

If the diver is perfectly neutral and wants to rise up above an obstacle or start their ascent they only need to breathe in slightly more than usual and the increased lung volume will increase their buoyancy and they will start to rise. Equally if they want to drop down then they can breathe out slightly more than the normal breath and the reduction in lung volume will reduce their buoyancy and they will start to descend.

Of course it is important to realise that the diver should not hold their breath for more than a few seconds when starting an ascent due to the risk of lung over expansion injuries.

Breath control can also be used to react to slight changes in buoyancy. If we find that we are becoming slightly positively buoyant and starting to drift up then we can breathe out more than the tidal volume, reducing the overall volume of air in the lungs and temporarily reducing our buoyancy. Of course this is just a temporary adjustment as we will have to breathe in again at some point but it can give us enough time to reach the dump on our BCD and dump some air so that, when we do take the next breath in, we will already have compensated. Equally, if we find that we are becoming slightly negatively buoyant and are starting to sink, we can breathe in more than the tidal volume, increasing the overall volume of air in the lungs and temporarily increase our buoyancy. Again we will have to breathe out again at some point but it can give us enough time to reach the inflator on our BCD and inject some air so that when we do breathe out we have already compensated.

In order for this technique to work the diver must recognise the change in buoyancy while it is still small so that they only need a slight increase to the size of the breath in or out. If they are only slightly to the right of the centre of the swingometer, i.e. slightly positive, they need only breathe out a little to regain the centre and neutral buoyancy. Equally if they are slightly to the left, slightly negative, then they can just breathe in and return to the neutral middle point. This means that they must be very aware of their buoyancy. If they wait until they have become very positive or negatively buoyant then the lungs on their own will not be enough to solve the problem. In terms of the swingometer this means that we want to be no more then a normal breath away from the mid point at any time.

Unfortunately many divers rely too much on their lungs for buoyancy. It is common for divers to be consistently negatively buoyant and to use their lungs to compensate. They do this because most divers would rather be slightly negatively buoyant rather than positively buoyant because on most dives the implication of floating up to the surface and having an unplanned ascent are worse than drifting down just a metre or so and hitting the bottom. As a result they tend to be negatively buoyant but then compensating by taking a slightly deeper than normal breath. They may still be breathing in and out the 0.5L tidal volume but this tidal volume is offset upwards and so the diver can be thought of as breathing in the top half of their lungs. Sometimes the opposite situation occurs. If the diver feels light they may breathe out more than normal and breathe in the bottom half of their lungs.

The disadvantage in this case is that the diver has lost the ability to adjust their buoyancy in one direction. If they are breathing at the top of their lungs then they cannot breathe in more in order to become more buoyant. Equally if they are breathing at the bottom of their lungs then they cannot breathe out any more in order to become less buoyant. Many divers do not even realise they are doing this.

A good test to see if you are breathing in the middle of your lungs is to stabilise in a neutral position and then breathe out more than the tidal volume. You should be able to sink half a metre and then take a big breath in to stop your descent. You should then be able to take in an even bigger breath and start to ascend back to your starting point.

A big breath out should bring you back to a stable position at your starting point. Then you should be able to reverse the process by breathing in and ascending, stabilising and then breathing out to return to the starting point. If you can move up and down from a stable position then this is a good indicator that you are breathing in the middle of your lungs. If you can only move down then you are breathing in the top half of your lungs. If you can only move up then you are breathing

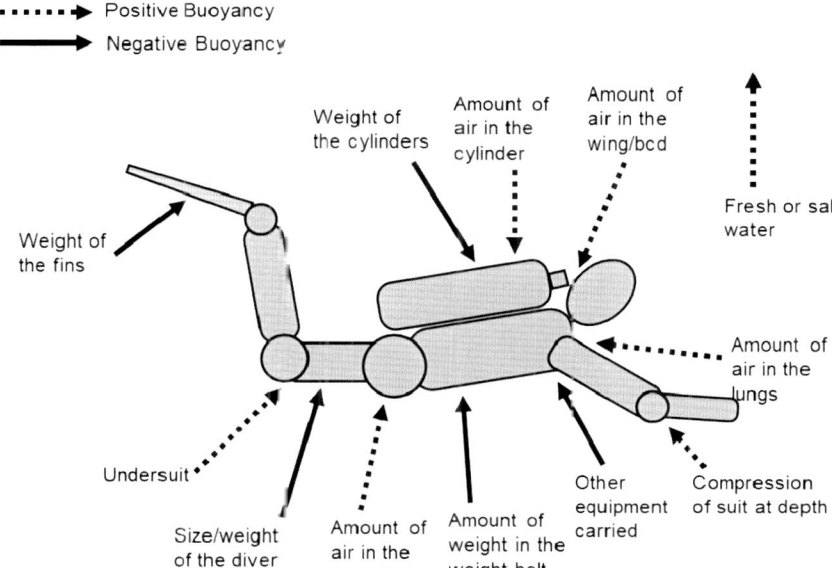

Diagram 5: Buoyancy Control

in the bottom half of your lungs.

Of course working hard will increase your breathing rate and you will breathe in a greater volume of air and then breathe out a correspondingly larger volume of air. This will inevitably result in a greater change in buoyancy than a normal breath. However, if the diver is correctly weighted and is breathing in the centre of their lungs, this will not cause any undue problems.

Hopefully it is clear that buoyancy control is a key skill that should be reviewed regularly by all divers. Reducing over weighting, regular weight checks, practicing buoyancy control exercises, being aware of the impact of new equipment and anticipating changes in buoyancy can all help to perfect your buoyancy control skills.

With increased buoyancy control you will be more comfortable in the water, use less air, reduce your risk of an uncontrolled ascent and generally enjoy your diving much more.

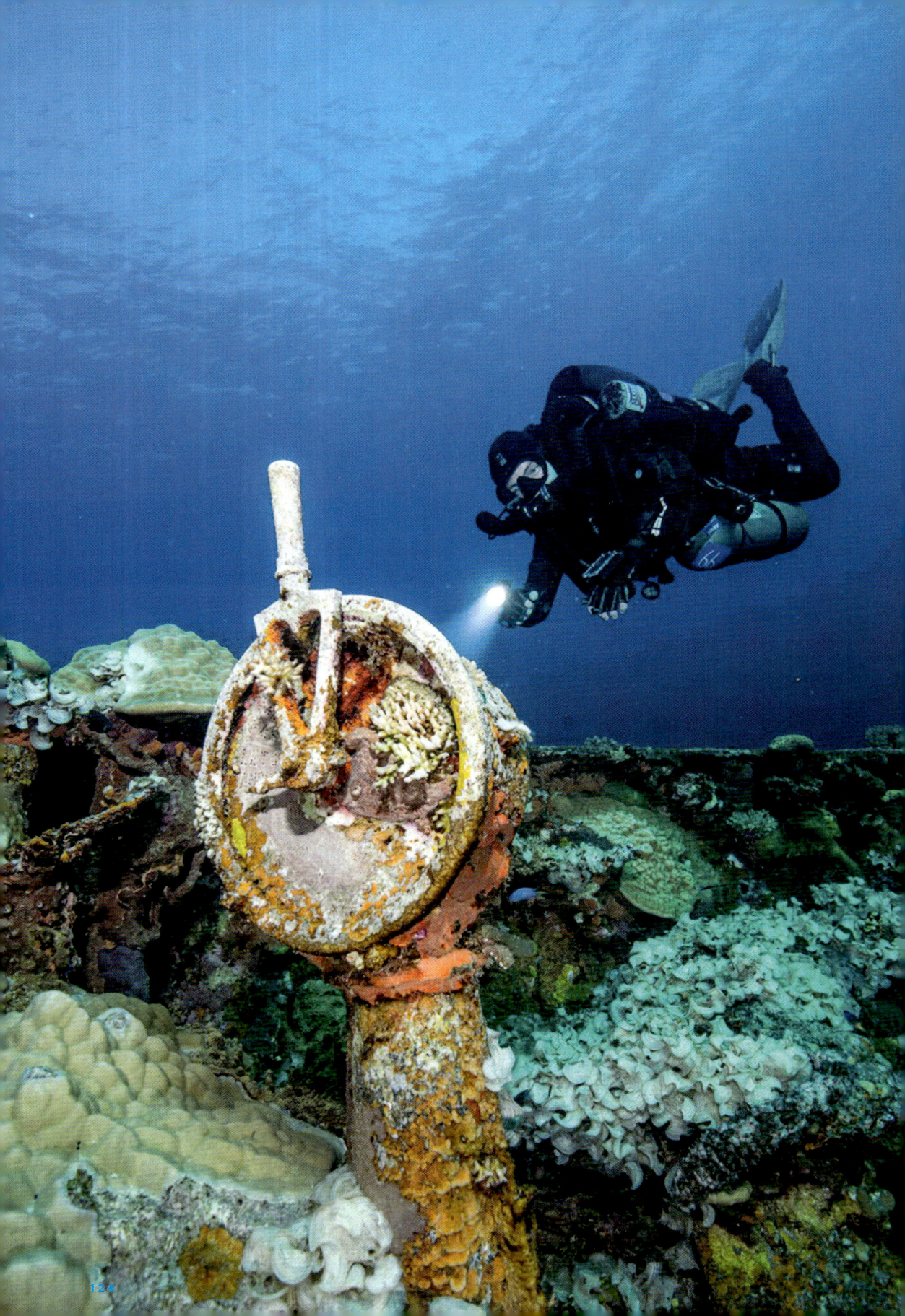

Trim

23

Buoyancy and trim are often discussed together as they are interrelated and struggling with one may show up as a problem with the other. The importance of buoyancy control is well known to most divers and is emphasised in the entry level training programs of all the major training agencies. Trim, on the other hand, is less well understood and is rarely mentioned, if at all, in many training courses. Many divers are not even sure what trim even means.

My Collin's English dictionary has 26 meanings of the word trim including the following three.

- The difference between the draught of the vessel at the bow and the stern.

- To maintain an even balance of a ship or aircraft by adjusting the position of the load or cargo.

- The attitude of an aircraft in flight when the pilot lets the main control surfaces to take their own position.[38]

Each of these has a bearing on the meaning of the word trim when we use it in diving. The most basic use of the word trim is similar to the first definition above and refers to our position in the water. If a line is drawn from the shoulders to the hips and continuing on to the knees of the diver then trim can be used to mean the angle of this line. This angle can be anything from completely vertical in the water to completely horizontal. This usage of the word makes no judgement about the ideal angle but is simply a measure of this angle. It is this measure that is then used in the other uses of the term.

A slightly different usage is related to the second definition above. This assumes that 'flat trim', where the diver is as close to horizontal in the water is desirable and upright trim is less desirable. In this case the diver can move equipment or use specific techniques to try to maintain an even balance and move into a horizontal position.

The last usage of the word trim is related to the third definition. Here it is used to mean the position in the water that the diver takes when they relax and do not use hands, fins or any other technique to maintain their position. It is primarily the distribution of weight and equipment rather than technique that will determine the position in the water.

As mentioned above, buoyancy and trim are often considered together because, although they are completely different effects, they are often used together by the diver. For example many divers never achieve neutral buoyancy and yet still maintain their position in the water column. They do this by having a head up trim position and then finning upwards.

---

[38] Collins English Dictionary

Their negative buoyancy is offset by the upwards finning which makes it appear that they have neutral buoyancy. In some cases, typically during the ascent, the diver becomes completely vertical and starts to fin harder in order to move upwards. In this case the diver is forced to have vertical trim in order to ascend. Less common is for divers to fin downwards in order to counteract positive buoyancy. There are many arguments amongst divers about whether the dry suit or BCD/Wing should be used as the primary source of buoyancy. However, for many divers it is actually their fins that are their primary buoyancy control device.

All of the major training agencies emphasize the importance of buoyancy in their training, even if the practical side of it is less well emphasized. Nevertheless there is very little detail on trim and many divers are not even aware of the concept. The reason for this is that for recreational diving buoyancy is very important and becomes even more important at the technical diving level. Trim on the other hand is not considered to be as important at the recreational level and only starts to be emphasized at the technical level. Despite this I believe that having good trim can provide benefits even for the recreational diver.

The first reason is that focusing on trim also forces the diver to concentrate on their buoyancy. With upright trim it is possible to get away with poor buoyancy because you can fin to compensate but if you try to get flat in the water you must also focus on getting your buoyancy control right. Of course this isn't easy. Trying to change the way you dive by changing two factors at the same time requires time and effort and many divers do not want to spend this amount of time on improving their technique. One of the main reasons why it is worth investing this time and effort is that in a difficult situation the fact that the diver is maintaining their position in the water by finning rather than buoyancy control can make the situation worse. When a diver is stressed and is focusing on one or more problems they are not focusing on their buoyancy and may stop finning while they deal with the problem. If this occurs then they will start to sink as it was only their finning that was keeping them in position. In this case they are still dealing with the original problem but now also have the added complication of sinking deeper at the same time. It doesn't even need to be a major problem or incident. Divers who are sending up a DSMB will often start to sink once their attention switches from buoyancy control to the DSMB. Therefore by improving your trim and reducing your reliance on finning to maintain buoyancy you can avoid this problem.

Another reason to improve your trim and reduce your reliance on your fins for buoyancy control is that the effort of finning uses up energy and will increase your breathing rate. So by improving your trim you can also reduce your breathing rate. This also has the effect of making you feel more comfortable in the water as you are no longer fighting to stay in the same position. This makes the whole experience of diving more enjoyable and comfortable which again is likely to reduce your breathing rate.

It is important to note that many divers do not have a horizontal position in the water but this does not mean that they have poor buoyancy control. Some of the most accomplished recreational divers and instructors in the world have a trim position that is far from horizontal and yet have perfect buoyancy. So a horizontal position is not essential for good buoyancy control although it is a good way to improve your buoyancy. For this reason a horizontal position has not been viewed as essential in recreational diving but rather it is a useful teaching tool or an optional extra. On the other hand for technical diving horizontal trim becomes much more important.

During decompression dives constant finning in order to maintain a deco stop is not practical. In order to do this the diver will have to maintain constant vigilance to ensure they do not drift down or up and any distraction, such as sending up a DSMB, switching to deco gas or checking their decompression schedule may result in them moving up or down. In addition constant finning on decompression stops means that they will be continuously drifting forward into their buddy, which can be very frustrating to both as well as likely to lead to twisted DSMB lines if there is more than one in the water.

In an overhead environment, such as a wreck or a cave, then good trim becomes absolutely essential. In many cases it is essential to be completely flat in the water in order to fit through small entrances and exits. Swimming through a doorway of a wreck that is lying on it's side is impossible unless you are completely horizontal. A diver in an upright position will simply not fit through the gap and even a slightly upright position is likely to result in them banging their cylinders on the top of the entrance or their knees and fins on the bottom of the entrance. The overhead environment diver cannot fin continuously or use their hands to control their position. By finning continuously they will be constantly moving which makes it impossible to stay stationary long enough to tie off their guideline. Drifting forward is not an option when there is a silty obstruction in front of you and moving your fins or hands to keep position can kick up additional silt.

There are a number of ways that you can change your position or trim in the water. The second and third definitions of trim give us an idea of what you can do and what you are aiming for. "To maintain an even balance of a ship or aircraft by adjusting the position of the load or cargo. The attitude of an aircraft in flight when the pilot lets the main control surfaces to take their own position." There are two main areas that you can focus on to improve your trim. The first is to move, change or modify your equipment in order to change your trim and the second is to change your diving technique to adjust your trim.

When we look at our diving equipment we have a number of items that are negatively buoyant; cylinders, weights, torches, etc. and a number of items that are positively buoyant; BCD/wing, dry suit, etc. For neutral buoyancy you just need to ensure that all of the negative buoyancy is counteracted by the positive buoyancy. As long as the two are equal then it doesn't matter where on your body you wear the equipment, you will still be neutrally buoyant. For trim, on the other hand, the correct positioning of the positive and negative pieces of equipment is essential in order to ensure a horizontal position. The position of a weight can make the difference between being feet heavy or head heavy. Switching weight from a weight belt to a v-weight (which is positioned between the cylinders and so moves the weight higher up the diver's body) will result in the diver becoming more head heavy while switching it to a tail weight (which is positioned below the bottom bolt of the twinset and so lower down the diver's body) will result in the diver becoming more feet heavy. Short dumpy cylinders will sit higher on your back and make you head heavy whereas taller and thinner cylinders will spread the weight along your length and make you more balanced. Many divers who have become accustomed to using ankle weights will find it very difficult to maintain a horizontal position as the ankle weights pull their feet down. The first step to achieving a horizontal position is therefore to lie completely still in the water without moving your hands or feet. You will then see if the distribution of weight is tipping your head down or feet down. You can then look at the distribution of the weight of your equipment and see if weight needs to be shifted around in order to compensate for the tipping.

The second way to control your trim is to modify your technique in the water. As well as your equipment, your trim is also dependant on the position of your body. By moving your body you can have a significant effect on your trim. Many divers do this by constantly moving their hands and feet. Divers with ankle weights usually fin continuously in order to keep their feet up. Others continuously use their hands to control their position. The disadvantage of both these methods is that when distracted the diver may forget to make these compensations. In addition, for technical diving these options are no longer viable. Constant finning on decompression stops or movement of hands and feet in an overhead environment are to be avoided. There are other techniques that you can use to control your position without constant movement. For example if you are head heavy then by pushing your arms forward you will move the positive buoyancy of your arms forward and bring your head up. Bending or straightening your legs as well as arching your back into a freefall parachutist position will affect your trim. Ultimately the goal of the technical diver is to be able to hold position in the water without any variation in their buoyancy and without tipping head down or feet down, all without any movement of the hands or fins

1

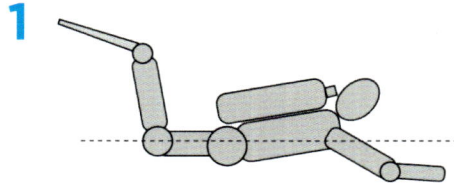

If a line is drawn from the shoulders to the hips and continuing on to the knees of the diver then trim can be used to mean the angle of this line. In this case the line is horizontal.

4

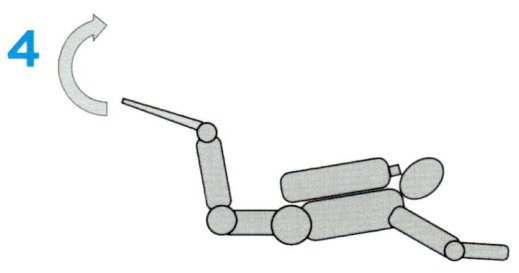

In this case, even though the diver is initially flat in the water, they are tipping head down, feet up. The diver will need to move weight down in order to maintain their position.

2

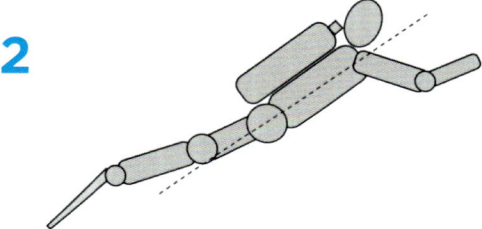

If a line is drawn from the shoulders to the hips and continuing on to the knees of the diver then trim can be used to mean the angle of this line. In this case the line is at approximately 45°.

5

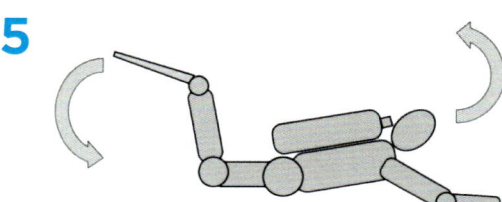

In this case, even though the diver is initially flat in the water, they are tipping head up, feet down. The diver will need to move weight up in order to maintain their position.

3

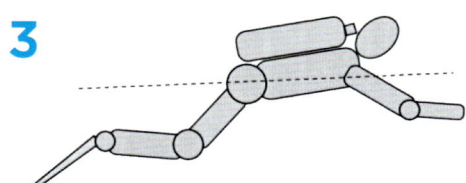

It is impossible to draw a line from the shoulders to the hips and continuing on to the knees of the diver in this case due to the fact that they are dropping their knees. Although the line from shoulder to hips is almost vertical the diver needs to lift their knees.

6

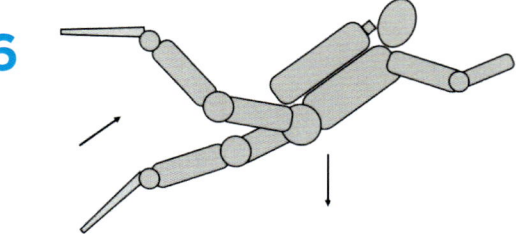

A head up trim position may be a result of a buoyancy issue. In this case the diver is negatively buoyant and is compensating by finning upwards to overcome the negative buoyancy and making it appear that they are neutrally buoyant

Diagram 6: Trim Position

Finning Techniques

24

"Don't be a fish; be a frog. Swim in the water and jump when you hit ground." **Kim Young-ha**

It's no surprise that technical diving involves different equipment. It has additional risks and uses different gases but just because you go a bit deeper do you really have to learn a whole new set of finning techniques? Don't you just kick your legs like you have always done?

Surprisingly many technical diving courses, supposedly the pinnacle of diving skills, go back to the basics of how to fin. On reflection maybe this shouldn't be such a surprise. The previous chapters have shown how the levels of buoyancy and trim required for technical diving are different to those for recreational diving and the same thing applies to finning techniques. The basic fin kick taught on all entry level courses is called the flutter kick. This involves a wide, slow, up and down motion, alternating legs with the knees straight and toes (fins) pointed. This has the advantage of being easy to learn and providing an effective use of power in propelling the diver forwards. For anyone who is familiar with the front crawl swimming stroke then it is very easy to pick up because it is the same leg movement that is used in the front crawl. A gentle flutter kick can produce a smooth movement through the water without exerting too much energy. The majority of recreational training agencies only teach this single technique. However for technical diving and indeed for many recreational diving situations a flutter kick is not always the best choice.

The greatest disadvantage of a flutter kick is that all of the power of the kick is directed downwards. This means that in silty conditions the power of the kick may disturb the silt even if you don't touch the bottom with your fins. A diver swimming a couple of metres above a silty bottom will still produce a cloud of silt if they use a flutter kick. Often it takes a few seconds for the power of the kick to reach the bottom and you have the situation where clouds of silt are appearing several metres behind the diver and several seconds after they have passed. They are not touching the bottom and think they are maintaining the visibility but, if they stop and look behind they will see a cloud of silt following them. In a silty overhead environment, such as when penetrating a wreck, this can be a serious safety issue but even for recreational divers on the outside of a wreck this can have an impact. They will reduce the visibility on the wreck by using this technique. We have all seen the situation where the visibility on a wreck deteriorates as the dive progresses; this is due to the amount of silt being kicked up.

Consequently even for recreational divers the flutter kick has some disadvantages. Despite this it is taught as the primary finning technique to most divers and many agencies do not teach any other techniques at entry level[39]. As well as the standard flutter kick the other options are modified flutter, frog kick, modified frog, helicopter turns and back finning. The modified flutter, involves bending the knees and kicking from the knees rather than the hips. This significantly reduces the power produced by the stroke and therefore it is less suited for swimming any significant distance. However, it has the effect of directing the force directly backwards rather than downwards. For enclosed or very silty areas this can be used to reduce the amount of silt disturbed.

Another finning technique which is widely used in technical diving is the frog kick. In the same way that the flutter kick is similar to the leg movement of the front crawl, the frog kick is similar to the leg movement of the breast stroke. In order to do a frog kick you need to float horizontally in the water and therefore buoyancy and trim already need to be under control. Your knees should be bent at right angles so that your fins are higher than your head. The most common mistake is to bend your legs at the hip as well but the legs need to be kept straight through the hips. This gives a position similar to a free fall parachutist in mid air. The legs are parted as in the normal breast stroke then brought together while straightening the knees so the fins go backwards as they come together. The ankles are rotated to try and bring the flat bottoms of the fins together. Then, when your feet are together, bend your knees up again. This has the advantage of directing all of the power of the kick directly backwards which provides a significant amount of forwards thrust but without kicking up any of the silt. Using a frog kick you can swim along almost touching the bottom but still without generating any silt. In an overhead environment this can be very useful but even in open water this can lead to a significant reduction in the amount of silt generated.

A variation of this is known as the modified frog kick which uses much smaller movements with most of the movement coming from the lower leg and ankles rather than the whole leg. This can be used in very confined spaces or for fine control of position. In addition to reducing silt the increase in control is one of the greatest benefits of mastering different fin techniques. This becomes even more clear when you stop thinking about moving forward but think about changing direction. If you want to turn around and are limited to using a traditional flutter kick then you have very few options. You can swim in a circle, can scull with your hands, can come upright and rotate in the water or you can grab hold of something and use this to turn yourself around. Neither of these is very efficient and have severe limitations if trying to turn around in a restricted area. Once you start to use a variety of other finning techniques then you quickly realise that if you have control over finning then you can also use this to control your position.

One of the most useful techniques for controlling your position is the use of helicopter turns. This allows you to pivot on the spot and turn within your own body length. In order to do a helicopter turn the diver starts in the same position as for a frog kick but only kicks with one foot while sculling backwards with the other. This makes the diver pivot on the spot. This is very useful when wanting to turn to look at your buddy without having to swim in a circle or when wanting to turn around in a restricted area. When starting out with helicopter turns it is sometimes easier to focus on using one fin at a time and then practice using them together.

The most difficult of the finning techniques is the back kick. Most divers, even some technical divers, go through their entire diving career without using a back kick however, if you can master it, then it can be extremely useful. A back kick allows you to swim backwards and effectively go into reverse. This is useful in a number of different situations. During decompression stops it is common for divers to drift in towards each other; a few strokes of back kicking can help you to keep a comfortable distance away from your buddy or even to continually back away if they have to fin to keep their legs up. Back kicks are also very useful for instructors as it

---

39 SDI is currently the only mainstream recreational agency that teaches a variety of finning techniques during their entry level courses

allows them to swim in to look at something, give a signal or make contact in some way with a student and then back away without having to turn their back on the student when turning around. It also allows you to back out of an area when there is not enough room to turn around. The back kick is particularly difficult for a number of reasons; the first is that it is quite an unnatural movement and the second is that it is a difficult technical manoeuvre. When watching someone do a frog kick or helicopter turn it is quite easy to see what they are doing and copy them. On the other hand with a back kick it's much more difficult to see exactly what they are doing and how it works. Once you start attempting a back kick it is made all the more difficult by the fact that the power part of the stroke is not very efficient but the recovery part, if not done correctly, is like a frog kick and can end up pushing you forward rather than back.

In order to do a back kick the diver has to be perfectly flat and with perfect buoyancy control, another reason why buoyancy and trim are the building blocks of good technique.

The diver starts with their feet together and their legs almost straight. They then scull their feet out to the side and bend their knees, effectively pulling their feet up towards their ears and using the side of the legs and their fins to provide the force. The tricky part is then to return the feet to the starting point without turning it into a frog kick. In order to do this they must bring their feet together and then slide them backwards while straightening their legs to return to the starting point. This makes it a three phase movement; kick, feet together and slide back. Trying to do it in two movements will just result in the diver moving forward rather than back.

At first you will probably do a good impression of an egg whisk and will undoubtedly end up going forwards rather than backwards. With more practice you will be able to get the power part of the stroke and may even go backwards a little although the recovery will still send you forward. After even more practice you will finally be able to move backwards and then recover without any forward movement. This is one technique that takes a lot of practice before it is possible to do it reliably every time. The key lesson is to have patience. Due to the inefficiency of the stroke you are not likely to start travelling backward at any great pace. The first stroke may have no obvious effect and the second and third may only result in a tiny movement. If you persevere you will build up momentum and by the fourth or fifth stroke you will be making reasonable progress backwards.

By expanding your repertoire of finning techniques recreational divers can gain a number of benefits. Using the right technique at the right time can help to reduce silt being kicked up on a wreck and as a result visibility of dives is increased. It can allow you to switch from using one set of muscles to another reducing fatigue and finally it can allow a much greater level of control over your position in the water. All of these can increase the enjoyment and comfort of a dive and that's something that should appeal to divers of all levels.

Advantages of various finning techniques	
Flutter kick	Uses strong thigh muscles Effective in strong currents
Modified flutter kick	Reduces silting compared to full flutter Good for restrictions with limited width such as hatchways in a wreck
Frog kick	Reduces silting compared to full flutter kick Efficient for long dives Good for restrictions with limited height
Modified frog kick	Reduces silting Good for restricted areas
Helicopter turn	Allows the diver to turn in any direction while maintaining horizontal trim Good for turning in restricted areas
Back kick	Good for maintaining position relative to your buddy Allows fine tuning of position Good for restricted areas where it is impossible to turn around

Table 8: Advantages of various finning techniques

Reaching Your Valves

25

"Success is due to our stretching to the challenges of life. Failure comes when we shrink from them." **John C. Maxwell**

Technical diving invariably involves using either a rebreather or a twinset. There are a number of common twinset configurations but the most common setup is to have the two cylinders connected together with a manifold and an isolation valve on the manifold. This allows you to use both cylinders without having to switch from one regulator to the other. The disadvantage of this setup is that in the case of a free-flow or other major leak the gas will drain from both sides unless the isolating manifold can be closed. If you cannot close the isolation manifold then you are not really diving a twinset but instead are diving one large cylinder which just happens to be split into two sections with a connection between the two.

This is the reason why the shutdown is such an important skill for twinset divers and the reason why it is emphasised on almost every open circuit technical diving course. The first step in doing a shutdown is being able to reach the isolation valve and the two cylinder valves. Many divers struggle with this task and often give up on reaching their valves as they believe it is impossible. Instead they may change to using independent cylinders so that they don't have the connecting manifold; or they switch to inverted cylinders so they can reach their valves more easily; or they use a remote isolator, commonly known as a 'slob knob'; or worst of all they just ignore the fact that they cannot reach their valves and hope that they never have a problem that will require a shutdown. In reality the vast majority of divers are able to reach their valves but have just never been shown how to reach them. Many technical divers, including many technical instructors, simply do not know the right technique to reach their valves.

The reason why so many people struggle to do this is that there are a number of things you need to get right in order to reach. Get them all right and it can be remarkably easy but get just one or two wrong and you will be struggling. The first area to look at is personal flexibility. Some people are simply more flexible than others, this can be due to body type, previous injuries or lack of stretching. In order to test your flexibility you should aim to reach behind your head and then down towards your shoulder blades. If you can touch your spine at the point level with the top of your shoulders when wearing a t-shirt or other normal clothing, then there is no reason why you should not be able to reach your valves. I have found that the vast majority of people can do this and that it is very rarely personal flexibility that stops them reaching their valves. There are, of course, exceptions; sporting injuries and motorbike accidents are amongst the common causes for reduced mobility and in these cases there is often nothing you can do to increase flexibility. In many cases though, gentle stretching exercises can make a significant difference to the level of flexibility.

Figure 28: If you can reach this far you can reach your valves

The next area to look at is equipment. There are a whole host of equipment factors that can help or hinder the task. The first is your undersuit, you may be able to reach your spine in a t-shirt but when you put on your undersuit this may restrict your movement. Many suits have a seam running under the arm, down the body all the way to the feet and this can restrict your movement. If this is the case a new undersuit or an alteration to the existing undersuit may provide enough movement. The same thing applies to the dry suit. Many have a seam that runs the same as the undersuit and can severely limit your movement. Repeat the same stretch while wearing your dry suit and this will show if you have enough scope for movement in your drysuit. Unfortunately, if it is the drysuit that is restricting your movement there is no easy or cheap answer and a new drysuit or an alteration to your existing suit may be required in order for you to reach the valves. You may have plenty of flexibility in your drysuit on dry land but when you kit up be careful that your weight belt or harness doesn't trap some of the material and restrict your flexibility. During the descent I usually stretch out my arms in front of me to ensure that none of the suit is restricted by the weight belt or harness.

Figure 29: A well fitting drysuit will not restrict your movement

The next pieces of equipment to look at are the cylinders. If they are too high or too low on your back then it will make it difficult to reach. This can usually be adjusted by changing the bands on the cylinder to move them up or down on your back. Some backplates have a number of holes so that they can be attached to the cylinders at a range of heights. The harness can also have a major impact on your ability to reach your valves. Some makes of harness have very bulky shoulder padding which can restrict your movement. An overly tight harness can also restrict your movement while an overly loose harness can allow the cylinders to slide around on your back and move the valves out of reach. A correctly fitting harness is therefore essential if you want to reach your valves.

On many twinsets you will notice the isolation valve is angled over towards the divers head. This makes it easier for you to get your hand on the valve as you don't need to come over and down onto it. Many divers replace the short, plastic valve with a longer rubberised version. The additional length makes it easier to reach and the rubberised or 'tactile' material makes it easier to grip and hence turn. Each of these aspects on their own makes it slightly easier to reach your valves but when taken together can make the difference between struggling to reach and turn the valve and easily reaching it.

If your equipment is set up correctly then the only other area to look at is technique. If this is what's stopping you then that is good news because changing equipment can be difficult and expensive but it is relatively easy to correct your technique. Most divers, when they are trying to do a shutdown, make the mistake of coming upright. This is because they are often more comfortable in an upright position. Be that as it may, this makes it even more difficult to reach your valves. As you come upright the cylinders slide down your back as a result of gravity pulling them down. Even if you hike them up they will just slide back down again. This makes it harder to reach as you have further to go before you reach the valves. Although many divers are more comfortable upright it is much easier to reach your valves when you are horizontal in the water. This is because gravity is not pulling your cylinder down your back when you are flat. If you hike them up while flat then they will stay there.

By far the most common mistake people make when doing a shutdown is to drop their head. Everyone does it to begin with; they think that if they drop their head they will have more room to reach their valves. In dropping your head you are not just moving your head but you are moving your shoulders away from the twinset. This has the effect of increasing the distance you have to reach in order to get to the valves. The most important thing to remember when doing a shutdown is to keep your head back. With your head right back your should just about be able to feel the first stages of your regulators on either side of the back of your head. You may even be able to feel the isolation valve in the centre. In this case, if you can touch the back of your head, then you should be able to reach the isolation valve. It is even possible to put your hand on the back of your head and then move your head back so as to push your hand onto the valve. A good way to check this is to think about where you are looking. If you are looking down at the seabed then you have dropped your head but if you are looking at your buddy in front of you then you know you have your head up.

Figure 30: An example of poor technique. An upright position and dropping the head makes it much more difficult to reach your valves

Figure 31: An example of good technique. With a horizontal position and the head back the head is much closer to the valves

Figure 32: It's easy to reach your valves when you have the right technique

The last aspect of technique to watch is how you reach back towards the valves. If your elbow is out to the side of your body then this restricts how far you can reach back due to the way the shoulder joint works. If you keep your elbow in close to the side of your head while reaching you can reach much further. The easiest way to do this is to first stretch your hand out in front of your face then bring it back past your ear and keep reaching back until your elbow also passes close to your ear. You will now find that your hand is in almost the perfect position for reaching your isolation valve. Just remember to keep your head back while you are doing this.

Many divers seem to be able to just about reach their isolator and right hand cylinder valve but then struggle with the left hand valve. There are two reasons for this. The first is that the majority of people are right handed and have more dexterity and stretch in their right arm and correspondingly less in their left arm. The second reason is that a shutdown drill starts with the isolator and right hand post and then moves on to the left hand post. Often the diver has a good position, i.e. flat and head back, when starting the shutdown but as it progresses they become more and more upright and their head drops as they struggle or get tired. By the time they get to the left hand post their technique has deteriorated so much that they inevitably struggle to reach the valve. This is why it is important to monitor your technique as you go through the shutdown and ensure that your position is not changing.

It may seem to be a lot to remember just to reach your valves but realistically it is very easy. You only need to set the equipment up correctly once and then from that point onwards it is correctly set up. Equally it may seem unrealistic to first get into a flat position, then remember to put your head back and finally to first reach forward and then back past your ear while you have gas venting loudly from a leak behind your head. The more you practice this the easier it gets until eventually you will be able to hold a flat position with your head back at all times. This makes it easier to then reach back and close your valves. In addition it is worth a little bit of effort in practice to remove the risk of not being able to reach your valves should an emergency ever occur.

	'Key steps in reaching your valves'
1.	Stretch regularly to ensure you have enough flexibility
2.	Ensure your drysuit and undersuit do not restrict your movement
3.	Review your cylinder bands, backplate and harness configuration to ensure that your cylinders are in the right place
4.	Stretch out your arms, drysuit and undersuit as soon as you get in the water
5.	Maintain horizontal trim to keep the cylinders high up on your back
6.	Keep your head up so that the back of your head is touching your first stages
7.	Maintain eye contact with your buddy or other visual reference to make sure you keep your head up
8.	Keep your elbow in close to your head when reaching back
9.	Do not drop your head while reaching back
10.	Use video to watch yourself trying to reach. This will help you see what mistakes you are making
11.	Book a day with an instructor who can help you identify what mistakes you are making
12.	Practice, Practice, Practice

Table 9: Key steps in reaching your valves

Shutdown Drills

26

"There is nothing in the intellect which was not first in some way in the senses," **Maria Montessori**

Once you are confident you can reach the valves the next question is "what do we do now in order to solve a problem?"

There are two types of problems that you might face. In some cases you know exactly where the leak is coming from and which valve it comes from. In this case a full shutdown drill is not necessary. If you know the right hand regulator is leaking and this comes from the right hand post then you would just close that post. Equally if it is the drysuit hose that has burst and that comes from the left hand post then you would just close the left hand post. However, things are not always this simple. It is very difficult to identify where a leak is coming from if it is behind your head. If there are hoses crossing behind your head you may have bubbles coming from the left hand side that are fed from the right hand post and vice versa. This also means that listening to try and tell which side the bubbles are coming from is useless, even more so as the sound properties of water mean that it is more difficult to tell direction underwater than on the surface. Finally, trying to use your hand to judge where the bubbles are coming from is also unreliable as you can feel bubbles on the right hand side from a burst backup regulator hose – which is fed from the left hand post.

Figure 33: It can be very difficult to tell where a leak is coming from'

Even if the leak is in front of you it is still very difficult to tell where it is coming from. A buddy of mine once had the medium pressure inflator hose feeding his wing burst during a dive. Even though the leak was in front of him, he had no idea of where the leak was coming from as all he could see were bubbles. It could have been his primary or backup regulator, it could also have been his drysuit inflator but he could not tell due to the bubbles. Even for me, looking directly at him, it was very difficult to identify where the bubbles were coming from. It is very foolish or arrogant to assume that you will always be able to tell where a leak is coming from. If you do not know where the leak is coming from then a full shutdown drill will be required.

Figure 34: Even your buddy might find it difficult to tell where the leak is coming from

There are a number of variants on the shutdown drill. Table 10 shows the six basic steps involved in the most common shutdown drill and the text below provides an explanation of each of the steps.

1.	Close central isolator a. Signal with torch to your team that you have a problem b. Switch to backup regulator
2.	Close right hand post a. Signal with torch to your team that you have a problem b. Purge right hand regulator c. Check if bubbles have stopped
3.	Reopen right hand post a. Check right hand regulator b. Switch from left hand to right hand regulator c. Transfer torch to right hand
4.	Close left hand post a. Signal with torch to your team that you have a problem b. Purge left hand regulator c. Check if bubbles have stopped
5.	Re-open left hand post a. Check left hand regulator
6.	Re-open central isolator
7.	Valve check

Table 10: The steps in a shutdown drill

1 - CLOSE CENTRAL ISOLATOR

The first step in the shutdown drill is to close the central isolator. The reason for this is that while the isolator is open gas will be leaking from both cylinders. Once the isolator has been closed you have saved at least half of your gas. At worst you could do nothing else and still have half of your gas available. This reduces the pressure and stress as you no longer need to worry about the possibility of losing all of your gas. The situation has changed from life or death to an inconvenience. This psychological advantage can provide a huge benefit. In order to close the central isolator we usually reach back with our right hand and close the isolator. In order to attract our buddies attention you can also use a torch to signal to them that you have a problem. For this reason it is common to have an umbilical torch with a Goodman Handle in the left hand. This means that while the right hand is closing the central isolator you can be signalling with the left hand by moving this torch from side to side to give the "attention" signal.

It also makes sense to turn towards your buddies at this point if you were not already facing them. This allows you to use them as a visual reference to avoid sinking or rising while doing the shutdown. By keeping an eye on your buddies it also forces you to keep your head up rather than dropping it which, as we saw in the previous chapter, makes it easier to reach the valves. By facing your buddies they can see what you are doing and can keep track of the progress of the shutdown just in case they need to step in and help you at some point. If they know where you are then they are less likely to accidentally turn off one post at the same time as you have turned off the other. Finally if you are facing them they will more easily be able to see the problem and may be able to tell you the source of the leak.

Once the isolator is closed then you know you have saved at least half of your gas but ideally we would like to save more than half. In addition shutting off the leaking valve reduces the level of stress on the diver and makes it easier to manage buoyancy control. The bubbles produced by a leak can significantly affect your buoyancy and can lead to rapid ascents. For this reason you can now move on to trying to identify where the leak is coming from and shut it down

Figure 35: Closing the right hand post

2 - CLOSE RIGHT HAND POST

It is common that the primary regulator and primary buoyancy control come from the right hand post and it follows that this is the one that has the most demands placed on it. For this reason it is more likely for the right hand post to be the one that is leaking and therefore you should start by shutting down this post. However, as you are breathing from the regulator attached to the right hand post, it is not a good idea to shutdown the regulator you are breathing from and so the first step is to switch to your backup regulator which comes from the left hand post. You can then reach back, again with the right hand, and close the right hand post. Again, you can use the torch in your left hand to continue signalling to your team if necessary. Once the right hand post is completely closed you can then see if the bubbles stop as the air in the right hand hoses will gradually leak out. If the leak is small, then this may take some time, so it is a better idea to purge the right hand regulator. If the bubbles stop then you know the leak was from the right hand side but if they do not, you know that it is coming from somewhere else and that the right hand regulator is not the problem.

3 - RE-OPEN RIGHT HAND POST

If the right hand post is not the problem then you have just shut down the working post and are breathing off the leaking post so you need to re-open the right hand post. Once this is done, check the regulator by purging it gently to ensure that it is working correctly and then switch back from the left hand regulator to the right hand regulator.

4 - CLOSE LEFT HAND POST

If the problem is not with the right hand post then it is almost certainly the left hand post and so you would close the valve on the left hand post. If you have a torch in your left hand then you will need to transfer it to the right hand before reaching back with the left hand to close the valve. Again you can signal to your buddies with the torch that is now in your right hand. Once you have shut down the left hand post you can purge the left hand regulator to check that the bubbles have stopped.

5 - RE-OPEN LEFT HAND POST

To complete the drill you should ensure that all valves are once again opened and you should start off by re-opening the left hand post. Check that the regulator is working by briefly purging the regulator.

6 - RE-OPEN CENTRAL ISOLATOR

Finally re-open the central isolator and you are back to the starting position. To confirm this, check the position of all valves to ensure that they are open.

7 - VALVE CHECK

Finally we check that all valves are in the correct position by performing a valve or flow check. Whenever anyone, including yourself, has been manipulating the valves, it is a good idea to do a flow check at the end to ensure all the valves are where they are supposed to be. This involves reaching back and checking that each valve in turn is full open. Once this is done you signal to the team that the drill is complete.

Of course you would hope that in a real situation you would, at some point, identify where the bubbles have been coming from and by turning off the relevant post you can stop the leak. At this point you have the isolator closed and are only breathing from one of the cylinders. One of the advantages of a manifold is that it allows the gas from one cylinder to pass from one side to the other and thus you can breathe from both cylinders through either post. This means that the gas in both cylinders can be accessed even if one of the valves is turned off. However, this is only possible if the isolator is re-opened. If the bubbles were coming from the right post then, once this has been turned off, you could re-open the isolator and breathe the gas from the left hand cylinder as well as the right hand cylinder through the left hand regulator. Equally if the leak was on the left hand post then once shut off you could re-open the isolator and breathe the gas left in both cylinders from the right hand regulator. Even if the leak has been stopped the buddy team should start the ascent as you now have no redundant source of gas and have probably also lost the feed to one of your sources of buoyancy.

On the other hand if you cannot stop the bubbles, that is to say you have shut down the right hand post, purged it and, after turning it back on, turned off the left hand post and also purged that without stopping the bubbles then you have a much more serious problem. The leak is not coming from one of the valves but is either coming from the manifold itself, the isolator or possibly from the cylinder valve. It is impossible to work out yourself which of the three possible positions are causing the leak. If your buddy is on hand they may be able to assist in identifying the source of the leak. The difficulty in this case is that you would be unable to stop the leak. The best you can do in this case would be to keep the isolator closed to maintain at least half your gas and start your ascent immediately.

As mentioned above there are other versions of the shutdown or valve drill. Some of these involve minor variations such as breathing down the regulator rather than purging it. Some agencies and instructors will be less interested in using the torch for signalling to your buddies. However the most significant variation is the GUE valve drill. This is discussed overleaf.[40]

---

40 I am not a GUE instructor and so this discussion is based on my own interpretation of this drill. There may be mistakes or misinterpretations in my description of this drill. If you want to learn the GUE drill then you will need to contact a GUE instructor.

VALVE DRILL VS WHAT YOU WOULD DO FOR REAL

1.	Get your team's attention a. Signal to your team you are going to perform a valve drill b. Wait until your team is in place and then continue
2.	Close right hand post a. Purge backup regulator b. Shut down the right hand post while simultaneously signalling you are manipulating a valve to your team c. When the post is shut down, breathe down the regulator until it "locks" d. Remove the regulator and replace with your backup regulator e. Clip off your primary regulator on the right chest D ring
3.	Open right hand post a. Open the right post b. Unclip the primary regulator and purge it c. Remove the backup regulator from your mouth and replace with the primary regulator
4.	Close the central isolator a. Shut down the isolator while simultaneously signalling you are manipulating a valve to your team
5.	Open the central isolator a. When the valve is closed, re-open the isolator
6.	Close the left hand post a. Move your torch to your right hand b. Shut down the left hand post while simultaneously signalling you are manipulating a valve to your team c. When the post is closed, purge the backup regulator until it "locks"
7.	Open the left hand post a. Open the left post and purge to confirm it is working b. Move the torch to your left hand
8.	Valve Check a. Check the position of your right hand post b. Check the position of your isolator c. Move the torch to your right hand and check the position of your left hand post d. Signal that your drill is complete

Table 11: The GUE valve drill

1 - GET YOUR TEAM'S ATTENTION

A fundamental aspect of the GUE drill is that it is a team oriented drill where the team is an essential part of the drill. This is very relevant for any non-GUE diver as in order to use this drill you must have a team that is similarly qualified and is aware of the drill and what you expect from them. In the same way as the previous drill you would get your team's attention by moving your torch from side to side to give the "attention" signal.

2 - CLOSE RIGHT HAND POST

As mentioned, it is common that the primary regulator and primary buoyancy control come from the right hand post. For this reason it is more likely for the right hand post to be the one that is leaking and so you should start by shutting down this post. The GUE drill closes the right hand post before the isolator. If it is indeed the right hand post then this will result in a greater saving of gas, however in the case of it being the left hand post then there will be a greater loss. This drill advocates breathing down the right hand regulator until the demand valve "locks". This is to ensure that there is no gas left in the right hand side of the system. In this case it is also important to check that the left hand regulator works by purging it slightly to avoid turning off the right hand regulator and then not being able to find the left hand regulator or finding that it has a problem. This purge does not remove the risk completely. The left hand regulator may purge but still have a problem or if the valve is turned on there may be enough gas in the hose to perform a purge but then none left when you put the regulator in your mouth. At this point your buddy would need to assist.

While shutting down the valve you would continue to signal your team moving your torch from side to side to give the "attention" signal. Once the right hand post has been closed the right hand regulator is clipped off to the right hand shoulder D-ring.

3 - OPEN RIGHT HAND POST

If the right hand post is not the problem you can re-open this post and then unclip the regulator from the right hand shoulder D-ring and purge it to make sure it is working. Then swap from the left hand regulator back to the right hand regulator.

4 - CLOSE THE CENTRAL ISOLATOR

By this point the rest of your team should be present and ready to help identifying the problem. This will determine the best course of action, As a result the rest of the drill is not what you would expect to do in a real situation and is aimed more at ensuring that you can reach all of the valves. The next step in the drill is to close the central isolator while signalling to your team.

5 - OPEN THE CENTRAL ISOLATOR

The next step would be to open the central isolator. It must be stressed that this is not what you would do in a real situation. Closing the central isolator after already determining that the right hand regulator is not the problem would slow down the loss of gas from both sides but reopening the isolator immediately afterwards completely negates this as you would once again be losing gas from both sides and have not progressed any further in identifying where the leak is coming from. The main point of this step of the drill at this point is to show that you can indeed close and open the central isolator.

6 - CLOSE THE LEFT HAND POST

If the problem is not with the right hand post then it is almost certainly the left hand post and so you would close the valve on the left hand post. As you have your torch in your left hand then you will need to transfer it to the right hand before reaching back with the left hand to close the valve. Again you will signal to your buddies with the torch that is now in your right hand. Once you have shut down the left hand post you will purge the left hand regulator rather than breathing it down to check whether the bubbles have stopped.

7 - OPEN THE LEFT HAND POST

You then re-open the left hand post and check that the regulator is working by briefly purging the regulator. Then move the torch back to the left hand.

8 - VALVE CHECK

Finally check that all valves are in the correct position by performing a valve or flow check. Whenever anyone, including yourself, has been manipulating the valves, it is a good idea to do a flow check at the end to ensure all the valves are where they are supposed to be. This involves reaching back and checking that each valve in turn is fully open. Once this is done you signal to the team that the drill is complete.

There are three main differences between the two drills described above. The first difference is that one starts with closing the central isolator while the other starts with closing the right hand post. The argument for starting with the isolator is that while the isolator is open gas will be leaking from both cylinders. Once the isolator has been closed you will have saved at least half of your gas. At worst you could do nothing else and still have half of your gas available. This reduces the pressure and stress as you no longer need to worry about the possibility of losing all of your gas. This psychological advantage can provide a huge benefit. In order to close the central isolator you usually reach back with your right hand and close the isolator. On the other hand the argument for starting with the right hand post is that it is more likely for the right hand post to be the one that is leaking and so you should start by shutting down this post. Furthermore, shutting the isolator does not move you any closer to identifying where the leak is coming from or stopping it. If it is indeed the right hand post that is leaking then going straight for this post will result in a greater saving of gas. Nevertheless in the case of it being the left hand post then there will be significantly more loss.

The second main difference is that the standard drill is designed to be exactly what you would do in the case of an unknown leak. This means that the process that is practiced is meant to be the process that is followed in a real situation. This builds on the concept that, in an emergency, frequently practiced skills are the ones that are most likely to be remembered. However the GUE drill is not what you would do in a real emergency and apart from closing the right hand post the actual steps taken will depend on the situation and the input from your team. The process of reaching the valves – the valve drill – and the actions to be taken in an emergency, are two different things and following the actual steps of the valve drill would not be the right course of action in a real situation. This is one of the disadvantages of this drill in that it breaks the principle of practicing, and building up muscle memory, of what to do in an emergency through practicing the actual steps to be followed. The danger is that you fall back on performing the steps of the valve drill. It has been shown time and time again that in a stressful situation we tend to do what we have been drilled to do and so by having a realistic drill it increases our chance of doing the right thing in an emergency. This is also one of the dangers of divers adopting practices they have heard about without understanding the reasoning behind it.

The last main difference is that the standard drill can be completed without assistance from a buddy or team. If they are available then they can help out but equally the diver can solve the problem on their own if necessary. It is also an advantage if you dive with a range of people who may or may not know a particular drill. The GUE approach, on the other hand, depends on having a team that understands the process and with which you have practiced. As a result the GUE drill should only be used within a well practiced GUE team.

It doesn't matter which drill you adopt as long as you are confident that you could execute it in a real emergency. A drill will only work if you practice it regularly. Knowing what to do in theory is only part of the solution. It is essential that technical divers practice this drill on a regular basis in order that if they do ever need to do a shutdown they are confident that they will be able to do it quickly and safely.

Individual or Team Diving

27

"All for one and one for all." **d'Artagnan**

One of the most contentious issues amongst technical divers is the difference between the self sufficiency and team diving approaches to diving. Like a number of other issues in technical diving it seems to polarize opinions, often along agency boundaries. This often leads to exaggerated positions that can take on a similarity to religious fundamentalism.

The self sufficiency mindset is where the diver is fully self sufficient and approaches the dive with the view that they can perform the dive on their own and would be fully able to complete the dive without a buddy. The approach is summed up by the mindset that if you can't do the dive on your own then you should not be doing the dive at all.

The other approach is team diving where strong team work and cooperation are the focus of the dive and you plan to dive with a team of divers and the team works as a well coordinated whole.

These two approaches seem to have a very different emphasis and many divers think that they are contradictory. That is you have to decide whether you have a self sufficient approach or a team based approach and that it is a choice of one or the other. Both approaches have their extremists who will go to great lengths to explain why their approach is right and the other approach is wrong.

In some areas technical diving has evolved into a culture of solo diving where many experienced technical divers dive solo. All equipment choices are made on the basis that you will be diving alone or that your buddy will be of no use. Gas planning is based on the principle that it is impossible or unlikely that your buddy will be any use in an emergency and so all procedures are based on individual action.

The team diving approach also has its extremists who focus on teamwork as the primary goal and consider self sufficiency to be a sign of weak teamwork. These divers will only dive with divers who follow the exact same team procedures.

In reality these two extreme positions are not very realistic and when taken to the extreme counteract the very point of the principles. This can cause significant problems as the advocates of self sufficiency can refuse to see some of the benefits of team diving and the advocates of team diving refuse to see any benefit in self sufficiency.

In particular the principle of self sufficiency does not mean the same thing as solo diving. For example, pioneering technical diving instructor Kevin Gurr says "Assume all dives are solo dives; do not get into the water if you feel you can't do it without someone else to rely on."[41] This is a clear endorsement of the self sufficient approach and many people have taken this to be a recommendation for diving solo. However Kevin then goes on to say "This does not mean you should not dive in a team, you should. Be prepared to be separated and to have to look after your self." Similarly those who advocate team diving do not mean that you should not be able to deal with situations on your own or need to rely on your team.

So despite initial impressions the self sufficient and team diving approaches are not as contradictory as they might at first seem. In fact they are just two sides of the same coin.

The best technical divers obviously have to have good individual skills. Building on your own level of buoyancy control, familiarity with kit and ability to deal with difficult situations are fundamental for anyone wanting to progress in technical diving. No diver who has thought about this question for more then a millisecond would ever suggest anything less. Team sports such as football, rugby or cricket are a perfect example of the team approach but players still ensure that they work on their individual skills. Players with weak individual skills would never make it into the team in the first place. Diving with someone who is not self sufficient is not team diving. If one of the team cannot deal with an emergency situation then they are going to weaken the overall team rather than strengthen it. This means that self sufficiency is clearly a prerequisite for team diving.

The self sufficiency extremists however go further than this. They claim that all divers should be self sufficient because you can never rely on a buddy to provide any assistance in an emergency. They will often cite examples of where an individual buddy has not been able or willing to provide assistance in an emergency and from this conclude that no buddy will ever be able to provide assistance. Furthermore, they argue that a poor buddy might cause an incident that would not have happened had you been on your own. As such their argument is that it's better to be completely solo and never have a buddy than to have a poor buddy. In some ways this argument has some merits in recreational diving as there are a whole range of abilities. Inexperienced or out of practice divers can certainly fit this description and many instructors and dive guides will tell you that they feel safer on their own. Certain recreational training agencies even support the concept of solo diving in the recreational area and provide training courses on self sufficiency and solo diving. However, this argument breaks down for technical diving. At this level any divers undertaking these types of dives require a higher level of skill and abilities. Divers who are unable to help their buddy are clearly operating at the limits of their own ability and therefore do not have enough self sufficiency to undertake that dive whether they are alone or with a buddy.

The best approach then is to aim for self sufficiency within a team environment. Each diver should have enough capacity to resolve any problems they may have and have enough spare capacity to be able to offer assistance to the other members of their team. If their buddies also have enough capacity to resolve their own problems and have enough spare capacity to be able to offer assistance to the other divers, then you have a very strong team.

The strongest teams usually consist of experienced individual divers with good self sufficiency and self awareness skills that have practiced working together in a team. Training and practice are essential in order for team diving to work successfully. Each member of the team should have similar views so they are following the same general approach. In addition good teamwork only comes with practice. You can see this with national sports teams. Each player is amongst the best player in the country yet unless they train together as a team they will not be able to perform well as an effective team.

When team diving is carried out by experienced, trained divers then it is a very safe way of diving. In the case of a problem you have more options available to help out; more gas available, more chance of spotting the problem and more ideas on how to solve it. In the case of an incident, one member of the team can be initiating a rescue while the other sends up a delayed SMB and another provides a visual reference to ensure the rest of the team can maintain depth. It is when problems occur that the benefits of diving in a team become apparent.

---

41 Gurr, K. (2010). Technical Diving From the Bottom Up.

Of course this is very easy to say and raises the question that if self sufficiency within a team environment is the goal how come it is not that common? The reason for this is that it's not easy to develop these two aspects. The time and effort required to master your own skills to the point where you are truly self sufficient and then the additional time and effort required to maintain those skills is more than most people can commit to. We all have jobs, families, other hobbies and commitments which are all competing for our time. It is entirely feasible to be a recreational diver and just dive a few times a year on holiday or on a couple of dive club trips. However, this is not the case for technical diving. If you are involved in decompression diving, trimix or rebreathers then it is essential to ensure that you put in sufficient practice to build up and maintain your skills. Some people may take to diving more easily than others but no one is born with all the skills and knowledge they need to become a technical diver. There are some people that may have more innate football skills than others but if you want to play for one of the premiership teams you will need to put in a huge amount of practice in order to refine your skills and reach the level required. Once you have reached that level you then need to put in even more effort to maintain those skills.

The development of a strong team also requires time and effort. If it is difficult to ensure that a single person can dedicate the time and effort it is even more difficult to gather a group or team to practice together. The individual commitments of each team member and the logistics of getting them together can be difficult. Notwithstanding the same principle applies. If you want to become a true technical diver then it requires a certain commitment in terms of time and effort. Irrespective of how good a football player is and how much time they spend working on their individual skills they spend more time in team training.

It is because developing strong self sufficiency skills and teamwork require such a commitment that alternative approaches have sprung up. If individual divers and their buddies do not have the individual or team skills required they take alternative approaches to try to overcome these problems. Teamwork is made more prescriptive so that it removes the emphasis on the individual diver. Alternatively teamwork is ignored alltogether and divers adopt a solo diving mentality. Each of these approaches might seem easier in the short term and more appealing to those who cannot commit the time and effort to develop their individual and team skills but it is a poor solution to the problem. In the case of emergencies the lack of personal skills and self sufficiency can cause problems for you and any buddies you are loosely teamed up with. Equally the lack of team skills may cause confusion and often makes the situation worse. Even though those alternatives might seem more attractive in the short term and may be acceptable for the majority of divers where nothing goes wrong, they are a poor long term solution as they can fall apart in times of emergency.

There is no getting away from the fact that for technical diving there is a need to invest time and effort in developing your personal skills and your team skills to a higher level than is normally required for recreational diving. Playing football in the park with our kids, or in a pub team is great fun. In this environment you will sometimes find very good players but the level of play is nowhere near the same level as in the Premier League. As technical divers we should use Premier League football as our model rather than a game in the park or the occasional pub team game.

Team Sizing

28

"Coming together is a beginning. Keeping together is progress. Working together is success." **Henry Ford**

Recreational diver training agencies have always encouraged divers to adopt the buddy system and always dive in buddy pairs. Diving in a group made up of more than two people has been described as undesirable while most agencies explicitly ban solo diving. The 2005 BSAC incident report explicitly raises the risks of diving in a trio and one of its four main conclusions is that "Fatal incidents associated with solo and trio diving continue to feature"[42].

This view must be balanced against the teachings of the technical diver training agencies who encourage divers to dive as a team and often cite three as the optimum team size.[43] Technical divers carry out a large number of challenging dives to depths well in excess of the recreational limit in this team format with obvious success. What makes them choose this style of diving if the recreational industry is so set against it?

There are a number of reasons for the apparent contradiction between recreational and technical training agencies. By examining these reasons we may be able to adopt some of the best practices from team diving for use in recreational diving. We will also see that many of the concepts of good buddy diving are the same as those of good team diving.

Team diving has a number of disadvantages if you are not familiar with diving in this way. Most recreational divers have little experience of this type of diving and usually express a dislike of diving in a three. This is not surprising as all recreational training focuses on diving in buddy pairs and for most divers their subsequent diving has all been focused on buddy pairs. It's no wonder then that diving in a trio is uncomfortable as you have never been trained or practiced diving in this way

In the recreational world a trio is often put together at the last minute due to odd numbers. Very little thought is put into who should be teamed up with whom and there is no preparation, planning or practice. In this case we end up with a haphazard trio which is certainly going to cause more problems than a traditional buddy pair. If an incident occurs then the third person adds confusion to the situation rather than helping to resolve it and there have been a number of cases where two divers become involved in a situation and subsequently become separated from the third. In these cases the divers are not following a team diving approach but are simple jumping in as a trio.

The buddy system also has its disadvantages. It can lead to

---

[42] BSAC incident report 2005
[43] TDI Intro To Tech Manual, TDI Advanced Trimix Manual, IANTD Normoxic Trimix manual and any GUE manual.

buddy dependence where we always assume our buddy is there to get us out of trouble. This is not always the case. In the case of a problem underwater buddies are often too far apart to be able to help each other or do not pay sufficient attention to their buddy to notice that they have got tangled up in fishing line or have experienced some other problem.

The buddy system is often followed in name only with so called "same ocean buddies" who jump in together and will spend time somewhere in the vicinity of each other without really expecting to stay together. These divers are effectively solo diving but without the equipment, training and experience to deal with a problem on their own.

Poor buddy skills often go unnoticed on recreational dives but for technical dives or on dives with three divers these buddy or team skills become much more important. It is possible to get away with poor buddy skills when there are only two divers but this becomes less feasible as the number of divers increases or the complexity of the dive increases. In this case additional techniques and training are required to ensure things go to plan.

Effective team diving clearly involves more than just diving with more than two divers. Team diving involves a style of diving where diving in a trio or larger group is a conscious decision which is planned in advance and where adequate training, practice and preparation has already been carried out. In a buddy pair you only have one other person to keep track of, this makes things fairly straightforward. When diving in a trio you now have two others to keep track of and therefore you spend more time looking for the third person. As you are unfamiliar with diving in a trio all three of you are likely to be moving around and looking for the other two which makes the task even more difficult. If you are diving in a four then you now have three other divers to look for and now you spend more time looking for the other divers than looking at

the wreck. It's no surprise that your first experience of diving in a three is likely to put you off ever doing it again.

This problem occurs because divers don't usually know where to look for the other divers, especially in a trio or more. One of the key principles of team diving is having agreed positions. This simplifies things immensely because if you know exactly where the other two divers should be, it's very easy to confirm that they are indeed in the spot you expected without having to look 360 degrees around and then above and below to find them.

Common positions when diving in a three are to dive in a line, either one in front of the other or side by side, or alternatively in an arrow head position. Swimming side by side works well for drift dives or well broken up wrecks where you are swimming over the top of the wreckage. In this case the person on the left only has to keep track of the person in the middle – no different to a buddy pair. The person in the middle has to keep an eye on the person to their left and right but equally has two people keeping an eye on them. The person on the right just has to keep an eye on the person in the middle.

Another option, one in front of the other works well for swimming along the side of wrecks, reefs, through restricted areas or on wall dives. In this case the person in front only has to keep track of the person immediately behind them – again no different to a buddy pair. The person in the middle has to keep an eye on the person in front and the person behind. This is more work but again they have two people keeping an eye on them. The person at the back just has to keep an eye on the person in the middle however this is the most exposed position as there is no one looking at them unless the person in the middle looks back to monitor them. Of course this is no worse than a buddy pair where one buddy is in front of the other.

An arrow head position can work in a number of situations. In this case one person is in front at the tip of the arrow head and the other two are side by side behind the lead diver. This is more like a buddy pair with one person in front and so may be more comfortable for divers used to buddy diving. This is preferable to the single person being behind the other two as in this case it is all too easy for the two in front to concentrate on each other and forget about the diver behind.

If diving in a four then diving in a line easily scales up to four or more divers. The first person still only has to keep an eye on the person behind and the similarly the last person also only has to keep an eye on the person in front. The divers in the middle have to keep an eye on two divers but they also have two divers watching them. The alternative is to have two pairs diving in a box formation. Again this may be more familiar to divers used to diving in a buddy pair.

In each case it is essential that each diver is monitoring the relevant member(s) of the team closely enough to stay in contact and to be close enough to assist should they get into trouble. A high level of awareness is required in order to achieve this. If this awareness is not present then the team can easily become separated leading to many of the problems associated with trios. The use of powerful torches for signalling can make keeping track of other members of the team much easier. If you can see the torch beam of the diver behind then you don't need to turn around in order to check that they are still there. In addition the diver behind can use their torch to signal the diver in front if they need to get their attention.

The strongest teams usually consist of experienced individual divers with good self sufficiency and self awareness skills that have practiced working together in a team. Training and practice are essential in order for team diving to work successfully. Each member of the team should have similar views so that they are following the same general approach. In addition, good teamwork only comes with practice.

Diving in a team becomes much easier if each member of the team standardises certain aspects of their diving practice. Communication is much easier if all signals are standardised further it is common to expand the standard signals to include others that may be relevant to the type of diving you are doing.

Standardizing gases is also common, if one of you is on air and the other is on nitrox then no-stop times are going to vary. The diver using nitrox will be unable to take advantage of extended no-stop times as they have to take into account the other members of the team. At a very minimum each member of the team should be on the same gas mixture and many teams standardize on set gas mixes for pre-defined depth ranges. Some teams even go so far as to completely standardise all of their equipment. Even if you don't go for identical kit then it is still worth standardizing on certain aspects, such as low pressure inflator fittings so that spares can be shared.

The idea of team diving can be further extended to all the divers on the boat enabling all dive teams to work together in terms of dive planning and surface support. For this type of diving the boat skipper and crew would also become an integral part of the team. This is essential for expedition or project based diving. This is discussed in a later section Chapter 41.

The skills required to be a good buddy are the same as those required to be a good team diver and vice-versa. By adopting some of the team diving methods used by technical divers you can become better buddies even if you are carrying out a recreational no-stop dive. Recreational dives with three divers can be made easier by adopting a fixed position and using torches for signaling. The other aspects of team diving can still be adopted, even if diving in a traditional buddy pair. Each buddy should be self sufficient but at the same time fully aware of their buddy and ready to help out should it be needed. Effective communication between buddies will help them stay together and avoid any potential problems. In this way you can take some of the aspects of team diving and increase your safety on all of your dives.

Problem Solving

29

"A problem, at its core, is really just an opportunity to learn and explore" **Stephen Coleman**

Despite initial impressions, most technical diving courses are not just about teaching you to dive to a specific depth but are rather all about teaching you about being able to dive to that depth and also deal with the multitude of problems that could potentially occur. Diving to depths in excess of 40m/130ft is not that difficult providing everything goes well but can be an order of magnitude more challenging when things are going wrong. As a result the technical diving mindset is not one of hoping that everything will go well but rather of expecting everything to go wrong and being prepared for it. One of the UK's Maritime Coastguard Agency diving liaison officers recently commented that they have less problems with technical divers because they are better prepared and practiced. However, when it does go wrong the consequences are often more severe.

This mindset starts with preparation and practice. The technical diver will prepare his equipment and procedures to try and avoid the potential for any problems. This can often be a surprise for experienced recreational divers who make the switch to technical diving. Some of their equipment configuration may need to change and they may find that they struggle with some of the problem scenarios. The reason for this is that many of the experienced recreational divers who come to technical diving may have hundreds, even thousands of dives. However, diving is comparatively safe and so many divers will have done hundreds of dives without encountering any problems. As a result they have lots of experience of dives going well but have never had any experience of dives going badly. If they are ever involved in an incident they do not necessarily have the skills or experience to resolve the issue. This is a major problem for divers who gradually progress deeper and deeper, getting into technical diving depths while still using recreational diving techniques and mindset. This can be seen every year in the BSAC or DAN incident report. Each year there are several cases of what appear to be very experienced divers who get into a slight problem which escalates into a major incident. Often the original problem was relatively minor and in itself, would not have caused a major incident. However, the diver is unable to resolve the initial problem easily and ends up in a more serious situation. For recreational diving depths the consequences of a rapid ascent may not be too serious but once we get into decompression diving the consequences of not being able to resolve the situation become much more serious. A rapid ascent from a decompression dive can result in a serious case of decompression illness, burst lung or worse.

This approach to problem avoidance or risk reduction involves a number of factors. The first is the use of standard procedures. By standardising the ways things are done technical divers can reduce the potential for things going wrong. In the same way that recreational divers perform a buddy check technical divers will perform a pre-dive check. Each agency has its own version of these checks and each tries to come up with a catchy abbreviation or mnemonic to help divers remember it. An example of one of these pre-dive checks is using START as the abbreviation. The key objective of these checks is to ensure that everything is ready before getting into the water. Once their training course is complete it is unusual to hear technical divers reciting these checks out loud but most will go through them explicitly or implicity wth their buddies or on their own before each dive. For rebreather divers it is even more important to perform the pre-dive checks before diving and some rebreathers even guide you through the pre-dive checks on the handset before the rebreather can be dived. Currently every rebreather manufacturer produces a checklist that can be used to ensure the rebreather is working correctly. In addition some agencies publish rebreather pre-dive checklists.

- **S** – S-Drill – Out Of air drill and bubble check
- **T** – Team – Buddy equipment check and team formation
- **A** – Air – Gas matching
- **R** – Route – Entry/exit and planned path
- **T** – Tables – Depth, duration, waypoints and schedule

Table 12: START can be used to ensure all areas of the pre-dive preparation are covered

Once in the water the procedural approach continues. By agreeing the procedures for each stage of the dive mistakes can be avoided.

For example all technical divers, both open circuit and rebreather, should perform a bubble check during the descent at 3-6m/10-20ft. This only takes a few seconds but can quickly identify any potential problems. At this depth it is easy to ascend back to the surface or even get back on the boat and resolve any potential problem and still jump back in and do the dive. On the other hand if a leak is not spotted at this point and instead isn't noticed until you get to the bottom, then it is no longer possible to ascend, resolve the problem and continue the dive. Even worse the problem may not be spotted until it causes a more serious issue at which point the divers are involved in resolving an incident rather than fixing a minor problem. After the bubble check the diver will carry out an S-Drill or Safety Drill. As a minimum this involves deploying the long hose to ensure it will come free if required in an emergency while at the same time switching to the backup regulator. This shows that in an out of gas situation the long hose will come free and is not caught up in the waist strap of the harness and also that the backup regulator is fully working. If either of these is not the case then it is better to find out during the S-Drill rather than when your buddy is swimming up to you at depth frantically giving the out of gas signal.

Switching onto a decompression gas is another operation where a specific procedure is used. For any technical diver switching to the wrong gas at the wrong depth is one of the most dangerous mistakes that can be made. Having a set procedure for ensuring that you switch to the correct gas at the correct depth is absolutely critical.

In most of the examples above the procedures used to prevent problems occurring are achieved by working as a team. As we saw in previous chapters, within technical diving there are two broad approaches. One is the solo diving or self sufficient mentality and the other is the team based mentality. With the team based mentality the other members of your team provide a double check on the procedures whereas with the self sufficiency mentality you have to ensure that you put in place additional procedures to double check your own actions. The team based mentality extends from prevention of problems to the actions in resolving a problem. It assumes that by working together as a team you will be better placed to resolve a problem. Team members are available as another set of hands and eyes, another source of gas, a visual

Figure 36: When technical diving goes wrong the consequences are often more severe

reference or just an additional brain to think through the situation. It is a common misconception that team members are reliant on the other members of their team. This is not true, all team members should be capable of resolving a situation on their own but the presence of their team members may make the process easier. If you are fully dependant on another member of your team then you are not functioning as a team and you should consider if you are ready for this particular dive.

The specifics of how our equipment is configured can also have a huge impact on the avoidance of problems. Many technical divers are accused of being obsessive with kit configuration and in many cases this accusation is entirely justified. The reason for this obsession is the realisation that having the correct equipment set up in the correct way can go a huge way to avoiding problems in the first place or making them easier to deal with if they do occur. For example, the placement of a D-ring can make the difference between being able to easily unclip a piece of equipment and struggling to reach that piece of equipment. A loop of bungy cord to clip on backup equipment in your pocket can make the difference between easily locating your backup equipment and struggling to find it. A long hose on your regulator can make an out of gas ascent a much less stressful event whereas a short hose can increase the difficulty and stress involved in the incident. In all of these cases the benefit of the particular configuration choice may not be apparent until a problem occurs.

One of the most effective ways to prepare for dealing with a problem is to practice that situation. Most technical diving courses include lots of practice of dealing with a range of emergency situations. In many cases the drills included in these courses are based on the lessons learned from previous incidents. It is typical that if we try something for the first time we will not be very successful at it. If the first time is also during an emergency situation then that increases the potential for it to go wrong. For this reason most of the emergency drills are practiced during training courses. For example carrying a backup mask is a good idea because if you lose your mask then it is very difficult to accurately carry out an ascent, stopping at the correct decompression stops and perform a gas switch. However, just carrying the back up mask is not enough, it is important that you know that you can get it out of the pocket or wherever you have stored it. If you have problems getting it out then it is of no use. For this reason switching to a backup mask, deploying your backup DSMB, disconnecting your dry suit or wing inflate, performing a shutdown and a whole range of other emergency procedures will be practiced during a training course. After the course divers are encouraged to keep practicing to ensure that these skills remain sharp and ready to use. It is amazing to discover the number of people who have never practiced basic skills since their initial training course. These skills are not things that you need to perform in order to pass a course they are skills that you need to perform in order to deal with a problem.

If a problem occurs then it is typical for divers who do not have experience of dealing with problems to focus entirely on the immediate problem.

They may resolve their immediate problem but cause a potentially more serious problem. Once the initial problem has been resolved they realise that they have lost control of their buoyancy and have sunk much deeper than their starting point or have had a rapid ascent. Equally they may find that in dealing with the problem they have become separated from their buddy or run low on gas. For this reason it is important to focus on a number of aspects. The first priority is your buddy. Even though you are dealing with a problem you should keep an eye on your buddy as they may also need help but they may also be able to help you. At the very least if they are level in the water then using them as a visual reference will help you maintain your buoyancy. This is the second focus as it doesn't matter whether you deal with the problem if as a result you end up losing control of your buoyancy. If your buoyancy is under control then resolving the problem itself becomes easier. For this reason the focus should be on your buddy, your buoyancy and then the task.

BUDDY BUOYANCY TASK

One aspect of dealing with problems in technical diving that is exactly the same as the techniques taught at recreational level is the use of the term Breathe-Think-Plan-Act. The first priority is to get your breathing under control. If you are breathing then the situation can't be too bad and by taking a breath or two it will calm you down. This will allow you to think about your options and to plan the best way to deal with the situation. Only then should you act to carry out your plan. By following these steps you are more likely to make the right choice and less likely to make decisions that make the situation worse. By thinking about the options you can prioritise the order in which you do things and deal with the most important problem first rather than focusing on less important aspects of the situation.

One of the most effective ways of dealing with a problem is to avoid it happening in the first place. You can increase your chances of avoiding a problem by practicing situation awareness. Put simply situational awareness is noticing what is going on around you and noticing when things are starting to go wrong. This may seem an obvious thing to do and something we do everyday but in reality we often miss many of the events and clues around us that would give an indication that a problem is developing. Situational awareness involves noticing what is going on around us, understanding what that means and predicting the outcome before it happens in order to take preemptive action.

While we may all think we are very observant it is very easy to miss things unless you are looking for them. For example, think back to the last time you bought a new car. As soon as you make the decision to buy that specific car you suddenly start seeing the same model everywhere. It's not that everyone else also went out and bought that same model overnight, those cars were there all along but they were not relevant to you so your brain filtered out your perception of them. Once you make a decision to buy that model, your brain realizes that those cars are relevant to you and you start to perceive them. Unless we force our brains to notice things it will filter out anything that it does not consider to be important. We can re-train our brain to be more attentive to relevant information. One way to do this is to focus on each individual area that we want to focus on. These can be thought of as gradually widening circles of awareness. Every minute or so I think about each of these circles in turn. Starting with myself, my equipment, my team, the environment around me and finishing by projecting the current situation into the future. I then start again moving through each of the circles. With time this becomes automatic and all of a sudden you start to notice tiny clues to developing problems that you would never have noticed before.

Me	How do I feel? What is my breathing rate? Do I feel cold/nervous?
My Equipment	Is everything working correctly? How much gas do I have? What is my depth, time and decompression obligation?
My Team	Can I see my team? Can they see me? Does their body language look unusual? How much gas do they have?
The Environment	What is the composition of the sea bottom? Is the depth increasing? What is the visibility? What is the strength and direction of the current? Where is our exit point?
The Future	How much gas will I have in five minutes time? What will be my depth, time and decompression obligation five minutes from now? How far will we have to swim back?

Table 13: Situational Awareness Considerations

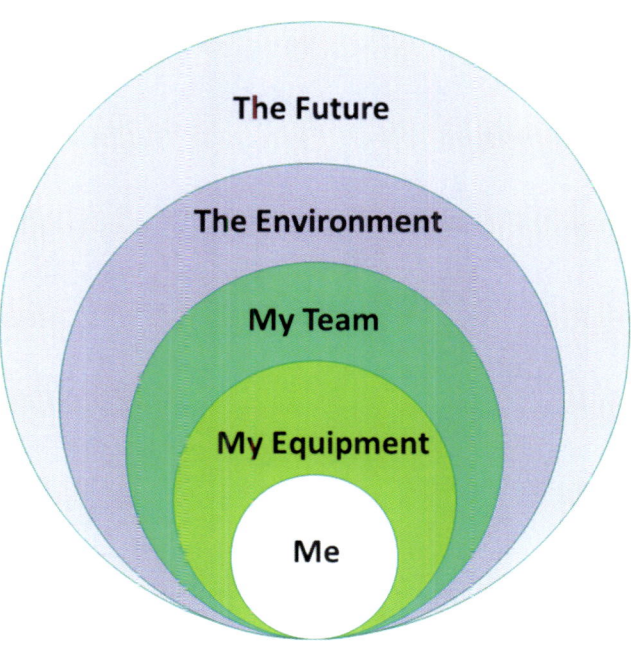

Diagram 7: Situational Awareness

Technical Skills

30

"There is no such thing as a great talent without great willpower."
Honore de Balzac

There are a number of differences between the mainstream technical diving agencies but in fact there are more similarities than differences. Although the syllabus for each agency will be different there are some skills that you will be expected to cover whichever agency you do your technical training with. In some cases these skills are rushed over as something you need to do in order to pass the course. However, if we understand a little bit more about the principles behind some of these skills, then it can help you perform the skill better but it can also reveal that very often the particular skill is being used to teach a wider concept. In this chapter will look at a number of skills that will probably be included in any technical diving course and look at the key principles behind them.

A common skill taught by a number of instructors is to get the team of divers to send up a DSMB each while neutrally buoyant. This is typical of the type of skill taught in that it is a useful skill in itself but also teaches a number of other aspects. Sending up a DSMB is an essential skill for any diver and even more so for a technical diver. Technical dives invariably involve decompression and as a result the diver is likely to drift further during the ascent than a recreational diver who, other than stopping for a few minutes for a safety stop, will be coming almost directly to the surface. During the decompression stop it is possible for you to drift a considerable distance. A DSMB is essential in order for the boat skipper to know exactly where the diver is. Some boat skippers will ask for one DSMB per diver on a decompression dive so that they know the exact position for each of the divers. Recreational divers often send up a DSMB from the bottom but technical divers will often do this during the ascent or on one of the earlier decompression stops. The reason for this is that sending up a DSMB up from the bottom eats into precious bottom time or looking at it the other way incurs additional decompression time. The deployment of the DSMB and the amount of time that it takes to get to the surface from a deep dive can add a significant amount of time to the decompression. As a result the technical diver will often not want to waste bottom time on sending up a DSMB. In addition, many reels do not have sufficient line to be sent up from the bottom. It is common to have between 30m and 50m (100-164ft) of line on a reel which is useless when the wreck is at 60m (200ft). As a result the ability to send up the DSMB in mid water while ascending at a controlled rate or holding position at a deco stop is essential.

In addition this skill also highlights a number of other areas. The first is teamwork. It is very common for a team of two or three divers to become so fixated on their own DSMB that they completely forget their teammates. I have often seen divers who have been keeping close contact and monitoring each other during the dive then turn their backs on their buddies while deploying a DSMB. The deployment takes up all their available concentration and they forget that they are still supposed to be diving in a team. This shows that they are operating at the limit of their comfort zone. This is particularly important because the end of the dive and in particular deploying a DSMB, is one of the most dangerous parts of the dive. Reels can get jammed, buoyancy can be forgotten, line can become tangled around regulators or other bits of equipment and so this time, almost more than any other, is when the divers should be aware of their team mates. The second aspect that is tested by this skill is buoyancy control. Divers can often manage their buoyancy very well as long as they are not distracted by anything else but as soon as they are distracted, by the act of deploying the DSMB for example, their buoyancy control starts to go and they start to float up or sink into the depths. So when we say we want to send up a DSMB what we really mean is that we want to maintain contact with our team mates, while maintaining our position in the water while sending up our DSMB. If a team can do this then it shows they have good team skills, good buoyancy skills and good DSMB skills.

Stage cylinder swapping is another skill that is useful in itself but also has a number of other purposes. If a diver is planning to use a rich nitrox mix in a stage cylinder, in order to accelerate their decompression, then this can significantly reduce the length of time they need to decompress. However, if there is a problem with the decompression cylinder, then this removes the reduction in decompression and they will need to spend much longer decompressing. If they have used sensible gas planning rules then they should have enough gas in their twinset to be able to do this but there are other options. Once their buddy has finished their own decompression they can potentially pass the remaining gas in the deco cylinder over to the diver with the problem. Of course decompression stops are usually done in mid water and so being able to do this without changing depth or dropping the cylinder into the depths is a very important skill. Once again though, there are other skills being practiced during this exercise. The communication and coordination required between the divers again helps to build teamwork. If the divers can identify the situation, communicate the proposed solution, agree on the course of action and then carry out the cylinder swap, then they are clearly acting as a solid team. If they cannot do this then it illustrates the weaknesses in the team and can be used to identify and then resolve these weaknesses. In addition it gives great buoyancy control practice. If this is done in mid water with no visual reference other than a third team member or a DSMB reel hanging at a fixed depth then it is a very difficult exercise and the first time it is carried out it is likely that even the most experienced recreational divers will have major buoyancy control problems. This will illustrate again how easy it is to get distracted from your buoyancy by a challenging task. By practicing this task it allows the divers to increase their buoyancy awareness and helps to teach divers how to manage their position in the water while at the same time carrying out a difficult task. This helps to build good awareness of depth and builds the ability to monitor depth even when other activities are going on.

The third skill which is taught and drilled on almost every course is an out of gas situation. It's obvious why being able to donate quickly and efficiently to an out of gas diver is an essential skill. However there is more to this skill. Most instructors test this skill when neither the out of gas diver nor the donor are expecting it. This shows the difference between a practice drill where both parties are expecting it and an unexpected situation. When both divers are expecting the skill the stress levels are much lower, there is less confusion and in my experience it very rarely goes wrong. However when the drill is sprung when it's not expected by either diver then it shows up a number of potential problems. For a start many divers spend large parts of the dive too far apart and in the case of an out of gas situation cannot get to their buddies in one breath. This shows how close you should be to your buddy in case of an out of gas situation. It also shows the importance of position. If the diver in front is out of gas then they can just turn around and the other diver can see them immediately. They will swim towards each other, effectively halving the distance between them. However if it is the diver at the back that is out of gas they need to catch up with the diver in front, effectively doubling the distance. They will then need to get their attention and signal that they are out of gas. This will obviously take significantly longer. As the time the diver is out of gas increases, even if it is simulated and they are just holding their breath, so their stress levels will increase. When the stress levels go up so does the urgency, and so does the likelihood that one of the divers will make a mistake. I have seen divers forget the drill they have been taught, react far too slowly or get their bungied long hose caught because they have fumbled the deployment. In each case the most important lesson is that a more realistic situation can create problems that are just not present in a nice relaxed simulated situation and so in a real emergency this is going to be even worse. It also shows that little things can become huge when a problem occurs. Convoluted solutions to gas donation inevitably cause problems in a real life situation and this is where the disadvantages of independent twinsets, bungied long hoses, inaccessible backup regulators and clutter can become glaringly obvious. As a result, an out of gas exercise can also be a very effective way to illustrate a problem in kit configuration.

Hopefully it is clear that in some cases these skills are taught because they are useful themselves but also because they teach other skills. There are additional challenges that are set on a technical diving course that appear to have no relevance to real life diving. In this case they are set in order to practice some other, more important skill. Often this is buoyancy control or team work. These additional exercises are used because in order to master certain skills we need to do more than just use those skills regularly on a dive. When people first learn many skills such as diving, skiing, typing, driving, playing a musical instrument, etc., they improve very quickly, until they reach a proficient level and the skill becomes effectively automatic. Buoyancy control is a perfect example of this. New divers quickly learn the basics of buoyancy control and get to a reasonable level of proficiency so that they stop having to constantly think about how to control their buoyancy. At this point, most people's buoyancy skills stop progressing, they reach a plateau. This is known as the "OK Plateau"[44] and most divers stay there not knowing how to progress to a higher level and in many cases not even realising that a higher level of buoyancy control is even possible. Even if they practice

their skills by diving regularly they will maintain this level but will not significantly improve their skills. Of course this is in contradiction to the idea that practice makes perfect, so why don't people who dive more, necessarily get better and better? And why do some people seem to be able to master a skill while others remain stuck on the OK Plateau?

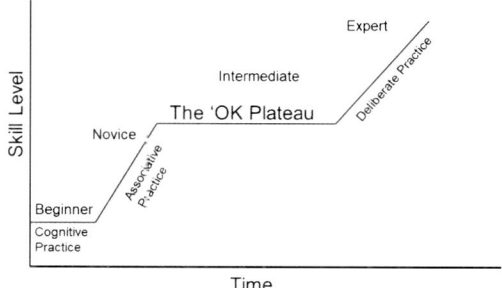

Diagram 8: The OK Plateau

What separates those who master buoyancy control or teamwork or any other skill, is that instead of just doing the activity they will focus on practice specifically aimed at stretching their skills, this is often known as "deliberate practice". Amateur guitarists, for example, are more likely to spend their time playing music, whereas more advanced guitarists will spend their time working through a specific exercise to improve their technique. With diving, it's very common to get to the OK plateau and just stop. However, the technical diver needs to aim further than this and increase their skills to a higher level. This can only be done by deliberate practice of key skills and exercises intended to stretch and fine tune those skills.

The exercises used for this deliberate practice should make you feel outside your comfort zone and allow you to make mistakes in a relatively safe practice environment. Technical diving courses start off this process and include a number of exercises designed to do just this in order to help push the diver beyond being just OK and towards really mastering the key skills.

---

44 Science writer, Joshua Foer, popularised the term 'ok plateau' in his book, Moonwalking with Einstein, on the subject of improving memory. It is used to describe that common autopilot state when you have habitually mastered the basics of a task, but despite being skilled you stop really improving to reach expert status; you simply plateau in performance.

PART 5
Rebreathers

Chapter 31. Rebreathers 171

Chapter 32. Rebreather configurations 181

Rebreathers

Many of the pieces of equipment used by technical divers look different to the equipment used by recreational divers. For most of the time the basic principles are the same. SCUBA regulators work on the same principles whether they are attached to a single cylinder or a twinset. Nevertheless the use of rebreathers in technical diving completely changes many of the basic principles that govern recreational diving. Some limits are removed almost completely but unfortunately other complications are introduced.

Although they look much more complicated than normal scuba, a rebreather works on a very simple principle. It is a way to reuse the gas breathed out by the diver by topping up the oxygen consumed by the diver's metabolism in conjunction with a method of removing the carbon dioxide produced.

While they are often considered a modern development, the rebreather predates the invention of open circuit scuba. The concept of a rebreather was first proposed in 1679 by the Italian mathematician Giovanni Borrelli who believed that re-circulating air through a copper tube cooled by seawater would allow impurities to condense and filter out the carbon dioxide.[45] Although the process he suggests for filtering out the carbon dioxide would not work the overall idea is identical to the way a modern rebreather works.

Diagram 9: Borelli's rebreather

The first working prototype rebreather was built in 1849 by Pierre Aimable De Saint Simon Sicard, and refined in 1853 by Professor T. Schwann in Belgium. It had a large back mounted oxygen tank and removed carbon dioxide using two scrubbers containing sponges soaked in caustic soda.

The first commercially available closed circuit rebreather was designed and built by the diving engineer Henry Fleuss in 1878.[46] His rebreather consisted of a rubber mask connected

---

45   Marx, RF (1990). The History of Underwater Exploration Courier Dover Publications. Page 88

46   Davis, RH (1955). Deep Diving and Submarine Operations (6th ed.). Tolworth, Surbiton, Surrey: Siebe Gorman & Company Ltd. p. 693.

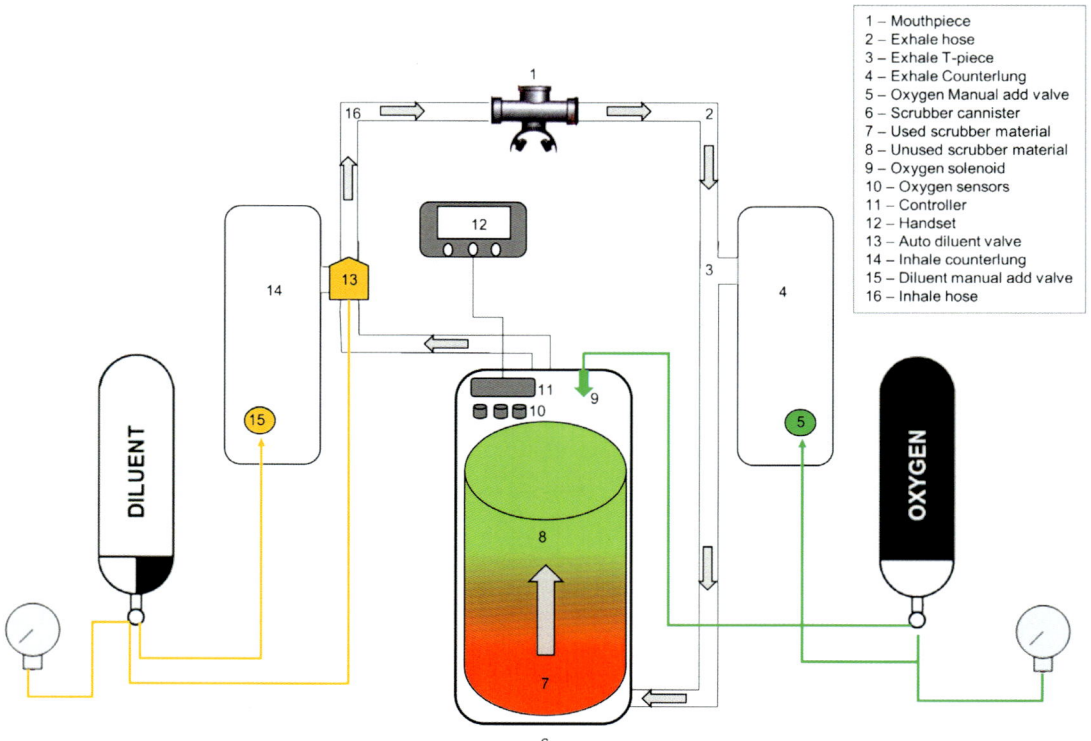

Diagram 10: CCR Schematic

to a breathing bag, with a nitrox mix containing 50–60% O_2 supplied from a copper tank. Carbon dioxide was removed using a scrubber consisting of rope yarn soaked in a solution of caustic potash; the system giving a duration of about three hours. Fleuss tested his device in 1879 by spending an hour submerged in a water tank, then one week later by diving to a depth of 5.5m/18ft in open water.

The Fleuss rebreather was used in 1880 by Alexander Lambert, the lead diver on the Severn Tunnel construction project, who was able to travel 300m/1000ft in the darkness to close several submerged sluice doors in the tunnel. This was after several attempts by hard hat divers had failed due to the danger of their air supply hoses becoming fouled on submerged debris, and the strong water currents in the tunnel.

Fleuss continually improved his apparatus, adding a demand regulator and tanks capable of holding greater amounts of oxygen at higher pressure. Sir Robert Davis, head of Siebe Gorman, perfected the oxygen rebreather in 1910 with his invention of the Davis Submerged Escape Apparatus, the first practical rebreather to be made in quantity. While intended primarily as an emergency escape apparatus for submarine crews, it was soon also used for diving, being a handy shallow water diving apparatus with a thirty minute endurance and as an industrial breathing set.

The main advantage of a rebreather is that it is much more efficient on gas usage. When breathing normal air at the surface we use up about 4% of the oxygen in the air for our metabolism and breathe out the rest of the oxygen as well as all the nitrogen. This means that 96% of the gas we breathe escapes with each breath. Hence traditional SCUBA is often referred to as Open Circuit or OC Diving. At depth, this is made even worse by the fact that we are breathing gas under much higher pressure, therefore each breath contains a much higher volume of air. At 40m/130ft we are breathing five times the volume of air with each breath compared to the surface and at 90m/300ft we are breathing ten times the volume that we would be on the surface. With every breath this gas escapes from our second stage and bubbles to the surface. This is inefficient as the body still only needs the same amount of oxygen but we are wasting ten times as much gas with each breath in order to obtain it. This is one of the reasons why for open circuit divers gas planning and breathing rate is so critical. The limiting factor for an open circuit dive to 90m/300ft is almost certainly going to be the amount of gas that needs to be carried for the dive. A rebreather avoids this problem by re-using the gas breathed out by the diver. As the majority of the gas isn't being wasted the diver doesn't need to carry as much gas in order to do the same dive. A rebreather works by catching this exhaled breath and instead of allowing it to escape, it reuses it in the next breath. The small fraction of oxygen that was used up by the body is replaced with more oxygen. This means that rather than wasting the vast majority of each breath we reuse all of the gas.

By reusing our gas this provides three key benefits to the technical diver:

1 - GAS DURATION

Firstly you don't need to use anywhere near as much gas as an open circuit diver. The amount of oxygen required by the body is roughly the same at any depth and therefore the oxygen will last the same at 100m/330ft as it will at 20m/60ft. The balance of the gas in the breathing loop, known as the diluent, is reused rather than wasted and so again you use the same amount at 100m/330ft as at 20m/164ft. This vastly decreases the amount of gas you will need to complete the dive and rather than twin 20L cylinders you can use two 3L cylinders.

On open circuit we breathe much more at depth due to the effect of pressure and therefore as we go deeper and deeper we have to take larger and larger cylinders. Despite taking these large cylinders they will still be used up very quickly and the amount of available gas becomes the most critical part of our dive planning. On a rebreather our gas supply is used up at the same rate irrespective of depth and so the amount of gas we are carrying is no longer the limiting factor. This means that running out of gas on a rebreather is much less of a concern than for an open circuit diver. Instead the critical factors become the amount of decompression we are incurring, the duration of our carbon dioxide absorbent and our risk of oxygen toxicity.

2 - GAS COSTS

One of the biggest factors that comes into the decision to switch to a rebreather is costs. This has two aspects, the cost of the rebreather, including buying and maintaining it, set against the cost of open circuit diving. One of the biggest disadvantages of open circuit trimix diving is the cost of the gas. A twinset of trimix can cost anything from £30/$40/€35 for a relatively weak mix for use in 40m/130ft to over £100/$130/€110 for a mix suitable for diving deeper than 100m/330ft. This makes each trimix dive an expensive proposition. On the other hand a rebreather uses much smaller cylinders because the gas is reused rather than wasted, as a result you use much less and the gas costs are much lower. You might only be spending £5-£10 for the same mixtures discussed above. As a result there is a significant gas saving when compared to open circuit diving. This can look very attractive when you are spending considerable amounts on each open circuit fill. Notwithstanding, this must be set against the costs of the rebreather. Depending on the model a rebreather is likely to cost between four and eight thousand pounds ($5,000-$10,000/€4,500-€9,000). If you go for an older second hand model then you may get one for less than this. In addition to the initial cost of the rebreather you will need to factor in training on the rebreather which is likely to add another thousand pounds ($1,250/€1,100). There will undoubtedly be additional costs to add on extra equipment to the basic rebreather. As a result it is not uncommon for the initial start up costs of a rebreather to be between six and ten thousand pounds ($7,500-$12,500/€6,600-€11,000). Obviously you will need to do a lot of trimix diving in order to save enough to justify this initial outlay.

The majority of divers do not do enough diving to clearly justify buying a rebreather based on savings in gas costs. Unless you are doing 20 or more trimix dives a year then it is not cost effective. If you also do a significant amount of recreational diving then each dive may actually cost you more on a rebreather. On open circuit you may only need to pay for an air fill but on even the shallowest dive you will still need to use pure oxygen in one of the cylinders and use carbon dioxide absorbent in the rebreather. The annual replacement of the three oxygen sensors and handset batteries also needs to be taken into account. This means that a shallow recreational dive may only cost £5/$7/€6 for an open circuit diver but £10-£15 ($13-$20/€12-€18) for a rebreather diver.

It is clear that unless you are doing significant numbers of deep trimix dives a year with little or no recreational diving then the gas savings from using a rebreather will not outweigh the initial start-up costs. But still there are a number of other reasons why a rebreather is an attractive option.

3 - GAS LOGISTICS

The third advantage that the improved gas usage provides is in simplifying gas logistics during longer dive trips. Open circuit divers may be using up twin 12L/85cf, 15L/108cf or even 18L/120cf cylinders on each trimix dive. In addition they may be using up to four stage cylinders for decompression gas for each dive. This requires lots of additional helium and oxygen each day. Filling these large back gas cylinders and decompression cylinders is expensive, time consuming and labourious.

The fact that a rebreather uses smaller cylinders makes the logistics of filling much easier. The volumes of gas needed are much smaller when filling a 3L/21cf cylinder rather than twin 12L/85cf and it becomes feasible to take enough gas with you for even a weeks diving. This contrasts with the situation when using open circuit where significant volumes of helium and oxygen will be required because the majority will be breathed out and wasted. This can make a big difference if you don't have a local dive shop that can fill trimix. If you have to drive 80km/50miles there and back to drop off a twinset for a trimix fill and then do the same thing the next day to pick it up, the logistics of this can be significant. Similarly if you are diving somewhere without easy access to a dive centre that can fill trimix, the ability to take your own gas simplifies the planning and logistics.

Of course, this assumes that the rebreather will always work as intended. Just in case there are any problems with the rebreather you also need to carry open circuit gas to get you safely to the surface. In this case you would need a bailout cylinder that you could start using at the maximum depth and would then need sufficient bailout to get to the surface completing all your decompression. Unlike the open circuit diver the rebreather diver will not use their stages unless there is an emergency but will still need to carry them. Whereas on open circuit the diver will use the decompression stages on each dive and these will be required to be filled each day.

4 - DECOMPRESSION OBLIGATION

The other advantage of a rebreather is that it can reduce the decompression obligation when compared to the same dive on open circuit. For a diver using a twinset and a stage cylinder they may plan their gas to have the optimum mix on the bottom, i.e. the highest oxygen percentage in order to reduce the amount of inert gas absorbed by the body. They will also make a choice of the decompression gas carried in the stage cylinder with a view to ensuring that they get rid of the inert gas as fast as possible during the decompression. However, the choice of each of these gasses will always be a compromise. The bottom gas will be chosen to be as rich as possible but with some margin for error in case the dive is a little deeper than expected. If the diver ascends up from the planned maximum depth then the mix is no longer the optimum mix. Equally the decompression mix will only be the most effective mix at the depth at which the diver switches to it. Prior to the switch, the diver could have switched to a leaner mix and at the later stops there will always be a richer mix that would have provided faster off-gassing. A rebreather avoids these problems by constantly adjusting the gas being breathed to ensure the minimum amount of inert gas is being breathed. The rebreather (or the diver in the case of a manually operated rebreather) adds oxygen to ensure that the minimum amount of inert gas is being breathed. At depth the diver can ensure that the breathing loop of the rebreather contains the maximum amount of oxygen and hence the minimum amount of inert gas. This will reduce the rate of on-gassing. As the diver ascends and completes his decompression stop they can ensure that the mixture again contains the maximum amount of oxygen which will accelerate the off-gassing and reduce the required decompression. In this way the rebreather is constantly providing the best gas for the depth the diver is at. To simulate this on open circuit a diver would have to switch to a new breathing gas every meter of the ascent in order to constantly have access to the best possible decompression gas. For this reason a rebreather is sometimes unofficially called a best mix generator.

when the exhaled gas passes through a scrubber which is packed with a suitable chemical designed to remove the carbon dioxide. Correctly packing the scrubber is one of the most important steps in preparing a rebreather as incorrect packing can allow carbon dioxide to be 'channelled' through the scrubber and cause a build up in the breathing loop and lead to carbon dioxide poisoning. This can cause headaches, lack of concentration, unconsciousness and death.

	Advantages	Disadvantages
CCR	Reduced gas requirements Reduced decompression obligation Warm air Simplified gas logistics	Risk of CO_2 Poisoning Risk of CNS toxicity High initial costs Additional complication Non standard equipment and procedures Need to relearn diving skills
OC	Simple equipment configuration Simple to set up Standard equipment allows for easier repairs Standardised procedures	High gas costs Gas consumption limits deeper dives Complicated gas logistics

Table 14: Advantages and disadvantages of rebreather and open circuit diving

We can see that rebreathers offer a number of significant advantages over open circuit diving. On the other hand a rebreather introduces a number of significant additional costs, risks and complications to any dive and should not be seen as a magic wand to solve all of the potential problems of deep technical diving. In the first place buying a rebreather is an expensive proposition. Prices vary from £3,500 to over £8,000 ($4,500-$10,000/€4,000-€9,000) for the unit alone. When combined with training and the inevitable extra bits of kit, it is a false economy to buy a rebreather in order to save money on gas fills. In addition to the cost there are a number of other risks introduced by using a rebreather.

Whenever we breathe out, as well as exhaling the remaining oxygen and inert gas, the body has also added carbon dioxide. If our breath is recycled without removing the carbon dioxide then the levels will build up and eventually you will succumb to carbon dioxide poisoning. This is one of the biggest risks of rebreather diving. In order to avoid this, the carbon dioxide must be removed by a chemical process. This takes place

Unfortunately the diver suffering from this condition may be unaware of the condition or may be so incapacitated as to be unable to respond to the problem. Overusing the scrubber material is another potential cause of carbon dioxide poisoning and for this reason it is vital to monitor the amount of time that the material has been used and to replace it at the appropriate time. If there is any doubt in the diver's mind that they may be suffering from carbon dioxide poisoning then they are taught to bailout to a known source of gas. For this reason rebreather divers carry open circuit bailout gas. Also many rebreathers are supplied with a Bail Out Valve (BOV) which allows the diver to switch from the rebreather loop to an open circuit regulator at the flick of a switch. Of course once the diver has bailed out to open circuit they are limited by all the same gas consumption issues that the open circuit diver has to face. This is one of the reasons why a rebreather is not necessarily the full solution for deep technical diving. You will need to carry enough gas in order to be able to safely ascend in the case of a problem with your rebreather and so you will have to carry the same amount of decompression gas as an open

circuit diver. The alternative approach, known as the alpinist approach, is to assume that any problem can be avoided by careful preparation of the unit or by managing the problem on the unit rather than by bailing out to open circuit.

In addition to excess carbon dioxide the other big danger that faces rebreather divers is an incorrect partial pressure of oxygen. In an eCCR, the rebreather itself maintains the partial pressure of oxygen within the breathing loop, while on an mCCR it is the diver's responsibility to maintain the partial pressure. Either way it is always the diver's responsibility to know their partial pressure at all times and this is one of the golden rules of rebreather diving. All rebreathers will have a display which shows the partial pressure of oxygen. This can be an electronic gauge which is often wrist or console mounted or can be a visual display using coloured LEDs. These Head Up Displays (HUDs) can provide instant warnings of incorrect partial pressure levels. During the dive a diver will usually aim to maintain a partial pressure of between 1.0 and 1.4 bar of oxygen. This is known as a 'set point'. Allowing the partial pressure to rise too high can lead to oxygen toxicity problems while allowing it to fall too low can lead to hypoxia and a blackout.

The equipment used in a rebreather is more complicated than open circuit and the procedures required are more detailed and intensive. Preparing a rebreather to dive will inevitably take more time than preparing open circuit equipment. The added complication of the kit also increases the chances of a problem occurring, either before the dive causing it to be aborted, or during the dive causing potentially more serious problems. These considerations are covered in extensive detail during any rebreather training course but one of the biggest dangers for rebreather divers is complacency. As they build their experience they start to take short cuts or start to neglect basic checks. It is typically divers who have around 50 hours of experience who tend to fall into this complacency trap.

BUT I WANT ONE

Even if you won't save money and don't need a rebreather for logistic reasons there are still other reasons to switch. Diving is a hobby and so doesn't always have to be justified on cost reasons. The cheapest option is not to dive but most of us don't consider this a possibility. In the same way that some people spend their money on motorbikes, horses, home cinemas, model helicopters or any other hobby there is no reason why someone shouldn't spend their money on a rebreather just because they want one. Other people may switch to a rebreather to challenge themselves to learn something new.

SHOULD YOU SWITCH?

As we have seen there are a number of reasons why many divers want to switch to a rebreather. Yet the risks of rebreather diving mean that there are some people who are better suited to rebreather diving than others.

Rebreathers are significantly more complicated pieces of equipment than an open circuit scuba set. While rebreathers do not require a huge amount of effort they do nonetheless require more care and maintenance than open circuit. For divers that throw their kit into the back of the car or into the garage and then don't look at it until the next dive this can cause a problem. This type of person is not really suited to rebreather diving unless they can discipline themselves to ensure they maintain the rebreather. On the other hand there are many divers who enjoy cleaning and maintaining their equipment almost as much as the dive itself. They get pleasure from adjusting the kit until it is just right and it is viewed as part of the hobby rather than an added chore they must do. This type of person is ideally suited to rebreather diving.

In addition to cleaning and maintenance rebreathers require discipline while diving them. There is a certain mindset that is required to ensure that the unit is assembled correctly each time and that all of the pre-dive checks are rigorously followed. Most rebreather accidents are caused by the divers not following the correct procedure. This includes not diving the unit if there is any problem with it. Many divers become complacent and will dive with known problems with their rebreather. They are confident that they can overcome the problem and in the majority of cases they manage to deal with the known problem. However if there is any problem during the dive the impact of the initial problem can be significantly increased by subsequent problems. It requires a significant level of discipline to call off a dive for what might appear to be a minor problem. Nevertheless becoming complacent about these failures is one of the most common causes of rebreather accidents. During the dive you must constantly monitor the unit to ensure it is operating correctly. This is summed up by the golden rule of rebreather diving "Always know your partial pressure". It doesn't matter if you are at 10m/30ft or 100m/330ft the level of monitoring is the same and because of this a 10m/30ft dive must be approached with the same mindset as a 100m/330ft dive. As such there is no such thing as a casual rebreather dive. Not all divers have the mindset to adjust to rebreather diving but without this mindset they should not consider rebreather diving.

In order to be a safe rebreather diver there are a number of skills that need to be mastered over and above the basic open circuit skills. Some of these are related to the normal operation of the rebreather and some are related to emergency situations. Like any skill it takes practice to master these skills and practice to maintain them. When moving from open circuit to a rebreather there are skills, like buoyancy control which must be re-learnt. This takes time and effort. For an experienced diver this means the frustrating process of going back to basics and building up their experience.

> **Unless you are prepared to put in the time to master the basic skills you will always be diving on a base of weak rebreather skills, even if you were previously a very experienced open circuit diver.**

These skills also need to be practiced regularly in order to ensure that they are maintained. This means that it is essential to dive a rebreather regularly in order to maintain the appropriate skill levels.

For these reasons not all technical divers have adopted rebreathers. It is clear that for some people a rebreather is a desirable and in some cases an essential way to progress their technical diving. For others the advantages do not necessarily outweigh the disadvantages. For depths between 30m/100ft and 80m/260ft open circuit technical diving is still a very feasible option and there will always be open circuit technical divers in this range. Beyond 80m/260ft then rebreather technology becomes the more common tool and it is likely that for dives in excess of 80m/260ft rebreathers will continue to be viewed as the tool of choice. For this reason it is a very personal decision and not one to be taken lightly. First you must decide whether there is a good reason to dive a rebreather and then whether you have the right mindset to be able to dive it safely. Like many things the correct decision will vary from one person to another.

OC	Open Circuit – Traditional SCUBA
CCR	Closed Circuit Rebreather
SCR	Semi closed Circuit Rebreather
eCCR	Electronically controlled Closed Circuit Rebreather
mCCR	Manually controlled Closed Circuit Rebreather
HUD	Heads Up Display, LED display of oxygen partial pressure
BOV	Bail Out Valve, open circuit bail out used in an emergency
Diluent	Gas used to make up the balance of the breathing loop, can be air or Trimix
Scrubber	Module used to remove carbon dioxide from the breathing loop
ADV	Auto Diluent Valve, automatically injects diluent into the counterlung to maintain the volume of gas.
MAV	Manual Add Valve, can be used to manually inject diluent into the counterlung

Table 15: Rebreather terms

Rebreather configurations

"Explore, and explore. Be neither chided nor flattered out of your position of perpetual inquiry. Neither dogmatize, or accept another's dogmatism." **Ralph Waldo Emerson**

Rebreather diving involves a very different approach to open circuit. Furthermore the differences between one rebreather and another can be much wider than the differences between various open circuit configurations.

Rebreathers are categorised into three main types. Oxygen Rebreathers, Semi Closed Rebreathers (SCR) and Closed Circuit Rebreathers (CCR). The simplest type of rebreather is an oxygen rebreather. This consists of an oxygen cylinder, a breathing loop and a scrubber. The diver breathes pure oxygen in the loop and the carbon dioxide that is produced is removed by a chemical in the scrubber. As the diver is breathing pure oxygen there is always enough oxygen in the breathing loop to sustain life. The diver then tops up the oxygen in the loop as it is metabolised. This means that there is no wasted gas and as no gas will be released from the system there will be no bubbles. The disadvantage of an oxygen rebreather is that it is depth restricted to 6m-9m/20ft-30ft due to the use of pure oxygen. Oxygen rebreathers have been used extensively by military divers for shallow water operations but are not suitable for sport diving applications.

Semi Closed Rebreathers (SCR) have a similar design to an oxygen rebreather except that instead of using a cylinder of pure oxygen they use a cylinder of nitrox. The nitrox is fed into the breathing loop at a constant rate designed to keep an appropriate partial pressure of oxygen in the breathing loop. The gas is then re-circulated to gain an advantage in gas usage over open circuit. The nitrogen in the nitrox mix means that an SCR can be used at greater depths than an oxygen rebreather. The disadvantage is that the nitrogen is not used up and the excess gas must be expelled at regular intervals and therefore an SCR is not completely bubble less. By re-circulating the gas in the breathing loop an SCR diver will use approximately one third of the gas of an open circuit diver. This means that the same size cylinder will last three times as long when used in an SCR than in an open circuit configuration.

The most sophisticated type of rebreather is a fully Closed Circuit Rebreather (CCR). A CCR works by adding a specific amount of pure oxygen into the breathing loop in order to maintain a certain partial pressure of oxygen in the loop. This is known as the set point. The rest of the breathing loop is then made up of a diluent gas whose role is to provide sufficient volume for the diver to get a full breath at ambient pressure by diluting the oxygen with sufficient volume of an inert gas. At depth the loop volume will remain constant and so the rebreather just needs to top up the oxygen that has been metabolised by the diver. This means that there is no wasted gas and no bubbles, hence closed circuit. It also means that the CCR diver only uses the oxygen that is metabolised by the body and is therefore very efficient with respect to gas usage.

Oxygen rebreathers were widely used by the military but have no real sport diving application. Some of the earliest sport diving rebreathers, produced by Draeger, were semi-closed rebreathers but until recently there were very few semi-closed rebreathers available and they were considered old fashioned and of limited use. The KISS GEM and the Hollis Explorer are more recent SCR models that have attempted to revitalise the SCR market. Nevertheless both of these units are firmly aimed at the recreational rebreather market. The majority of technical diving rebreathers have been CCR and this seems the best technology for deep technical diving. Even within the CCR market there are a whole range of options as to how a CCR should be configured and how it works.

The first major variation between different types of rebreather is whether they are manually controlled or electronically controlled. No matter what type of rebreather you use it is essential that the partial pressure of oxygen (ppO_2) that you breathe is maintained at a consistent level. This is achieved by injecting oxygen into the breathing mixture in the breathing loop to maintain the partial pressure irrespective of depth. With a manually operated closed circuit rebreather (MCCR) this is achieved by the diver, whereas with an electronically operated closed circuit rebreather (ECCR) it is the rebreather that maintains the partial pressure. Many manually operated rebreathers will have a constant flow of oxygen which is then just 'topped up' by the diver. This has the disadvantage that it requires specific action on the part of the diver in order to maintain the ppO_2. It also has the associated advantage that as the diver is an essential part of the control process it forces them to take a more active role in monitoring their ppO_2.

With an ECCR the diver does not have to maintain the partial pressure, the rebreather senses it using a range of oxygen cells and when it drops below a set level the rebreather will automatically inject additional oxygen into the breathing loop to maintain the ppO_2. This removes the need for the diver to be an active part of the process although it is still important for them to know their partial pressure at all times.

The approach taken by MCCR and ECCR systems is completely different in terms of the approach taken but also the philosophy behind them. The MCCR makes a virtue of simplicity, one make of MCCR is named the KISS to emphasize this idea. The lack of electronics and electronic injectors simplifies the whole system and reduces the number of components. In addition the fact that the diver is an essential part of the process to maintain the correct partial pressure means that they must be more closely involved in monitoring this process. The disadvantage of course is that there is more effort required in the process. An ECCR on the other hand works by automating this process. The rebreather will automatically maintain the correct partial pressure for the diver. This simplifies the operation for the diver, allowing them to focus on other things. The down side of this approach is that the system is more complex with more potential for error. In addition some less diligent divers may neglect to monitor their partial pressure as they assume the rebreather will take care of it.

Supporters of MCCR point to the much lower rate of fatalities on this type of rebreather than on ECCR as evidence that simplicity and manual operation provide a greater level of safety. This must be balanced against the fact that the vast majority of rebreathers in use are of the ECCR variety and therefore this may affect the statistics.

The next difference between different types of rebreather is whether the counter lungs are back mounted, front mounted or over the shoulder mounted. When a rebreather diver breathes out the exhaled gas is collected in a counter lung, scrubbed of carbon dioxide and re-circulated, hence the name rebreather. In order to do this the gas must be held in a counter lung which is of a similar size to the diver's own lungs. Due to the pressure of water acting on these counter lungs the positioning of them can make a big difference to the ease with which the diver can breathe. This work of breathing (WOB) will vary depending on whether the counter lungs are back mounted, front mounted or over the shoulder mounted combined with the diver's position in the water. If the diver is upright then the position of the counter lungs is less important because they will be at the same level in the water as the diver's own lungs. If the diver has a horizontal (face down) position in the water then back mounted counter lungs will be above the level of the diver's own lungs while front mounted counter lungs will be below them and over the shoulder mounted counter lungs they will be at the same level as them. If the counter lungs are at a different level then the water pressure acting on them will be slightly but still noticeably, different to the pressure acting on the diver's own lungs.

For example, for back mounted counter lungs when in a horizontal swimming position the pressure difference between the counter lungs and the centre of the diver's own lungs, may create a lower pressure difference which the diver has to suck against in order to take a breath. In this case the work of breathing when breathing in (inhale) would be higher in order to counteract this pressure difference than when breathing out (exhale). Front mounted counter lungs have the opposite effect in the same swim position so breathing in is easy but when breathing out the diver has to force the air out. Over the shoulder counter lungs have much less of a pressure difference in this position and would have a more equal work of breathing between inhale and exhale breaths

Figure 37: An APD inspiration with over the shoulder mounted counter lungs

From a work of breathing point of view, over the shoulder counter lungs would appear to have a big advantage and were initially adopted by the most popular rebreather design, the Ambient Pressure Diving Inspiration and Evolution range. There are nonetheless some disadvantages to them. By having to be mounted on the shoulders and upper chest the counter lungs are exposed to wear and damage. They are also quite bulky and create a feeling of clutter in the chest area. Front mounted counter lungs share the same disadvantages. On the other hand back mounted counter lungs avoid these disadvantages by mounting the counter lungs behind the diver, either within the case of the rebreather or between the diver and the wing. Within the case they are protected from damage and by removing them from the front of the diver they reduce clutter from the chest area and can increase streamlining of the diver in the water. This is the approach adopted by the KISS, Sentinel/RedBare and rEvo. Even if they are outside the case and mounted between the diver and the wing they reduce clutter from the chest area and can increase streamlining of the diver in the water and are still less exposed than on the front. This is the approach that has been adopted by Ambient Pressure Diving for the back mounted version of the Inspiration as well as the JJ-CCR, XCCR and a number of other manufacturers.

We have already seen that it is essential that a rebreather diver knows their partial pressure of oxygen at all times. Too high a partial pressure and oxygen toxicity is a risk whereas too low a partial pressure and the diver may lose consciousness due to hypoxia or lack of oxygen. Many of the first commercially available rebreathers such as the Inspiration and KISS were supplied with handset displays that showed the current partial pressure. These could be wrist mounted or clipped onto the chest area. The diver would then check their handset on a regular basis to determine their partial pressure. During training divers were taught that they should be checking their handset every 30 seconds or so and more often during critical periods such as ascents and descents. Despite this it is all too easy to forget to check your handset and to leave it a minute or more between checks. In order to provide an additional safety check a number of independent manufacturers began supplying head up displays (HUD). These displays were LED driven displays that would sit just in front of the diver's mask and provide a visual check that the partial pressure was within an acceptable range or whether there was a problem. These HUDs were not designed to replace the need for a handset but merely to give an early warning or to prompt the diver to look at their handset in order to find out what the specific problem was. In time rebreather manufacturers began to offer HUDs as optional extras and then as part of the standard configuration. Now the majority of rebreathers come with a HUD as standard.

Other than making the rebreather slightly more complicated there are very few disadvantages to the HUD system. The only other possible criticism is that it may make the diver lazy in that they will only look at their handset if the HUD indicates a problem. More recent HUD designs such as the Shearwater NERD or APD HUS have moved away from simple LED displays and now offer full displays presenting as much information as normal handset displays.

Figure 38: CCR Diver carrying a separate open circuit bailout cylinder

If there is any problem with a rebreather then the diver has the option of coming "off the loop" and "bailing out" to open circuit. This means switching to an open circuit regulator connected to a scuba cylinder. How this is achieved provides a number of configuration options. The diver can use a separate open circuit regulator or can use an open circuit regulator built into the rebreather mouthpiece. The regulator can then be connected to the rebreather's diluent cylinders or to a completely separate bailout cylinder. If the diver uses the rebreather's diluent cylinder then this restricts the amount of gas available as most rebreathers only use a 2L/14cf or 3L/21cf cylinder. This will not provide an adequate gas supply for any but the most shallow dives. This approach has the advantage of keeping the set up simple and many divers who are confident in the reliability of their unit and their own ability to resolve any problems adopt this approach, known as the alpinist approach. Other divers will always carry sufficient open circuit bailout, in the form of stage cylinders, to ensure they can get to the surface even in the case of a complete failure of the rebreather.

Alpinist divers develop good procedures for ensuring their units are meticulously prepared because they know any mistake in preparation is likely to be fatal as they have no open circuit backup. They are also very careful about anything that could damage the breathing loop such as penetrating a wreck with sharp edges that could tear or rip the breathing hoses. Again this is because they know that a loop flood will leave them with no other way to get to the surface. Alpinist divers are often critical of divers who plan on using bailout to deal with any situation as they believe that this develops bad habits and a lack of understanding of the unit. Despite these good precautions the alpinist style has fallen out of favour. This is primarily because it doesn't matter how many precautions you take or how much confidence you have in your rebreather there is always the potential for something to go wrong. The safest approach is to prepare your unit and dive as if you were alpinist but to also carry sufficient bailout.

The open circuit regulator used to bailout can be a standard scuba regulator attached to the bailout cylinder or can be built into the rebreather mouthpiece. When using a standard scuba cylinder the rebreather diver has to deploy the scuba regulator, close the rebreather mouthpiece and then switch to the scuba regulator. In an emergency, this sequence of events may be a considerable strain. On the other hand a scuba regulator can be built into the rebreather mouthpiece. This is known as a bail out valve (BCV) and in this case to switch to open circuit the diver just turns a leaver and is automatically switched from the rebreather loop to the open circuit regulator.

Given the number of configuration options anyone looking to start rebreather diving is faced with a bewildering set of decisions. Should they go for back mounted counter lungs or over the shoulder? Electronic or manual control? Alpinist or external bailout?

Given each of these options is there such a thing as the best configuration? Unfortunately the best option for one reason may not be the best option for another and hence any decision will inevitably be a compromise. The compromise that is chosen will depend on what factors you consider to be most important. This means that the best rebreather for one diver may not be the same as the best rebreather for another diver as they may have different views on the compromises to be made. One day we may see a single rebreather that resolves all the issues perfectly but that may still be some time off.

PART 6
Aspects

Chapter 33. Extending your diving – Longer rather than deeper 189

Chapter 34. Decompression Diving 193

Chapter 35. Nitrogen Narcosis 205

Chapter 36. Trimix 209

Chapter 37. Oxygen Toxicity 213

Chapter 38. Dive Planning 217

Chapter 39. Wreck Penetration 225

Chapter 40. Cave Diving 229

Chapter 41. Expeditions 235

Chapter 32. Missed Decompression 239

33
Extending your diving – Longer rather than deeper

"We shall not cease from exploration. And the end of all our exploring will be to arrive where we started and know the place for the first time" **T.S. Eliot**

If you ask the majority of divers to define technical diving you will probably end up with a definition at least partly based on depth. Although the ability to dive deeper than recreational limits has always been one of the major aspects of technical diving it is by no means the only aspect. Technical diving is about extending your diving and this extension can develop along a number of different dimensions.

One of the greatest advantages to using technical diving techniques is in extending the length of the dive rather than the depth. For example a recreational diver with a Deep Diver speciality is certified to dive to 40m/130ft. However 40m/130ft recreational dives don't make a lot of sense. The no-stop limit for 40m/130ft is between 3 and 10 minutes depending on the tables you use[47]. If you have spent 3 hours driving to the coast and another 2 hours on a boat to get out to a wreck then that is a round trip time of ten hours for a ten minute bottom time. That's an hour travelling time for every minute on the wreck. Similarly if we add up the cost of the fuel for the drive, cylinder fills, charter fee for the day, possibly overnight accommodation and all the other costs then t results in a huge cost for each minute spent on the wreck. Of course the ten minutes also includes the descent time so we often end up spending only 5 minutes on the wreck itself. f the tide is running or you are dropped on a part of the wreck where there are no interesting features then this can be reduced even further. If we know that we only have a few minutes on the wreck then we tend to rush more and as a result may miss interesting points. The temptation to rush the descent in order to get more time on the wreck combined with the overall time pressure also increases the risk of nitrogen narcosis. Thinking back to my own experience of 40m/130ft no-stop dives, can remember lots of enthusiasm and excitement before the dive followed by a feeling afterwards that the dive didn't quite live up to expectations. I always felt that I hadn't really seen the wreck and had no feel for how t

---

[47] For the examples in this section I will use standard Bühlmann tables to illustrate the decompression times.

was lying and the structure of the wreck. There was always a feeling that although that dive was a bit of a disappointment the next dive would be better and I would get a better view of the wreck next time. On those dives where we were lucky and had fantastic visibility there was a huge feeling of regret that we couldn't stay longer on the wreck.

Technical diving and specifically decompression diving offers the possibility of significantly increasing the time you can spend on the wreck with only marginal increases in cost, effort or risk. Once you are properly equipped and trained for decompression diving then the no-stop time disappears as a limitation of your diving. If you are prepared to undertake a certain amount of decompression stops on the ascent then you can pass that no-stop time and enjoy a significantly increased time on the bottom. For example if you increase your bottom time from 10 minutes to 20 minutes then in effect you more than double your actual time on the wreck as the descent time stays the same. This means that you are getting more than twice as much time on the wreck for the same cost, the same travelling time and almost the same effort. This extra 10 minutes will give you much more time to explore the wreck and get a feel for the layout. You can certainly see more of a wreck in a single 20 minute dive than you will in two 10 minute dives. Now the price of this extra time is that you will have to perform decompression stops on the way back to the surface. In this case a 20 minute bottom time will give you 11 minutes of decompression stops. This seems to be well worth the effort. An additional 11 minutes of decompression at the end of the dive doesn't seem to be an unreasonable cost to pay for the increased time on the bottom. After all getting time on the bottom is why we dive.

As you increase the time on the bottom the amount of decompression also increases. If you do a 30 minute bottom time then you will have to do 30 minutes of decompression on the way back up. While 30 minutes on a wreck is very appealing 30 minutes of decompression is now starting to become a significant price to pay. For many divers 30 minutes of decompression is a significant amount and they start to think that the benefit to cost relationship is starting to swing too far towards the cost. In addition as the decompression obligation increases the gas reserves that are required start to increase. However there are additional ways that technical diving techniques can start to help.

The above examples were all worked out assuming that the diver is breathing air. However, by changing our breathing gas you can gain a further advantage. For no-stop dives at 40m/130ft the advantage of nitrox is minimal. The risk of oxygen toxicity means that you can only use relatively weak nitrox mixtures which have a minimal effect on no-stop times. Using EAN28 at 40m/130ft increases your no-stop time from 8 minutes to 12 minutes. Although this is a 50% increase the additional cost of a nitrox fill for four minutes extra on the bottom is often judged to be not worth it. However, for decompression dives the advantage becomes more noticeable. In the example above, a dive to 40m/130ft for a bottom time of 30 minutes resulted in 30 minutes of decompression if you are breathing air. On the other hand the same dive, using EAN28 rather than air, gives only 17 minutes of decompression. Although this is less than the 50% advantage on the no-stop dive a saving of 13 minutes is much more noticeable and is often considered to be well worth the cost and effort of using nitrox rather than air. We have already established that you can see more of the wreck in a single 20 minute dive than in two 10 minute dives and this principle is even more applicable for a 30 minute dive. You have the time to properly explore the wreck, to investigate certain areas in detail and even to start to penetrate into the interior of the wreck. You can often swim the length of a wreck and see the bigger picture of the shape, condition and layout of the wreck. It's not until you start to do longer dives on a 40m/130ft wreck that you can even start to get an overall feel for the wreck and really start to get to know the wreck. For wreck researchers this length of bottom time is very valuable in providing time to be able to start identifying features and begin the process of identification.

In addition to using nitrox as your main breathing gas technical diving techniques also allow you to switch to a second nitrox mix during the decompression in order to further optimise your decompression. Decompression stops allow time for dissolved nitrogen to come out of the body. You cannot ascend any higher until a certain amount of nitrogen has been allowed to escape, if you do ascend before the required amount of nitrogen has been allowed to escape then it will form bubbles which is the cause of decompression sickness (DCI). When you switch to a second nitrox mixture with a higher percentage of oxygen and by implication a lower percentage of nitrogen, the nitrogen dissolved in your body comes out faster and so you don't need to wait as long before you can move up in the water. This is why the technique is known as accelerated decompression, although some people prefer the term optimised decompression. By using EAN50 as a decompression gas you can reduce your decompression to 13 minutes and by using EAN80 or even 100% oxygen you can reduce it to just 9 minutes. Alternatively you could further increase your bottom time to 35 or even 40 minutes until you reach the maximum amount of decompression time you were happy to do. Of course you don't get anything for free and using this technique introduces a number of other considerations that the diver will need to take into account. In particular, much more detailed gas planning and the risk of oxygen toxicity must be considered. This is why specialised training is required in order to make use of these specific tools. In particular the decompression times and dive practices contained in these examples should not be taken as correct and are only provided for illustration.[48]

It should now be starting to become clear why some qualifications limit the time as well as the depth of the dive. There is only so much trouble you can get into on a no-stop dive whereas there is more potential for problems on a decompression dive. Recreational dive qualifications limit divers to no-stop times to limit the risks they are exposed to. Some other courses limit the diver to 15 minutes of decompression and are sometimes referred to as advanced recreational courses rather than full technical courses. As the diver progresses to full technical courses then the skills they will learn and the planning techniques they will use means that there is no limit on the amount of decompression a diver can carry out as long as they stay within the safe limits of gas availability, CNS and all other planning variables. In many cases it will be the divers own personal limits rather than any external factor that determines the maximum amount of decompression they want to do.

The skills contained within technical diving courses that allow divers to extend the time they can spend on the wreck are also a way to extend your diving. Many people undertake this training so that they can be safer and more skilled at the depths they are currently diving at rather than to progress any deeper. The skills required for technical diving can also make you a significantly better recreational diver. Having better buoyancy control, awareness of your situation and of your buddy will all help to make you a better diver. Together with better self rescue and buddy rescue skills they will also make you a safer diver no matter what depth you are at.

---

48   That should keep the lawyers happy.

34
Decompression Diving

"There's no such thing as a casual deco dive" **Rob Palmer**

One of the clearest differences between recreational and technical diving is that recreational diving involves dives that are within the no-stop limits whereas technical diving involves deeper or longer dives. This inevitably means carrying out dives that involve mandatory decompression stops. Decompression introduces a different set of concerns and requires a different way of thinking about your dives. At the very least divers involved in decompression diving need to understand a little about what is going on in their body when they dive.

Any dive whether it is a reef dive in 18m/60ft or a wreck dive at 80m/260ft will result in the body taking on an increased loading of inert gas such as nitrogen. The increased pressure at depth means that there is a higher pressure of nitrogen in the air you breathe. During the dive this nitrogen moves from the lungs into the blood and slowly spreads into the tissues of the body. Longer or deeper dives will result in a higher loading of nitrogen. For trimix divers, who use a mixture of oxygen, nitrogen and helium, their bodies will also have an increased level of helium as this is also an inert gas.

At the end of the dive the diver ascends and this dissolved inert gas starts to come out of the body. If the gas comes out too quickly then bubbles will form and Decompression Illness[49] (DCI) is likely to occur. For recreational no-stop dives the limited bottom time means that there is only a comparatively small amount of nitrogen in the body. During the ascent this gas starts to travel back to the lungs where it is exhaled. Providing that the correct ascent rate is followed there is little chance of DCI. This has lead to no-stop dives sometimes being called no-decompression dives. This is incorrect as we can see that every dive involves decompression to some extent. This means that there is no such thing as a no-decompression dive. No-stop dives are just dives in which the ascent time provides enough time for the nitrogen to escape and drop to a safe level. Of course this means that a rapid ascent, where the correct ascent rate isn't followed and there is not sufficient time for the nitrogen to escape can cause DCI, even on a no-stop dive.

If you stay longer at depth than the no-stop time, you will have absorbed more nitrogen than can safely escape during a

---

49 It used to be common to distinguish clearly between decompression sickness (DCS), also known as the bends, and pulmonary barotraumas, known as burst lung. This was found to be counterproductive as the symptoms and treatment of the two are the same as far as first aid is concerned. As a result the term decompression illness (DCI) was introduced to refer to both. In this chapter and the next I am primarily talking about "the bends" but I will use the term decompression illness (DCI) for consistency.

direct ascent to the surface. In this case you will need to carry out a mandatory decompression stop. This stop provides the time required for the higher levels of nitrogen to fall to a level where you can continue to the surface. For longer or deeper dives there will be increased nitrogen loading and it will take longer for the nitrogen levels to fall to a safe level. In this case the decompression stops will get longer and longer.

A common analogy for decompression is the process of opening a bottle of fizzy drink. If the bottle is opened too quickly then it will fizz up and overflow the bottle. On the other hand if the bottle is only opened a little and then closed the bubbles subside and it can then be opened a bit further.

Once a diver incurs a mandatory decompression stop then they can no longer ascend directly to the surface without risking DCI. For this reason the decompression stop depth is sometimes known as the virtual overhead or glass ceiling. Unlike a cave diver or a diver entering a wreck, the overhead is not visible but is still very real. This virtual overhead means that decompression diving requires a change of mindset, compared to the mindset of recreational divers. Going to the surface is no longer an option because the diver must have the ability to resolve any problem in the water. They must also have the buoyancy control to ensure they do not break this virtual overhead. Recreational divers who do not have the buoyancy control to accurately hold a safety stop or the skills and equipment required to resolve problems underwater, should not consider decompression dives involving mandatory decompression stops.

Most recreational divers have only a limited understanding of what is happening in their bodies as they dive. They follow their dive tables or dive computers and assume that they will be safe as long as they follow the rules. Given the huge number of recreational dives that are safely carried out using standard tables and dive computers this is not an unreasonable assumption. For divers involved in decompression diving this is not necessarily the case. There is far less knowledge about the safe limits of decompression diving and several competing theories as to what happens to our bodies during this type of diving. For this reason technical divers tend to learn more about decompression theory and take a more active interest in what is happening during the dive.

TRADITIONAL DECOMPRESSION

Most traditional dive tables and personal dive computers use a variant of the Bühlmann algorithm, named after Professor Albert A. Bühlmann. This in turn is based on the work of John Scott Haldane who developed a theory of decompression behaviour in order to create decompression tables for the Royal Navy. Haldane published his findings in 1908 and his work continues to influence decompression theory to this day. Haldane's work was modified in the 1940s and '50s by researchers from the US Navy. Then during the 1960s and '70s Bühlmann further refined the model and extended it in certain areas to deal with additional problems such as diving at altitude and using trimix rather than air or nitrox.

The traditional decompression model is also known as a dissolved gas model. This is because it assumes the inert gas is dissolved in the body until a certain critical point is reached. Once this point, known as the Maximum Value or M-Value, is reached the gas comes out of solution and forms bubbles which are the trigger for Decompression Illness. This model assumes that a relatively fast ascent from depth to a much more shallow depth, while still keeping the pressure change below a specific maximum value, will allow the maximum amount of nitrogen to be released or off-gassed from the body, while at the same time preventing bubbles from forming. As a result the ascent for a traditional decompression profile brings the diver rapidly up from depth to one or more decompression stops in shallow water.

This approach is based on the assumption that decompression sickness is caused by the formation of bubbles in the body. The conclusion from this is that a dive which does not result in decompression sickness cannot have caused any bubbles to form. We now know that the behaviour of the body is not quite as black and white as the traditional model would imply. The ideal of a critical limit where one side of the limit is safe and no bubbles are formed and yet the other side of the limit bubbles immediately begin to form is over simplistic. In fact even the idea that bubbles cause decompression sickness is an oversimplification. In the 1970s Doppler bubble detection showed that in fact bubbles are commonly found in divers who have been diving well within the no-stop limits of recreational tables. This contradicts the traditional Haldane approach but it shouldn't have been a great surprise. The body just doesn't work in absolutes and to suggest that on one side of an arbitrary limit no bubbles are formed but as soon as that line is crossed bubbles will start to form should have set alarm bells ringing for anyone with a passing knowledge of physiology.

Clearly there is more to DCI than just bubble formation. This has lead to the use of the term 'silent bubbles' or 'asymptomatic bubbles'. These are bubbles which do not lead to the traditional signs and symptoms of decompression sickness but which can routinely occur on even no-stop dives. These silent bubbles are the reason why some divers suffer an excessive level of tiredness or fatigue after diving. In addition an excess of silent bubbles can cause problems for repetitive dives. Although the silent bubbles are not sufficient to cause DCI they are still enough to give the body something to think about. The immune system starts to attack the bubbles and this can cause feelings of tiredness.

In recent years there has been a push towards slower ascent rates and an increased emphasis on safety stops. Ascent rates of 10m/min(33ft/min) are now preferred to anything faster and many dive computers include an automatic three minute safety stop. Even on no-stop dives these minor changes can have a significant impact on the number of bubbles in the body.

For decompression dives the effects of silent bubbles become more pronounced with longer and deeper dives producing more symptoms. For this reason many technical divers have looked at other options to try and reduce the risks of decompression diving. A number of 'tweaks' have been applied to the traditional Haldanian approach to try and reduce the formation of bubbles during otherwise uneventful dives. Most of these result in the introduction of much deeper initial stops or, for no-stop dives, the inclusion of additional deeper safety stops. As a result the term 'deep stops' has become a generic term for stops introduced to avoid the formation of silent bubbles. These are stops which start considerably deeper than a traditional decompression model would predict. The idea behind these deep stops is that they give the gas dissolved in the tissues a chance to escape from the body before it starts to form bubbles. Returning to the example of opening a bottle of fizzy drink this can be thought of as momentarily closing the top of the bottle to give the gas a chance to settle before once again opening it up.

DEEP STOPS

There are a number of ways that deep stops can be introduced into a decompression profile. The best known version of deep stops is the approach developed by Richard Pyle and as a result the term 'Pyle stops' has been used almost as commonly as deep stops. [50]

Richard Pyle is an experienced diver and marine biologist. Specifically he is an ichthyologist, although he describes himself as a 'fish-nerd'. Pyle regularly dives to depths of 60m-100m/200-330ft in order to study and collect specimens of the various fish species that live at these depths. While diving to these depths Pyle noticed that after some of his dives he felt overly tired and lethargic, a classic indication of asymtomatic DCI and silent bubbles, whereas after other dives there were no such indications. He realized that the feeling was related to decompression rather than just the physical exertion of the dive as a dive to 60m/200ft for a total time of an hour would give more of a feeling of tiredness than a dive of 4-6 hours at a much more shallow depth.

Pyle tried to identify the factors that separated the dives on which he felt good from the ones in which he felt overly tired. He considered a whole range of factors including obvious ones such as the length of the dive, depth, current, hydration levels, whether he had felt seasick during the journey, extra time added to the last deco stop, water temperature, how well he had slept the night before, etc., as well as less obvious factors such as the clarity of the water, days or dates of the month on which the dives were carried out, etc.

---

50 For more information on deep stops and other aspects of decompression the following are recommended.
Powell, M. J. 2008. Deco for Divers. AquaPress
Baker, E.C. 1998. Clearing up the confusion about deep stops. Immersed. Vol. 3, No. 4, 23-31.
Marroni A, Bennett P.B, Cronje F.J, Cali-Corleo R, Germonpre P, Pieri M, Bonucelli C, Balestra C. "A deep stop during decompression from 82 fsw (25m) significantly reduces bubbles and fast tissue gas tension" Undersea and Hyperbaric Medicine Journal, Volume 31 No 2.(2004)
Pyle, RL. The importance of Deep Safety Stops: Rethinking Ascent Patterns From Decompression Dives. Deep Tech, Issue 5

After looking for patterns in the dives which produced no signs, he eventually realized the common factor was that on dives on which he was catching and raising fish specimens from depth he was much less likely to get signs of asymptomatic DCI than on dives where no specimens were collected. This was a surprising result as initially there seemed to be no explanation as to why these dives would produce less symptoms. The major difference in these dives was that, in order to prevent damage to the fish from the gas in their swim-bladders expanding upon ascent, he would use a hypodermic syringe to extract air from their swim bladders during the ascent. The pause in the ascent required to carry out this procedure was usually much deeper than his first prescribed decompression stop, for example on a 60m/200ft dive, the first decompression stop would usually be around 15m/50ft, but Pyle would pause to remove air from the swim-bladder at around 40m/130ft. This meant that whenever he was collecting fish, his ascent profile would include an extra 2-3 minute stop much deeper than the first decompression stop required by a traditional decompression model. Using a traditional decompression model this approach doesn't make sense as the traditional model predicts that by stopping deeper you are not off-gassing effectively in some of your tissues and are allowing additional gas loading in other tissues. A traditional model would indicate that these stops should increase the symptoms of sub clinical DCI rather than reduce them.

Despite being at odds with traditional decompression theory Pyle concluded that it was these 'deep stops' which were reducing the signs of lethargy. As a result he began to include these 'deep stops' in all his deep dives with a subsequent reduction in signs of sub-clinical DCI.

Through an empirical process Pyle developed the following process for calculating deep stops.

PYLE DEEP STOPS PROCESS:

1. Take the distance between the depth when you start your ascent and the first required decompression stop and find the mid point. This depth will be your first deep safety stop and should be 2-3 minutes in duration.
2. If the distance between your first deep safety stop and your first required stop is greater than 9m, then add an additional deep safety stop at the midpoint between the first deep safety stop and the first required decompression stop.
3. Repeat as necessary until there is less than 9m between your last deep safety stop and the first required stop.

Table 16: Pyle Deep Stops Process

Some versions use a difference of less than 6m/20ft between the last deep safety stop and the first required stop. This is more common for dives of less than 40m/130ft. Other versions recommend a stop of 1-2 minutes rather than 2-3 minutes. Divers using a dive computer will find that the computer will recalculate the decompression stops and depending on the make and model of the computer, may add additional decompression time and even additional decompression stops. This can increase the overall length of the ascent as many current dive computers use a traditional algorithm which penalises the additional time spent at depth during the dive. This additional time on the total dive can be considered an additional safety margin. An example is shown in Table 17.

PYLE DEEP STOPS – A RECREATIONAL EXAMPLE

When carrying out a no-stop dive to 40m/130ft we will not incur any mandatory decompression, however we can consider the recommended safety stop at 5m/16ft to be the equivalent of the first decompression stop.

Take the distance between the depth when you start your ascent	40m
and the safety stop	5m
and find the mid point	(40+5)/2 = 23m
This depth will be your first deep safety stop and should be 1-2 minutes in duration	
If the distance between your first deep safety stop and your safety stop	23-5 = 18m
Is greater than 6m	Yes it is
then add an additional deep safety stop at the midpoint between the first deep safety stop	23m
and the safety stop	5m
Which is	(23+5)/2 = 14m
If the distance between your latest deep safety stop and your safety stop	14-5 = 9m
Is greater than 6m	Yes it is
then add an additional deep safety stop at the midpoint between the first deep safety stop	14m
and the first required decompression stop.	5m
Which is	(14+5)/2 = 9m (rounded up to 15m)
If the distance between your latest deep safety stop and your first required stop	9-4 = 4m
Is not greater than 6m	No it isn't
Then carry on to the first traditional safety stop	

Table 17: An example of Pyle stops

Therefore in this example we would end up with Pyle stops at 23m, 14m, 9m as well as a traditional safety stop at 5m.

Pyle met considerable scepticism when he initially discussed his approach. This is not surprising as his findings directly contradicted established decompression theory. Nonetheless later decompression research into 'bubble models' calls for initial decompression stops that are much deeper than those suggested by traditional neo-Haldanian decompression models. Although calculated in completely different ways they were very similar to the deep stops generated by Pyle's empirically derived method. This gave credence to the empirically derived method generated by Pyle. As the decompression modeling community as well as the growing ranks of technical divers began to appreciate the implications of 'Bubble models' Pyle's empirical approach began to be acknowledged as having some scientific basis. Although an over simplification in some cases, it certainly provided the easiest way to incorporate deep stops in decompression practice and 'Pyle Stops' has become a commonly used term.

GRADIENT FACTORS

Another option is to use a technique known as Gradient Factors. This provides an approach which modifies the specific calculations of the traditional dissolved gas model. The basic concept behind gradient factors is that if there is a danger of bubbles forming even within the traditional critical limit, then to increase safety we can simply stay further away from this limit. Gradient Factors are just a way of controlling how close we are prepared to get to the limit.

Gradient Factors are expressed as a percentage of the critical or M-Value limit or in other words as a percentage of the way into the decompression zone. So a 0% GF means that we have not travelled any distance towards the limit while 100% is right on the M-Value limit. A gradient factor of 20% would be 20% of the way to the limit. From this explanation we can see that a higher gradient factor is closer to the M-value limit whereas a lower gradient factor is further away from the limit.

Gradient factors are used in pairs with a lower limit, known as the gradient factor low or GF(Lo), and a higher limit, known as gradient factor high or GF(Hi). The GF(Lo) and GF(Hi) can be thought of as an additional set of lines between the ambient pressure and M-Value lines. This is shown graphically in Diagram 11.

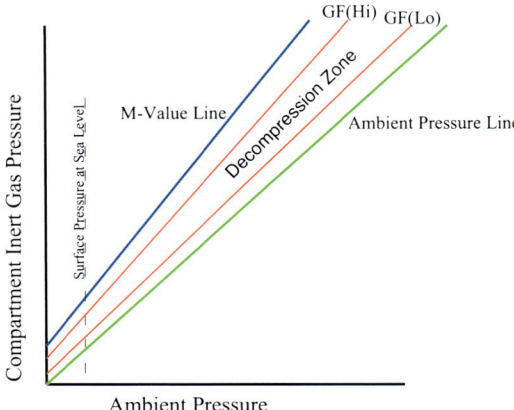

Diagram 11: Gradient factors shown graphically

The GF adaptations to the Bühlmann model work by inserting a stop during the ascent when we reach gradient factor low. So, for example, with GF(Lo) set to 30% a stop will be inserted when the leading compartment reaches 30% of the way to the M-Value line. Subsequent stops allow the maximum gradient factor to move from the low to high limit.

GF(Hi) determines the how close we are to the limit on surfacing. You would stay at your final stop until you can ascend to the surface without any of the tissues exceeding Gradient Factor High or GF(Hi). The value of GF(Hi) determines the length of the final stop with a lower value resulting in a longer final stop and a higher value resulting in a shorter final stop.

A GF ascent with GF(Lo) set to 30% and GF(Hi) set to 80% would give you an ascent as shown in Diagram 12. Once you reach the GF(Lo) limit, in this case 30% the model calculates the maximum gradient factor required to move from the GF(Lo) point to the GF(Hi) on reaching the surface. This is also shown in Diagram 12 as the purple line connecting the 30% and 80% lines.

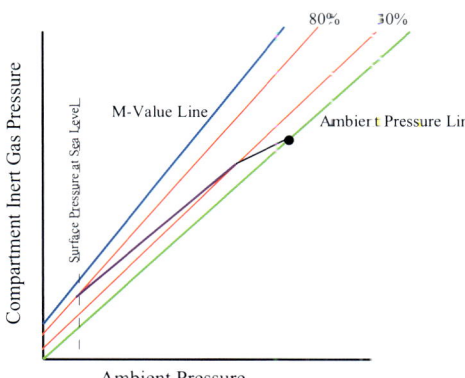

Diagram 12: Gradient factors applied to a Bühlmann model

In this example a Gradient Factor ascent would then keep you at the first stop depth until your can move up to the next stop depth without any of your compartments exceeding the recalculated maximum gradient factor, i.e. without breaking the purple line. The ascent from the lower gradient factor towards the maximum gradient factor that is, from 30% towards 80%. On the last stop the model will keep you at the stop depth until you can ascend to the surface without any of your compartments exceeding 80% of the limit. The full ascent using these settings is shown in Diagram 13.

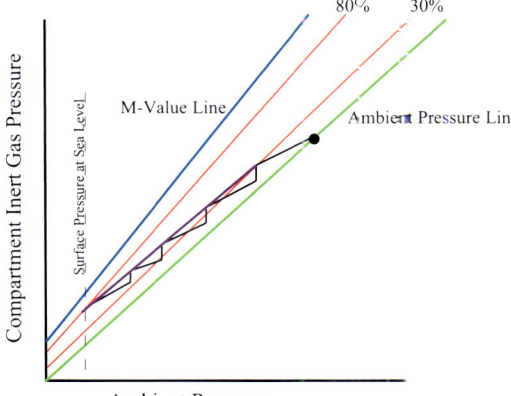

Diagram 13: A gradient factor based ascent

The values used for GF(Lo) and GF(Hi) are not fixed. They can be chosen by the user and altered to procuce a profile which suits their individual preference. The choice of settings for GF(Lo) and GF(Hi) will make significant changes to the decompression profile and the depth and length of decompression stops. The lower the value of GF(Lo) the deeper the first stop will be. For example if GF(Lo) is set to 1% then only a very slight ascent is required to reach this limit and so the first stop may only be a few metres above the bottom. On the other hand a higher setting for GF(Lo) will result in a much later or more shallow first stop depth, as the diver can ascend to a lesser depth before reaching the specified percentage of their leading tissue M-Value. Equally the setting for the GF(Hi) will determine the length of the last stop as the diver will have to stay at their last stop until their surfacing tissue tension is less then the value for GF(Hi). Lower values of GF(Hi) will result in longer final stops whereas higher values will result in shorter final stops.

Setting the value of GF(Lo) too low can cause problems as a certain level of supersaturation is required in order to allow off-gassing. By setting it too low we will introduce stops at a depth where the leading compartments are not off-gassing to any great extent but at the same time the slower compartment are still on-gassing at a significant rate. This on-gassing in the slower compartments will need to be offset by longer decompression during the shallower stops, which can add significantly to the overall decompression time.

BUBBLE MODELS

The last method of incorporating deep stops is to use what are known as bubble models. Traditional models assume that bubbles occur only when some threshold is crossed and that these bubbles then cause DCI. The aim of a traditional model is to prevent bubbles from forming. Bubble models, on the other hand, assume that bubbles form on almost every dive and that the key task is to balance the gas dissolved in the tissues with the gas in bubble form. The aim of a bubble model is to control the number and growth of bubbles to stay within a certain limit. Bubble models use complex mathematics to calculate this balance and as such require a desktop PC or sophisticated dive computer to create a dive profile. None of the standard recreational dive computers use a full bubble model algorithm although specialised technical diving computers are now starting to include these algorithms.

Pyle stops, gradient factors and bubble models all produce a decompression schedule that has much deeper initial stops than a traditional model. Although it is possible to use a dive computer which allows decompression diving or buy a decompression planning program from the internet to create one of these programs, you must be aware of the limitations of the planning tools and the implications of the decompression schedule. All of these approaches are at the leading edge of decompression theory and should not be used without specialized training.

BENEFITS OF DEEP STOPS AND BUBBLE MODELS

In order to investigate the claimed benefits of deep stops DAN performed a series of dives to study the impact of ascent rates and deep stops on bubble formation[51]. A series of dives were carried out to 25m/80ft for 25 minutes followed, after a surface interval of 3 hours and 30 minutes, by another dive to 25m/80ft for 20 minutes. Ascent rates of 18m/60ft, 10m/33ft and 3m/10ft were performed on each of the dives. Each ascent rate was combined with a direct ascent to the surface, a traditional safety stop of 5 minutes at 6m/20ft and finally a deep stop of 5 minutes at 15m/50ft combined with a traditional safety stop of 5 minutes at 6m/20ft. The only exception was that a direct ascent was not performed with an 18m/minute (60ft/minute) ascent rate as this was considered too risky. After each dive Doppler bubble detection was used to calculate a Bubble Score Index (BSI) which indicates the number of bubbles formed during that dive. The results of the research showed that the bubble score for the ascents with no-stops was higher than with a stop or 6m/20ft or a stop at 15m/50ft and 6m/20ft. The results for the ascents incorporating a deep stop at 15m/50ft as well as a stop at 6m/20ft clearly show a significantly lower BSI. This seems to confirm that the incorporation of a deep stop has a positive effect on bubble formation, even on recreational no-stop dives in the 25m/80ft depth range.

From Diagram 14 you can also see that an ascent rate of 18m/min (60ft/minute) gives a higher bubble score (where carried out) than the 10m/min (33ft/min). Interestingly you can also see that the 3m/minute (10ft/minute) ascent rate gives a higher bubble score reading than either the 18m/minute (60ft/minute) or 10m/minute (33ft/minute) ascents. This shows that a slow ascent rate is beneficial but that there is such a thing as an ascent rate that is too slow. The best combination is a 10m/minute (33ft/minute) ascent rate combined with a deep stop at 15m/50ft and a traditional safety stop at 6m/20ft.

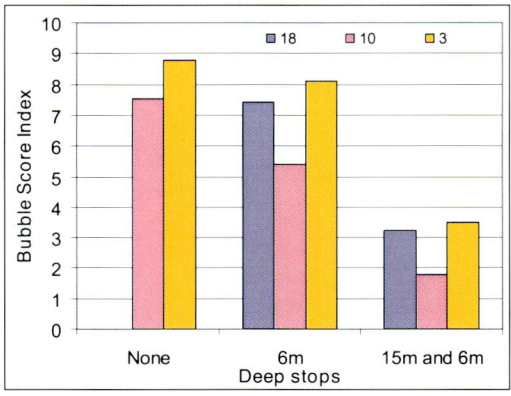

Diagram 14: Impact of deep stops on bubble formation

In the technical diving area the idea of deep stops and bubble models have become combined so that the terms are used almost interchangeably. The term deep stop is sometimes used to mean a stop calculated using Pyle's method or any stop deeper than a traditional Bühlmann stop. Similarly the term bubble model is used to include a decompression model that specifically models the formation and growth of bubbles as well as the much more general idea of any model that incorporates deeper stops in order to prevent or manage bubble formation. The concept of including deeper stops, whether they were added using Pyle's method or a true bubble model, gained a huge amount of support from the late 1990s right up until very recently. Stops were introduced deeper and deeper and major savings on the overall decompression time were claimed as a result of deep stops.

The emphasis on deep stops has started to swing back in recent years. The theory sounds very plausible and many technical divers were bordering on evangelical about deep stops, but is there any proof that the theory works? In reality most of the research into deep stops has been inconclusive at best. A study in 2005[52] failed to find any significant benefit, another study in 2010 found that bubble models resulted in a

---

51 Marroni A, Bennett P.B, Cronje F.J, Cali-Corleo R, Germonpre P, Pieri M, Bonucelli C, Balestra C. "A deep stop during decompression from 82 fsw (25m) significantly reduces bubbles and fast tissue gas tension" Undersea and Hyperbaric Medicine Journal, Volume 31 No 2.(2004)

52 Blatteau JE, Hugon M, Gardette B, Sainty JM, Galland FM.(2005) Bubble incidence after staged decompression from 50 or 60 msw: effect of adding deep stops. Aviat Space Environ Med. 2005 May;76(5):490-2. Ljubkovic, M. Marinovic, J. Obad, A. Breskovic, T. Gaustad, SE. Zeljko Dujic, Z. (2010) High incidence of venous and arterial gas emboli at rest after trimix diving without protocol violations J Appl Physiol 109: 1670-1674 Doolette, DJ; Gerth, WA; Gault, KA. (2011)Redistribution of decompression stop time from shallow to deep stops increases incidence of decompression sickness in air decompression dives US Navy Experimental Diving Unit Technical Report 2011-06. RRR ID: 10269

worryingly high level of bubbles, even though bubble models are supposed to control the level of bubbles. However, it was a US Navy study in 2011 that caused us to start to rethink bubble models. This study seemed to indicate that bubble models caused more problems than a traditional model. The study caused a huge amount of discussion which is still ongoing. Partly because it was not a great study, it didn't really do the sort of deep stops that divers actually do and there were a number of other questions about the structure of the study that called into question the results. However, it did get people talking about the idea. Although the study is not great and is just a single study which could have been discounted if it was the only study indicating this result, when combined with the other studies with similar results it starts to form a body of evidence that deep stops may not be the panacea that we previously thought. An unpublished study carried out for one of the Scandinavian Navies seemed to confirm the same results. Unfortunately, like many things public opinion has been all or nothing and this result has been taken as meaning that deep stops are bad.

The question we must ask is why did the deep stops seem to fail in this case? The obvious answer is that the deep stops are too deep. This study does not prove that deep stops are bad although it does, along with the other evidence, seem to indicate that you can have deep stops that are too deep. This raises the question what is "too deep" or what is a "good" deep stop and what is a "bad" deep stop?

Part of the problem is that the term deep stop is very vague, to the point that it is meaningless. In the Pyle stop example above, with a max depth of 40m/130ft and a first traditional stop of 9m/30ft then, in theory, anything deeper than 9m/30ft would be considered a deep stop. A stop at 39m/127ft, just 1m/3ft up from the bottom would be a deep stop while a stop at 12m/40ft, just 3m/10ft deeper than the 9m/30ft stop would also be considered a deep stop. Clearly, there is a big difference between a deep stop at 12m/40ft, and a deep stop at 39m/127ft but they could both be referred to as deep stops. The question is how deep is too deep?

In order to be a bit more objective, the table below shows the result of a dive planning program for a rebreather dive to 60m/200ft. It shows the stops resulting from using gradient factors of 30/80 and a range of others. I have chosen a 60m/200ft dive as the deeper the dive the more pronounced the effects become on the dive. I have also planned it as a CCR dive to remove any potential changes to the ascent profile caused by gas switches.

Low	High	Depth First	Length Last	Run Time
10	80	39m/128ft	36	104
20	80	36m/118ft	35	102
30	80	33m/108ft	34	99
40	80	30m/98ft	34	97
50	80	27/88ft	34	95
30	100	33m/108ft	24	81
30	90	33m/108ft	29	89
30	80	33m/108ft	34	99
30	70	33m/108ft	41	110

Table 18: Deep Stop Table

The first thing to say is that small changes in the gradient factors do not make a big difference but when we look at the whole range we can start to see the patterns. First of all let's keep the High GF constant at 80 while we change the low GF from 10 up to 50. Remember that the LOW GF affects the DEPTH of the FIRST stop and we can see this in the table. In this example every 10% change in the low GF results in a 3m/10ft change in the depth of the first stop. This is exactly as expected. However, if we now look at the Low GF in the range 30-50 we can see that the length of the last stop is constant at 34min. As the low GF is decreased even more, and stops are introduced at 36m/118ft and 39m/127ft, we can see that the time of the last stop increases to 35min and then 36min. The reason for this is that the additional stops at 36m/118ft and 39m/127ft are resulting in more on-gassing in the medium and slower compartments which then requires more decompression in the shallows. From this, we can see that a Low GF below 30 is making the situation worse, not better.

Of course, it should not be a surprise that it is possible to do deep stops that can be too deep. While we are doing the deep stops some of the medium and slow tissues, which were not saturated, will still be on-gassing. If we were to carry out very long deep stops or stop at very deep depths then this could cause a problem as the increased on-gassing in the slow tissues may result in longer decompression later in order to allow these tissues to off-gas. Any deep stop or bubble model must balance out the advantages of deeper stops in reducing bubble growth against the increased on-gassing in the mid to slow tissues.

When we keep the Low GF constant at 30 and change the High GF from 100 down to 70 we can see that the LENGTH of the LAST stop increases from 24 min up to 41 min. It is clear from this example that reducing the High GF forces the model to wait for more inert gas to be off-gassed before the diver is allowed to ascend and hence lower values of the High GF setting are clearly more conservative than higher numbers.

From this example, we can see that deep stops are complicated and it is not always easy to get simple answers.

Overall there are a number of conclusions we can draw from recent studies and discussions. The first is that 'deep stops' is a misleading term that does not always help the discussion. Maybe it is time to move away from using this term in favour of being more specific as to exactly what sort of stops we are talking about. The next conclusion is that it is definitely possible to stop too deep as shown by some of the examples given. Some of the advice given over the past few years has clearly been introducing stops that are too deep. However, a knee jerk reaction to say that 'deep stops are bad' is swinging too far the other way and we should be careful that we do not throw the baby out with the bathwater. The inescapable conclusion is that we do not know all the answers and we must be wary of anyone that tells you they know exactly what is the 'correct' decompression profile. Our knowledge of decompression theory is developing, even if it is sometimes at a very slow pace and it is important to keep up with the latest thoughts on decompression theory to ensure that you are not using out of date ideas.

DECOMPRESSION GASSES

In addition to the main gas carried by technical divers, usually in a twinset on their back, they will often carry additional gas mixes in stage cylinders. These decompression cylinders contain a rich nitrox mix that is used to reduce the amount of decompression the diver has to carry out. The rich nitrox mix contains a high percentage of oxygen and a correspondingly lower percentage on nitrogen. The lack of the nitrogen in the decompression mix means that the nitrogen in the diver's body will travel from the tissues into the blood and back to the lungs faster than would otherwise be the case. This increases the rate that the body 'off-gasses' and so reduces the total amount of decompression time. This is known as accelerated decompression. In some cases a single decompression gas can halve the amount of decompression that needs to be carried out. Multiple decompression cylinders can be carried so that the diver can switch to progressively richer mixes and further accelerate their decompression as they get closer to the surface.

Decompression diving can open up depths that are not available to the recreational no-stop diver. It can also allow increased bottom times which allow much greater scope for exploring the wrecks which are often better preserved at depth. However, decompression diving, as with many other aspects of technical diving, should not be undertaken lightly. Lack of buoyancy control or the inability to deal with a problem can result in missing decompression and a potential case of decompression illness. Any divers considering decompression diving should ensure their skills equipment and training are suitable for this type of diving.

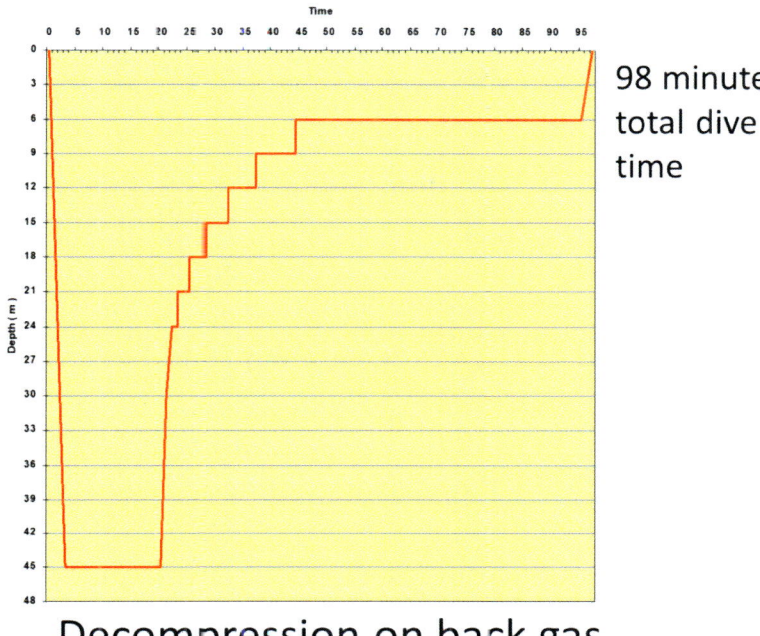

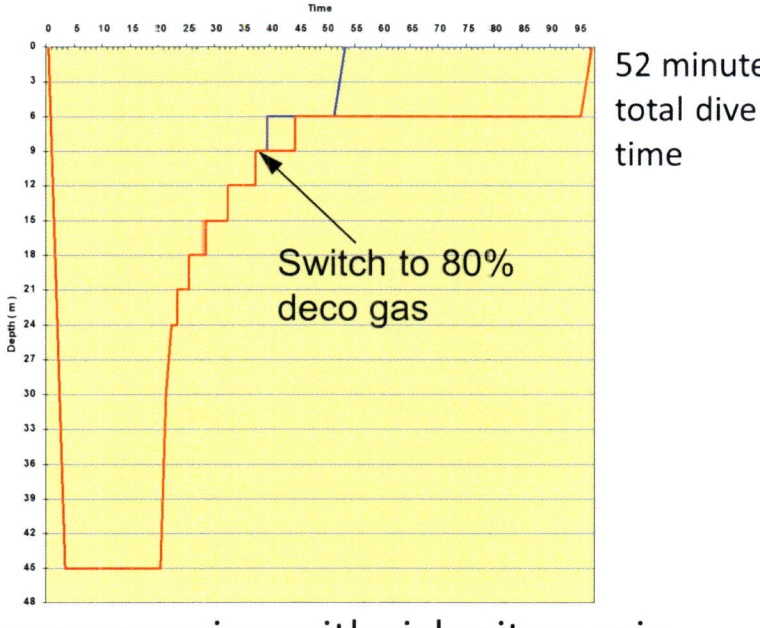

Diagram 15: The advantages of using a rich nitrox mix for decompression

Nitrogen Narcosis

"l'ivresse des grandes profondeurs" **Jacques Cousteau**

Of all the physiological factors that affect us as technical divers nitrogen narcosis is the most common but also the most widely misunderstood. Narcosis occurs as we dive deeper and becomes more severe the deeper we go. It has several side effects all of which serve to impair our ability to carry out basic tasks. Narcosis was most famously described in Jacques Cousteau's book, *The Silent World*, where Cousteau describes the symptoms and named it the "Rapture of the Deep".

The cause of narcosis has not been definitively proven although it is widely believed to be caused by the anaesthetic properties of certain gases at raised partial pressures.[53] Many divers incorrectly consider narcosis to be a black and white issue, either they are suffering from narcosis or they are not. Furthermore many divers claim that they have never suffered from narcosis. This shows a misunderstanding of the properties of narcosis and a lack of understanding of the symptoms.

If, as we believe, narcosis is caused by the anaesthetic properties of gases at increased partial pressure, then the level of narcosis experienced should be proportional to the depth. As the diver descends the narcosis should build up gradually. Those divers who claim never to have experienced narcosis have just never noticed the effects.

There are many effects of narcosis. The two most widely known are the extreme feelings of either euphoria or panic. In many ways the diver who experiences these feelings of panic and doom is lucky in that this type of narcosis is acting as a failsafe and preventing them going deeper and experiencing more narcosis. The diver who experiences euphoria is potentially at more risk as they are more likely to take risks or act dangerously. However, these two symptoms are not the only effects of narcosis.

There are a wide range of other effects. These may not always be as obvious as a feeling of overwhelming panic. Their symptoms can be much more subtle and so are not always immediately obvious. Divers suffering from narcosis often show a lack of judgement. They don't always make the best decisions or in some cases take an inordinate amount of time to make what should be a simple decision. I once watched a diver on a wreck penetration course take several minutes deciding which of two points to use to make a tie off. By the time he had finally made his mind up the team had run out of bottom time and had to turn around and start to

---

[53] Bennett PB, Rostain JC. (2002) Inert gas narcosis. In: Bennet PB, Elliot EH, eds. Bennett and Elliott's Physiology and Medicine of Diving. London: Saunders

exit. Until this was pointed out later by the rest of his team he didn't realise that he had taken this long to make the decision.

Narcosis appears to affect our memory. Divers who report no other symptoms of narcosis frequently show a lack of memory of certain parts of the dive. I spoke to a diver a few years ago who had just done the same dive as me. I was on trimix and they were on air. They confessed that despite a 20 minute bottom time they couldn't remember any specific detail of the dive.

Tasks which are easy in shallow water for some reason tend to become more difficult at depth. Loss of dexterity or motor control is a frequent symptom of narcosis. On many occasions I have seen someone send up a DSMB from 10m/33ft in just a few seconds only to have exactly the same task take several minutes at depth.

Narcosis often causes perceptual narrowing or task fixation. Divers become obsessed with completing the task they have begun, even when other tasks have obviously become a much higher priority. Divers suffering from narcosis often respond slower than they would in more shallow water. These extra seconds can make a vital difference at depth.

It is interesting that many of these additional symptoms of narcosis are not noticeable unless a problem or emergency occurs. If everything is going well then the fact that tasks take a little longer is no problem, especially as both parties are likely to forget many of the details of the dive anyway. However, narcosis becomes much more of an issue if a problem occurs. In this case the diver now has to assess the situation, make a judgement and act on it. All three of these are things that may be affected by their levels of narcosis. This means they are much less able to deal with a problem due to their level of narcosis.

Those divers who claim never to have experienced narcosis have just never noticed the effects.

We are lucky that the vast majority of dives do not involve an incident of any kind. During the dives that go well we can tolerate the level of narcosis that we experience. It is only when dives don't go well that that level of narcosis becomes dangerous. Unfortunately I still haven't been able to reliably identify in advance the dives when things will go well and those when an incident will occur. Until then I will remain wary of narcosis.

Divers that claim never to have experienced narcosis are focusing on the obvious symptoms and are ignoring, or forgetting, the more subtle symptoms. If you can feel that you are affected by narcosis then the symptoms probably started at a depth 10-15m/30-45ft less than when you noticed them.

For any given breathing mixture the level of narcosis is related to the depth of the dive, with technical diving we are almost by definition involved in deep diving. However, there is more to it than that. Depth is only one of the factors involved. The environmental and personal factors also play a significant part in narcosis. Environmental factors can increase your susceptibility to narcosis and can increase the symptoms at any given depth. Visibility is one of the biggest factors in susceptibility to narcosis. Consider a dive where you have 20m/60ft visibility and plenty of ambient light but then a week later you do the same dive but this time the visibility is less than a meter and there is no ambient light. The second dive is much more likely to produce symptoms of narcosis than the first.

Current can also be a major factor in bringing on narcosis. If you are fighting against a current and breathing faster than usual due to working hard to swim down a shotline, then you are at a higher risk of experiencing narcosis. Minor equipment problems can also induce narcosis. A slight equipment problem which, in itself will not cause any issues, may be enough to induce narcosis. This is related to other psychological causes of narcosis. Concern over the dive, diving with unfamiliar equipment or unfamiliar buddies, cold, drugs, fatigue, stress, motion sickness and motion sickness medications have all been linked to an increase in the likelihood of narcosis.

All of this means that the depth in itself is not the only factor that determines your level of narcosis. As such it's impossible to draw an arbitrary line where you can say air/nitrox is safe at this depth but no deeper.

It is clear that psychological factors affect narcosis. There have been a number of studies which have attempted to show the psychological aspect of narcosis. Tom Mount and Dr Gilbert Milner carried out a study in 1965 that demonstrated that divers tend to experience a level of narcosis that is consistent with the level they expect to experience.[54] A more recent study carried out for the HSE by the Diving Diseases Research Centre and Plymouth University supported the importance of psychological aspects in addition to the biophysical impact of narcosis.[55] One of the conclusions from this study was that narcosis is not simply an objective measurable phenomenon; it also has a subjective facet.

Until very recently it was commonly accepted that the use of nitrox would reduce narcosis. On the face of it this seems to make sense. If an increased partial pressure of nitrogen causes narcosis then if we replace some of the nitrogen in the breathing mix with oxygen we will reduce the partial pressure of nitrogen at a given depth. The majority of nitrox courses taught exactly this reasoning until quite recently. However, it is now believed that it's not just nitrogen that causes narcosis but that different gases result in varying levels of narcosis. Nitrogen has a high level of narcosis but is not the only narcotic gas.

As there is no definitive explanation for the causes of narcosis, it is difficult to prove which gases have more or less potential to cause it. The best estimate for the levels of narcosis is derived from a theory that says the level of narcosis caused by an individual gas is related to the solubility of that gas in a fatty substance. This is known as the Meyer-Overton hypothesis. Using this measure oxygen should be more narcotic than nitrogen. If this is the case then nitrox will not reduce our levels of narcosis as we are just replacing one narcotic gas with another.

It would be nice if we could prove this argument one way or the other by comparing the narcotic effects of air and nitrox. Unfortunately it's not that easy. In order to ensure that we have a measurable level of narcosis we would need to be at a significant depth. At these depths the risks of CNS oxygen toxicity mean that we would have to reduce the amount of the oxygen in the breathing mixture to the point where it would be too small to be able to distinguish between the effects of air and nitrox. The result is that the question of whether oxygen is more or less narcotic than nitrogen can generate some interesting discussions but is effectively irrelevant for recreational technical divers.

As we dive deeper the effects of narcosis become more and more significant. We have seen that using nitrox does not help in reducing narcosis. Furthermore the increased levels of oxygen limit the depth that we can dive using nitrox without risking CNS oxygen toxicity. So for deep diving we must look at another solution.

We know that different gasses have different narcotic properties and the best solution is to find a gas that is considerably less narcotic than either nitrogen or oxygen and use this to replace some of the nitrogen in the breathing mix. Helium and neon both have properties that predict that they would be considerably less narcotic than nitrogen and experiments have shown this to be the case. Neon is prohibitively expensive and it follows that helium, though still expensive, has been used as the gas of choice for deeper diving.

---

54 Mount, T., & Milner, G. (1965) In Mount, T. (Ed.) (1999) Technical Diver Encyclopædia. IANTD
55 Harding, S, Bryson, P & Perfect, T. (2004) "Investigating the relationship between simulated depth, cognitive function and metacognitive awareness" HSE Research Report 256

Trimix

36

"Thinking clearly and effectively is the greatest asset of any human being." **Harry Lorayne**

It is becoming increasingly popular for divers to use helium based mixtures, usually called trimix, for deeper dives. The main reason for this is to reduce narcosis. Helium is considerably less narcotic than nitrogen and so as we replace some of the nitrogen with helium we are reducing the overall narcotic effect of the combined gas. As we increase the amount of helium in the mixture and so further reduce the amount of nitrogen present, we further reduce the narcotic level of the overall gas.

Commercial and military divers often replace all of the nitrogen in their breathing mixture and just use a mixture of helium and oxygen. This is known as Heliox. This produces virtually no narcosis but due to the cost of helium is a very expensive option. Recreational technical divers tend to use a mixture of helium, oxygen and nitrogen, known as trimix. By adjusting the level of the three gases the diver can select a mixture that has the desired level of narcosis.

A trimix diver can perform a dive to 80m/262ft but can choose his breathing mixture so that they experience a level of narcosis that is the same as if they were breathing air at 35m/115ft. On a subsequent, deeper dive to 90m/295ft they may be 10m/33ft deeper but can choose a breathing mix that still gives the same level of narcosis. This is known as the Equivalent Narcotic Depth (END). In this case a trimix diver at 90m/295ft may be experiencing less narcosis than a recreational diver at 40m/131ft on air.

With trimix relatively easily available these days there is really no reason for divers to risk diving deep on air and inducing symptoms of nitrogen narcosis.

The reduction in narcosis introduces a number of advantages. A clearer head allows the diver to enjoy the dive and actually remember what they see down there. There is little point in exploring a wreck if you don't remember the experience later.

In addition the reduction in narcosis removes the lack of judgement, loss of coordination and inability to resolve problems. This can give the technical diver a huge safety advantage. As they go deeper and the risks increase, they can help to reduce those risks by reducing their level of narcosis. With trimix relatively easily available these days there is really no reason for divers to risk diving deep on air and inducing symptoms of nitrogen narcosis.

In the same way that the general name nitrox can be used to describe any mixture of nitrogen and oxygen, the term trimix is used to describe any combination of oxygen, nitrogen and helium. Specific types of mixes are also given names as the characteristics of each are very different.

A trimix which has between 18% and 21% oxygen is referred to as Normoxic Trimix. The term Normoxic refers to 'normal' levels of oxygen. In other words, a similar level of oxygen to normal air. The helium content in Normoxic Trimix is likely to be between 20-45%. This type of trimix is used to reduce narcosis in the 45-60m/150-200ft depth but does not change the oxygen levels significantly and so is limited to 60m/200ft by oxygen toxicity considerations.

For deeper dives the amount of oxygen in the mixture needs to be reduced and for this a Hypoxic mixture is used. Hypoxic means a reduced level of oxygen such that the mixture will not sustain consciousness at the surface. Oxygen levels below 18% are usually considered hypoxic for diving. The helium levels in a Hypoxic Trimix will be much higher because it is being used to reduce the amount of oxygen as well as being used to reduce the amount of nitrogen therefore helium levels between 40-60% are common.

In recent years it has become increasingly popular to add helium to the breathing mix for dives between 30-45m/100-150ft. In this case it is possible to use a weak Normoxic Trimix but it is also possible to have a higher level of oxygen, just as if diving nitrox but with the addition of some helium. This would be called Hyperoxic Trimix, due to the higher than normal levels of oxygen, but this name is not commonly used in order to avoid confusion with Hypoxic Trimix. Hyper means high levels and Hypo means low levels. Any trimix with a higher level of oxygen than air was originally called Helitrox when NAUI launched the first training course and TDI has stuck with this name. Other training agencies have used the term Triox or Recreational Trimix to refer to the same thing. Helitrox will typically contain between 10-30% helium.

Common Name	Alternatives	Description
n/a	Hypoxic Nitrox	Nitrox with less than 21% oxygen. Of no practical use in diving
Air	Normoxic Nitrox	Normal air with 21% oxygen and 79% nitrogen
Nitrox	EANx, DNAx, Hyperoxic Nitrox	Any mixture of nitrogen and oxygen
Heliox	n/a	Any mixture of helium and oxygen
Trimix	n/a	Any mixture of helium, nitrogen and oxygen
Trimix	Normoxic Trimix	Trimix with between 18-21% oxygen content
Trimix	Hypoxic Trimix	Trimix with less than 18% oxygen content
Helitrox	Triox, Recreational Trimix, Hyperoxic Trimix	Trimix with greater than 21% oxygen content

Table 19: Various classifications of potential breathing gasses

There are, however, some downsides to using helium. These mostly stem from the physiological aspects of helium. Helium is a very small molecule and is a very light gas. Amongst other things this means that it conducts heat much faster than air. As a result, a diver using a helium based gas to fill their drysuit will feel colder than a diver using air or nitrox. For small helium percentages this is not too noticeable but as the helium percentage increases this becomes more and more noticeable and hence for helium mixes above 20% it is recommended that a separate suit inflation cylinder is used specifically for filling your drysuit. This suit inflation cylinder is usually worn either mounted on the side of the twinset, attached to the backplate or on the waistband. A simple first stage provides an inflator hose for suit inflation. No second stage is attached but instead an over pressure relief valve is attached in case of a problem with the first stage.

The physical properties of helium also make decompression more complicated. This doesn't necessarily mean that trimix decompression is longer or shorter, better or worse than nitrox, just different. The reason for this is that with trimix we are dealing with two inert gasses rather than just one. There may be times when the body is taking in one inert gas while releasing the other. In addition, the small size of the helium molecule means that it is a fast gas, in other words it on-gasses faster than nitrogen but also off-gasses faster. All of this combines to make trimix decompression more complicated than air or nitrox decompression.

When it comes to dive planning using trimix there are a number of options. It is possible to buy trimix decompression tables but there are so many possible combinations of trimix together with combinations of deco gasses that it is not a very practical option. Until recently many divers have used PC planning programs such as V-Planner, Multi-Planner or Decoplanner to plan their dives. These tools allow the diver to calculate a decompression schedule together with gas requirements and oxygen toxicity levels. A range of plans can be generated which can be used to cover a number of alternative scenarios as well as providing backup plans in case the dive is deeper or longer than anticipated. Together with a bottom timer this is a very easy and cost efficient way of planning trimix dives.

Increasingly we are seeing a range of dive computers that can handle trimix as well as air or nitrox. The VR3 was the first successful commercial trimix computer and this has now been joined by computers from a range of other manufacturers. Some manufacturers focus on the extreme end of the technical diving market while other manufacturers have produced computers aimed at those divers using Normoxic Trimix or Helitrox. Suunto's HelO2 has brought trimix computers to the mass market and has done much to popularise this type of diving. These computers can be programmed with the details of your mixture together with any decompression gasses and will work out your decompression based on the combination of helium nitrogen and decompression gasses.

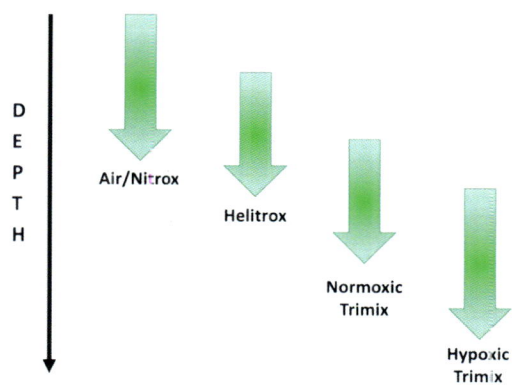

Diagram 16: Different depth ranges require different gases

The last disadvantage of using trimix is the cost. There is no doubt that a trimix fill is more expensive than nitrox but when compared against the cost of the boat fees, petrol to get to the dive site, accommodation and a drink in the pub it becomes less significant. Many divers will happily spend £40/$50/€44 on a night out but would not spend the same amount on trimix. If that £40/$50/€44 can help you remember the dive then it seems good value and if it can help you deal with a potentially dangerous situation then it becomes incredibly good value.

Many divers will happily spend £40 on a night out but would not spend the same amount on trimix

Oxygen Toxicity

37

"The convulsions are very violent.... They last about two minutes and are followed by flaccidity. I wake in a state of extreme terror, in which I may make futile attempts to escape from the steel chamber." **JBS Haldane**

Technical divers will often spend hours discussing the merits of different decompression approaches, the value of Bühlmann versus bubble models or deep stops versus gradient factors. On the other hand the topic of oxygen toxicity doesn't seem to generate as much discussion. This is strange as in reality oxygen toxicity is much more of a serious concern than DCI. The reason for this is that DCI often tends to occur once the diver is on the surface. DCI can result in long term damage, paralysis or death but if it is treated quickly after being identified there is a good chance that a full recovery will be made. Oxygen toxicity on the other hand tends to occur in the water where dealing with the situation is much more difficult than with dealing with DCI on the surface. Oxygen toxicity can result in a number of symptoms but the most dangerous is fitting and unconsciousness. While oxygen toxicity in itself is unlikely to cause any long term damage the fact that it occurs in the water makes it much more of a concern. Fitting and unconsciousness in the water are very dangerous as they are likely to lead to drowning which is a lot harder to treat than DCI. In general we can say that we are more concerned with oxygen toxicity in the water but once we are on the surface it is no longer an issue and now DCI is a greater concern.

The topic of oxygen toxicity is often discussed only briefly, if at all, during recreational scuba training. The reason for this is that if we are breathing air then oxygen toxicity doesn't become a problem until beyond the regular recreational diving depths. For depths less than 50m/164ft it is not a concern. Nitrogen narcosis or DCI are much more of an issue for the air diver. For recreational divers who start to use nitrox then all of a sudden oxygen toxicity is introduced as a real concern. With more oxygen in the breathing mixture the depth at which oxygen toxicity starts to become a concern is much less. The more oxygen we have in our mixture the more shallow the depth at which it becomes a concern. For a nitrox mixture with 28% oxygen the depth limit is 40m/130ft whereas for a mixture with 38% oxygen the depth limit is only 26m/85ft. One of the key messages on any nitrox course is that you should never go deeper than your maximum operating depth (MOD). Provided that this advice is followed the risks for nitrox divers using a single nitrox mix are almost non-existent. The main danger is complacency and accidentally going below the MOD.

One of the main differences between recreational and

technical divers is that technical divers will often carry one or more separate decompression gasses for use on their decompression stop. This additional gas is intended to speed up the rate of decompression and is achieved by using a richer nitrox mix. Mixtures such as 50%, 80% or even 100% oxygen are common. This is quite a different situation to the recreational nitrox diver who never goes deeper than the maximum operating depth for their gas. In the case of technical divers the majority of the dive will be carried out deeper than the maximum operating depth of the deco gas. If the diver were to switch to their decompression gas at depth an oxygen toxicity incident would be very likely. For this reason technical divers are extremely careful to never switch to their decompression gas at the wrong depth. A number of precautions are taken to ensure that this doesn't happen. One of the most common is to ensure that the decompression cylinder is turned off until it is required. Some divers will use different shaped mouthpieces or regulators, differently coloured regulators, gags or mouth guards over the regulator or clips to prevent accidental deployment of the regulator. All of these can reduce the chance of breathing the wrong gas at depth. One disadvantage of relying on this type of approach though is that if the diver has to use a different regulator, or has to switch their regulators for any reason they may become confused. The only guaranteed way of ensuring that the diver doesn't switch to the wrong gas is to mark up the cylinder with the maximum operating depth and ensure that the diver and their buddy double checks that they are switching to the right gas at the right depth.

Most training agencies recommend the use of 1.4 as the partial pressure of oxygen to be used with 1.6 as an absolute maximum. This is of course to reduce the overall exposure but also to allow some margin for error. Technical diving agencies still recommend 1.4 for the main cylinder or back gas as they refer to it but they often allow the use of up to 1.6 partial pressure of oxygen for decompression gasses. One reason for this is that it provides more effective decompression although for divers used to using 1.4 it sometimes causes concern that they are increasing their exposure. However for decompression stops we rarely spend more than a few minutes at this maximum partial pressure, as we move up to the next decompression stop the partial pressure drops. The exception to this is if we use 100% oxygen. The MOD of 100% is 6m/20ft which is also usually our last stop. This means that when using 100% at 6m/20ft we are right on the 1.6 limit for an extended period of time as the last stop is always the longest. Again this shows the importance of being able to hold a stop at exactly the right depth when using rich nitrox mixes.

The risk of switching to a deco gas by accident is another reason why technical divers prefer to use a long hose on their main regulator and have their backup on a bungee around their neck. With a typical recreational octopus setup the octopus regulator is normally stored somewhere around the chest or stomach area. A stage cylinder is usually worn on the side which means that the regulator tends to also be in the chest or stomach area. In an out of air situation there is always the risk that the out of air diver will take the stage cylinder regulator rather than the octopus. If the diver always donates the one in their mouth then they know it is breathable and they know that their backup is right beneath their chin.

For a diver with a single stage cylinder the main challenge is to ensure that they can switch to their stage cylinder while maintaining their buoyancy. If they drop during the gas switch they may drop below the MOD for the deco gas and put themselves at risk of oxygen toxicity. Equally they must be able to maintain their depth during the deco stop and be able to manage any tasks or issues that arise without changing their buoyancy. This is why the ability to hold a decompression stop to within half a metre of the intended depth is essential. Provided that a diver can hold their decompression stop to within an acceptable range and does not switch to the deco gas at the wrong depth then the risks of oxygen toxicity are still low. With a single decompression cylinder it is difficult to accumulate enough of an oxygen exposure to risk oxygen toxicity due to the fact that you are at a high partial pressure for only a short time and are limited by the gas volumes of a single cylinder.

For dives requiring two, three or more decompression gasses the exposure becomes much greater and the risk of exceeding a safe dose becomes higher. Unlike with a single decompression cylinder you can increase the partial pressure of oxygen up to the maximum each time you switch to a new decompression gas. In addition the fact that you have multiple decompression cylinders allows you to carry out much longer decompression and so significantly increase your exposure to oxygen. The risk of oxygen toxicity increases with higher partial pressures and also with the length of exposure and you are increasing both of these factors. This might mean that you start to approach the safe oxygen toxicity limits even without going below your MOD. For deeper dives the decompression required increases significantly and therefore you want to try to accelerate this decompression as much as possible by using rich nitrox mixes, often including 100% oxygen. While this may decrease your decompression requirement and as a result the amount of decompression gas you have to carry, it also increases your oxygen exposure and so dive planning becomes a balance between gas volumes, decompression and oxygen toxicity.

For deeper and longer dives there comes a point where the amount of decompression required means that the oxygen exposure reaches the recommended limit. When dives exceed this limit the only option is to include air breaks into the decompression schedule. An air break is when the diver switches from their decompression gas back to a gas which has a much lower partial pressure of oxygen. This can be their back gas or one of their other decompression gasses with a much lower percentage of oxygen. The idea is that this break gives the body a chance to recover from the high partial pressure of oxygen and can prevent or at least delay the onset of oxygen toxicity. One of the problems with this approach is that, like many other aspects of oxygen toxicity, there is very little hard scientific proof as to how effective the process is or what effect it has on the overall situation. Despite the lack of hard proof it has become common practice to use air breaks. Typically when using 100% oxygen or when approaching CNS limits a diver will switch back to their back gas and from then on alternate 15-20 minutes on oxygen followed by five minutes on back gas.

So far I have been focusing on Central Nervous System (CNS) oxygen toxicity. This is where the high levels of oxygen interfere with the functioning of the brain and central nervous system. In addition there is also pulmonary, sometimes called whole body, oxygen toxicity. Pulmonary toxicity is only of concern for very long exposures to oxygen, of the order of several hours. Most agencies teach that if you look after the CNS toxicity then pulmonary is not going to be a problem. It is really only with very long decompression dives or cave dives that there is any risk of pulmonary toxicity. Some divers do complain of chest irritation similar to a chest infection after very long dives or after several days of carrying out long dives. This may be more of an issue for rebreather divers who are breathing consistently raised partial pressures of oxygen for extended periods. It is certainly an area that a number of technical divers doing very long dives are starting to monitor

As we have already seen there is very little hard scientific evidence to justify the procedures we use to avoid oxygen toxicity. Much of the work on oxygen toxicity goes back to the Second World War[56] and the period immediately following it and there has been very little research since then. The limits that have been adopted for recreational and technical divers are extremely conservative.

Tests have shown that there is a range of times before subjects experience the signs and symptoms of oxygen toxicity and current recommendations are based on the most conservative end of this range This does mean that current limits are very conservative but given the dangers of an oxygen toxicity hit underwater that is no bad thing.

Oxygen Pressure Time Limits (Minutes)			
PO_2 (ATA)	Single Dive	% CNS/Min	Daily
1.6	45	2.22	150
1.5	120	0.83	180
1.4	150	0.67	180
1.3	180	0.56	210
1.2	210	0.48	240
1.1	240	0.42	270
1.0	300	0.33	300
0.9	360	0.28	360
0.8	450	0.22	450
0.7	570	0.18	570
0.6	720	0.14	720

Table 20: NOAA CNS Oxygen Limits

---
56 Donald, K (1992 Oxygen and the diver.

Dive Planning 38

"What the £*@& are you doing running out of gas" **Mark Powell**

Plan the dive and dive the plan has long been the mantra employed in all areas of diving. Technical divers in particular spend more time planning their dive than many recreational divers. This is due to a number of factors including increased risks, greater depths, high gas usage at depth, increased decompression obligations, increased oxygen toxicity loading and a host of other reasons. For many recreational divers dive planning has become a lost art but technical divers still place a large emphasis on the value of dive planning. Despite this the methods of dive planning have changed to take advantage of changes in technology and equipment. In this article we will look at how dive planning for technical divers has evolved and how we can best make use of modern technology while still maintaining safety.

In the early days of technical diving there were no PC planning tools or dive computers suitable for technical dive planning. The only option for planning a dive was to look up a decompression schedule using pre-generated tables. Initially, not even the pre-generated tables, were publicly available and the very earliest technical divers had to use commercial diving tables or work directly with decompression researchers if they wanted to obtain a set of trimix tables. The decompression schedule would be copied out on a dive slate with fixed decompression stops and run times. CNS and OTU loading would be calculated by hand and gas usage would be calculated for each phase of the dive and the rule of thirds used to add in a safety reserve.

The dive would then be executed by following the dive plan run times written on the slate with depth and time being monitored using a bottom timer.

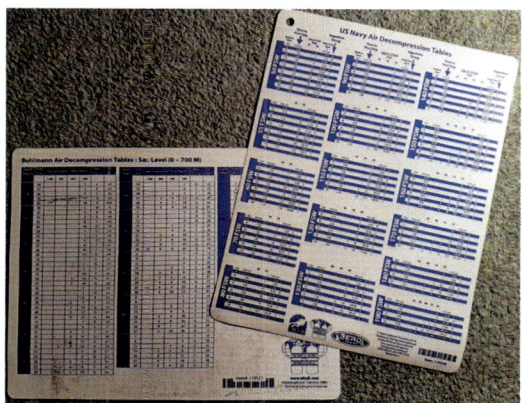

Figure 39: Hard copy diving tables

For most recreational divers gas planning is very straightforward. The only goal is to make sure they are back on the boat with 50 bar/700 psi still in their cylinder. With some experience they learn, for a 20-30m/60-100ft dive, that if they leave the bottom on 70-80 bar/1000-1100 psi then they will have around 50 bar/700 psi left by the time they do their ascent and safety stop. This approach works well for recreational diving and additional gas planning is not really required. The reason why this works is that for a recreational no-stop dive we can ascend directly to the surface and because a 20-30m/60-100ft ascent doesn't take very long.

However, for technical diving gas planning becomes more involved. We may have learnt that we need 20-30 bar/290-435psi in our cylinder to get to the surface after a 30m/100ft no-stop dive but how much do we need in order to ascend when we need to do multiple decompression stops for varying lengths of time at different depths? How much will we need when some of the ascent and stops are done using the gas in our twinset and when some are done using the gas in a stage cylinder? This question can only be answered by calculating our gas usage during the various parts of the dive.

Two of the most common reasons for undertaking technical diving are to go deeper or to spend longer at depth. Both of these increase our gas usage. As we go deeper we breathe in more with each breath. At 20m/60ft we are breathing three times as much gas with every breath when compared with the surface. At 40m/130ft we use five times as much gas, at 60m/120ft it is seven times as much and at 100m/330ft it is 11 times as much as at the surface. If we want longer bottom times then we will of course also be using more gas than on a shorter dive. When these two factors are combined, by going deeper and spending longer at that depth, we get the combination of the two effects and we need significantly more gas than for a shallower or shorter dive.

Gas planning is also critical for decompression diving because once we go into decompression then we have a 'virtual overhead environment' and direct ascent to the surface is no longer possible. This means that running out of air and heading for the surface is no longer an option. As a result, we have to make sure that we have enough breathing gas for each part of the dive.

Once we remove the no-decompression limit on our diving then it will usually be the amount of available gas that will limit the length of our dives and because of this we often start our dive planning by looking at how much gas we will need before looking at any other considerations. In order to work out how much gas we need we first need to know our breathing rate. Our Surface Air Consumption rate (SAC) is the amount of gas, measured in litres, that the diver will consume per minute at the surface. Knowing your SAC rate is a critical ingredient of effective gas management.

To determine our SAC we measure how much gas we use over a set period of time at a set depth. From this we can work out how many litres we have used in total. Then by dividing by the time and then dividing by the pressure at depth we can get a measure of our surface air consumption rate. It is worth doing this while finning at a normal rate to calculate our working SAC and then doing the same again while resting to get our resting SAC. We usually use the working SAC to calculate our gas requirements during the bottom part of the dive when we are active and swimming around but then use the resting SAC to calculate our gas requirements for the decompression stops where we are just floating in the water.

Your SAC rate can vary hugely due to a number of other factors. Additional or unfamiliar equipment, temperature, fitness levels, experience, level of buoyancy control, stress levels, current workload and a variety of other factors can all influence your breathing rate and therefore you need to consider these conditions when calculating your gas requirements.

Diagram 17: Gas requirements rule of thirds

Once you know your SAC you can work out the amount of gas you will need for each phase of the dive. You can work out the amount you need for the bottom time, the ascent and the decompression stops. This is done by multiplying your SAC rate by the length of each phase and then by the absolute pressure at that depth. This will give you the amount of gas you will need under normal circumstances. In order to be able to deal with any unexpected situations all technical divers will then add a reserve on to this amount. The most common method of doing this is to use the rule of thirds. This comes from cave diving where cave divers will use a third of their available gas on the way into the cave and will turn the dive and start swimming out once they have used the first third. They plan to use a third on the way out and to exit the cave with a third of their gas still remaining. The reason for this is that if there is a problem at the furthest point from the exit then they still have two thirds of their gas left and so they have enough gas to get themselves and their buddy back to the entry as they will breathe one of the remaining two-thirds and their buddy will breathe the second of the remaining two-thirds. The same principle is used for wreck penetration dives where you only plan to use one third of your available gas.

For normal sea dives where you are not planning to enter a cave or wreck you do not have the same 'in' and 'out' portions of the dive. Here you can use the rule of thirds to just add a third reserve on to the total amount required for the dive. This can be done easily by calculating how much you need and then multiplying the result by 1.5 to give you a third extra as contingency. This reserve is then available for your buddy if they should run out of air or for yourself if you have to work harder than expected, stay longer than planned or any other situation where you may need to use more of your gas.

The rule of thirds works well for back gas but doesn't work well for deco gas. The worst case situation with deco gas would occur if you turned the deco gas cylinder on and the regulator failed immediately. Here you would need your planned amount of deco gas and your buddy would also need their planed amount of deco gas. In this case having a third reserve of your deco gas would not be sufficient. You would need the same amount again as a reserve and can calculate the reserve on deco gas by doubling the planned amount of gas. In this way you would always have enough deco gas for yourself and your buddy if they should need it and your buddy has enough deco gas for himself and you if you need it.

Backup plans would also be prepared just in case the diver goes slightly deeper, stays slightly longer or, in the worst case, goes both deeper and stays longer. With pre-prepared decompression tables 'slightly deeper' was usually taken to mean the next depth increment, which on many tables was 3m or 10ft deeper. 'Slightly longer' would be taken to mean anything from three to five minutes longer. Finally, a backup plan would also be prepared showing the decompression schedule if the diver loses their decompression gas and has to complete their deco using back gas.

With the increased availability of personal computers, it became feasible to generate custom tables using a PC planning tool. This allowed divers to use a number of different gasses, decompression models and conservative settings. The overall process of planning a dive remained the same, just using a planning tool instead of tables. The planning tool would generate the decompression schedule, CNS and OTU loadings as well as gas requirements. The only difference would be that the PC planning tool would do the laborious arithmetic required to calculate gas requirement, CNS loading, etc. rather than the diver doing it by hand. When used correctly these PC planning tools removed the risk of the diver making a silly arithmetical error. The computer generated schedule would then be transferred to a slate just as when the plan is generated by hand. In the water the dive would be executed in exactly the same way with the diver using their bottom timer to monitor the run times written on the slate.

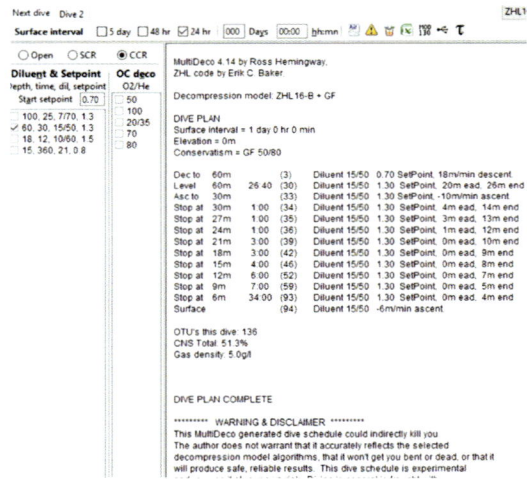

Figure 40 – Using a PC planning tool to generate a dive plan

In time, personal dive computers became available that could handle decompression diving, trimix or rebreathers but they were still expensive and often unreliable. As a result, it was common to use a written plan on a slate with a computer as backup in case of going off the plan or in case of an emergency.

This was not an ideal situation as divers would have to spend a significant amount of money on a dive computer without being able to make full use of it. This led to the difficult situation where the diver would have to forego the flexibility offered by the dive computer and stick to a fixed depth and time in order to be able to fall back to their written backup plan in the case of a computer failure. This difficult decision made many divers and agencies question the suitability of dive computers for technical diving.

Figure 41 - Using slates and wetnotes for dive plans

Nonetheless as computers became more common, reliable and affordable, this gradually changed. Divers would still use a planning tool to generate a deco schedule to write on their slate just as before. The change was that this schedule was now used as a backup to the computer which became the primary method of running the dive. Despite this, the plan would still primarily be predetermined in terms of a fixed bottom time, in order to still be able to fall back to the written plan. However, the actual ascent time would now be determined by the deco schedule on the computer.

Now computers are much more available and reliable. Also, the costs have reduced so much that many people have backup computers. The flexibility offered by the computer is in contrast to the rigid nature of tables. Unfortunately, when your backup is based on written tables you can't make full use of this flexibility. However, when you have a backup computer, suddenly this flexibility comes into its own and this is where significant changes to planning styles started to be adopted.

When you have a fixed deco schedule, working out the gas usage for that schedule is very straightforward. The disadvantage of having flexibility in the deco schedule is it now becomes impossible to calculate exactly how much will be required in advance. This is where a shift in the approach is required. If we think about the point of gas planning it is to ensure we don't run out of gas, even in an emergency situation. Specifically, you want enough gas to get yourself and your buddy to the surface, or to the next breathable gas source, even in a stressful situation. This is known as minimum gas. We can calculate our minimum gas in advance for our maximum planned depth. This is based on combining the breathing rates of our buddy and ourselves and then doubling this figure to take into account the stress of an out of air emergency. This is then multiplied by the time it will take to resolve the immediate problem, stabilise the situation, start the ascent and ascend to the first gas switch stop. We can then multiply this by a figure to account for the increased pressure at depth to give us the total volume of gas required in litres. Finally, we can convert this total volume into a bar pressure by dividing by the size of your cylinders. Let's say that after performing this calculation we know that our minimum gas is 70 bar/1000psi. This means that at any point in the dive, as long as you have at least 70 bar/1000psi you know you have enough gas to get to the next source of breathable gas, even if your buddy has a catastrophic gas loss. Once one of you reaches 70 bar/1000psi, you must then start the ascent. Using minimum gas rather than fixed usage gives you the flexibility in back gas planning to match the flexibility in deco schedules provided by the dive computer.

Minimum gas calculations will cover the gas required to get to the first gas switch but what about the gas required for the deco stops? The traditional approach has been to work out exactly what is required and see how much is available and ensure that the amount required, plus a contingency, is less than the amount available. The alternative is to use a planning tool to find the maximum amount of deco that can be done on the gas available, without exceeding the safety reserve. You now know that you can do this amount of deco, and this can be converted to a total time to surface. Again, you know that this time to surface can be done within the gas available. This means that as long as the total time to surface is less than this maximum amount you know you have enough gas available.

Putting these two concepts together the procedure is to first calculate the longest dive that can be done at the target depth within the deco gas limits. This can be used to find the maximum time to surface (TTS). We then calculate the minimum gas required to get the diver and their buddy up to their first gas switch. Provided the dive is around the target depth, the diver just needs to monitor their available gas and their time to surface. The actual bottom time becomes less important. The dive is terminated when either of these limits is reached: either the available gas reaches the minimum gas limits or the total TTS reaches the maximum amount.

If dive with a regular buddy and always use the same size cylinders and the same gas mixtures then this means that the minimum gas and time to surface will always be the same for each dive at that depth. As a result, you only need to calculate these number once for any given dive depth. With a PC planning tool, it is very easy to calculate these two numbers for a range of dive depths. This can be turned into a table in your wet notes that then contains all the required information you need for dive planning.

Depth	Min Gas	TTS
45m/150ft	70	62 mins
50m/165/ft	75	64 mins
55m/180ft	80	67 mins
60m/200ft	85	72 mins

Table 21: Sample dive planning table showing min gas and TTS for a range of depths. Note these are not real numbers and should not be used for dive planning

For most dives it will be gas usage, either back gas, deco gas or, in the case of CCR, bailout gas, that will determine the limits of the time. Other factors such as CNS should also be considered but when the dive plan is generated using the PC planning tool the CNS can be reviewed and, provided it is well within safe limits, can be considered as a secondary consideration to the real limiting factor.

The technical diver is very aware of their gas usage while planning a dive but should also be aware of their usage during the dive. It is very useful to develop an understanding of how much gas we would expect to have at various points during the dive. This means that when a technical diver looks at their pressure gauge they should already have an idea of how much gas they will have left and are just using the gauge to confirm what they already know rather than to find out something they don't know. You can practice this easily by trying to estimate how much gas you have left before you check your pressure gauge. You can then check it and see how close you were. Over time you will find that you become better and better at anticipating how much gas you should have at each point and will find that when you check your gauge you already have a good indication of what it will say. Once you have this skill then if there is a significant discrepancy between what you anticipate and what your gauge is telling you then you know that there is a problem. Maybe you are breathing harder than you expect, and may need to cut the dive short, or maybe there is a problem with the gauge. Either way you are instantly alerted to the fact that things are not going exactly as planned.

We can extend this habit by anticipating how much gas we will have at various waypoints on the dive. We should have an idea of how much gas we will have once we reach the bottom of the shot line, ten minutes into the dive, twenty minutes into the dive, when we start the ascent and so on. With this level of awareness there is really no excuse for running out of gas on a dive.

The discussion above has mainly been concerned with open circuit diving but CCR diving has progressed along a similar path. Modern rebreathers almost always have a built in decompression computer integrated into the handset and most divers have a backup computer. However, gas planning is very different on a rebreather compared to open circuit. A CCR has almost unlimited gas and if nothing goes wrong with the CCR, it is likely to be scrubber duration or CNS limits that will determine the maximum length of the dive. The only time that gas usage becomes an issue is in the case of a bailout where gas availability becomes critical. In reality, it is the bailout scenario that will normally be the limiting factor for most CCR dives. This means that bailout planning will determine the limits for TTS. This is done by using a planning tool to calculate the maximum CCR bottom time that can be done without then exceeding the available bailout gas when the diver bails out at the end of the planned CCR bottom time. The CCR TTS at this point becomes the end point of this dive as we know that as long as we stay within this CCR TTS the corresponding bailout ascent is achievable with the bailout available.

Overhead environment diving also introduces a number of

other factors. For cave and wreck penetration the minimum gas and time to surface calculations will have to include the time required to exit the overhead environment as well as the time to ascend and so the planning become more complicated.

For more advanced dives, when the depths are greater than 80m/260ft more planning factors come into play. Team logistics become the more important factor and although time to surface and minimum gas calculations can still be used, there are a whole range of additional factors such as the use of support divers, surface support emergency planning.

Technical training tends to follow the evolution above with new divers starting with written plans, generated from pre-printed tables or PC planning tools. This ensures that the diver understand the principles behind decompression schedules and gas planning. It also ensures that the diver can manage ascent rates and display the discipline required to follow the dive plan on the computer accurately. They then move on to using dive computers with tables on a slate as a backup before eventually planning using the TTS and minimum gas approach.

Using TTS or minimum gas does not remove the need for planning. You still need to do the planning in order to know your minimum gas or TTS but the details of the decompression profile can be calculated 'on the fly' by the dive computer. By understanding the minimum gas and time to surface concepts, the combination of dive planning using a PC planning computer and the use of a dive computer to intelligently manage the execution of the dive provides the best of both worlds.

The dive is still planned to ensure more than adequate safety, the diver still has to understand the details of their dive plan and are not 'blindly' following their dive computer but at the same time can make use of the flexibility offered by modern dive computers.

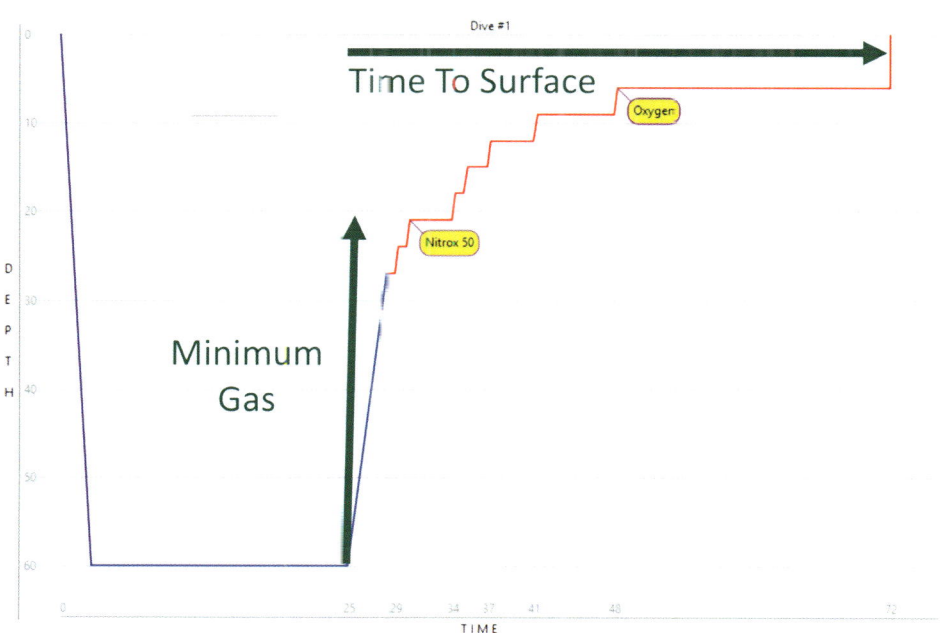

Diagram 18: Minimum Gas and Time to Surface

Wreck Penetration

39

"Everyone is an explorer. How could you possibly live your life looking at a door and not open it?" **Robert D. Ballard**

There are many reasons why people carry out technical diving, if you talk to technical divers then one reason for diving deeper or staying longer does seem to stand out as the most common. That reason is the desire to visit deeper wrecks or to spend more time on wreck dives. For divers who enjoy sea life there is relatively little reason for going deeper. Most of the sea life is in the first 20m/60ft and so for fish huggers there is little point in going beyond this zone. On the other hand, for wreck divers, diving deeper has a number of significant attractions. Wrecks in deeper water tend to be more intact than more shallow wrecks. Shallow wrecks are more exposed to wave action and storms therefore the forces of nature often result in these wrecks being very broken up. Wrecks in shallow waters are also a potential hazard to shipping and have often been broken up by the Navy to reduce the risks to other ships.

Wrecks in deeper water are much more protected from the elements. A ferocious storm on the surface will have comparatively little effect on a wreck in 60m/200ft. In addition a wreck at this depth is of no risk to other ships and is unlikely to have been dispersed by explosives. For this reason it is possible to find wrecks which are much better preserved at depth than similar ships in more shallow water.

The depth of the water also reduces the potential number of visitors to a wreck. This increases the sense of exploration. On some popular 30m/100ft wrecks it is not uncommon to have several boats all with divers visiting the wreck at the same time. The wreck may be spectacular but when there are over 40 other divers on the wreck at the same time it can spoil the feeling of exploration. For deeper wrecks it is much less common to see other divers and you can dive wrecks that only a handful of other people have seen before. One of the goals of most wreck divers is to be the first to dive an undiscovered wreck. Unfortunately there are very few opportunities to find undiscovered wrecks in 20-30m/60-100ft, the deeper you go the more undiscovered wrecks there are.

Because these deeper wrecks are more intact it is possible to get a feel for the size and layout of the ship. Many of the lower decks may still be intact and accessible. This means that swimming into the wreck is more than just a swim through with light at both ends. Instead it may be possible to penetrate considerable distances into a wreck. Divers can often access the holds of a ship and via hatchways or hull damage can penetrate into the interior.

It is a unique experience to swim through the corridors of an almost intact battleship, a vessel that has played a crucial part in the history of the twentieth century. Or to explore one of the merchant ships that played such a critical role in winning the Battle of the Atlantic. Or to explore the remains of a unique historical wreck such as *HMS Hermes*, the worlds first custom built aircraft carrier. Even a relatively modern freighter or factory fishing ship can be a breathtaking site when it looms out of the darkness below you.

You must always consider that on many of these wrecks the sailors and crews of the ships paid the ultimate price and the fact that you are visiting the site of a tragedy should never be forgotten. War graves or any wreck where there were fatalities should be treated with respect. Penetration is not allowed on many such wrecks.

Once inside a shipwreck the diver is now in a true overhead environment. That is to say there is no clear route to the surface. In the case of an emergency the diver may have to retrace his route and take ten minutes or more exiting the wreck before he can even begin his ascent. Also, the depth of the wreck may mean that his decompression obligation is increasing and even once he exits the wreck he still has the virtual overhead of his decompression ceiling. For this reason wreck penetration is very similar to cave diving and shares many of the same techniques. Despite the reputation of cave diving as being one of the most dangerous activities known to man, wrecks have just as many if not more dangers than caves.

Even the most intact wreck is a complicated tangle of passages, bulkheads and plates. Ships can be a confusing place at the best of time but when everything is at an angle and parts of the wreck have started to collapse, it can be a very disorientating place. With damage to the ship and the effects of rust on plates and other metalwork, every piece of metal becomes a sharp edge ready to cut line, puncture dry suits and snag on any loose piece of equipment.

One of the biggest risks in wreck penetration is entanglement. Wrecks are often filled with loose lines, collapsed pipes and wires as well as other debris. It is very easy for any of these to tangle around a valve, fin, or any other loose piece of equipment. This is the reason that wreck penetration divers are fanatical about ensuring there are no dangling pieces of equipment to get snagged. Although deeper wrecks may be more intact than their more shallow counterparts, the effect of the damage that caused the initial sinking combined with corrosion from years of immersion, means that there is always a risk of collapse. Bulkheads can give way and machinery bolted to the floor in a wreck on it's side or upside down can become loose and fall. As well as falling on a diver, collapsing wreckage can block exits or at the very least can fool divers who believe that they know the layout of a wreck they dive regularly.

There is often very little current running through the interior part of a wreck, which means that silt tends to build up within the wreck. Inexperienced divers can easily kick up this silt and reduce visibility to zero within seconds. The confusing layout of wrecks together with the potential for a silt-out can make it very easy for a diver to become lost and disorientated within the wreck. Many divers have lost their lives after becoming lost inside a wreck and being unable to find their way to safety.

In the same way that training and techniques developed for cave diving to try and reduce the risk of accidents, wreck divers have developed their own training and techniques. In many cases cave diving and wreck penetration techniques are very similar but in other areas they are subtlety different in order to be able to accommodate the specifics of the cave or wreck environment.

The biggest risk for any wreck penetration diver is getting lost within the wreck. For this reason you should always lay a guideline which gives a route back to safety. In the past several alternatives to line-laying have been suggested. One of the more common approaches was to gradually learn the layout of the wreck and memorize every detail of the route in and out. The diver would become familiar with one section of the route before moving on to the next passageway or room. There are several obvious disadvantages to this method. Firstly, it would take a large number of dives to learn the layout of even a modest size wreck but secondly and more importantly, in the case of reduced visibility it is far too easy to get disorientated and lose your way. For these reasons this approach has largely been consigned to history

Wreck penetration training now focuses on the use of line-laying as the only reliable way to find your way back to an exit. A line is attached to a solid point outside the wreck and special techniques are used to position the line in a safe way that won't subsequently become a risk to the diver. Using the right technique is essential because line-laying is a double edged sword. Although the line is our guide back to safety, a poorly laid line can tangle up the diver and become the very thing that stops them getting out of the wreck.

In addition to line-laying skills, the other key skill required by overhead environment divers is buoyancy control. Of course, buoyancy control is important to all divers but in wreck penetration it is much more important. The diver needs to be able to maintain absolute control at all times. When swimming through a passageway there may be just a few inches of space above, below and either side of the diver. If they sink just a few inches they will kick up years of silt on the bottom of the passageway and reduce the visibility to zero. If they rise just a few inches they will knock the ceiling and potentially dislodge pieces of debris or get entangled in wiring or other hazards. The diver needs to be able to swim, turn, tie off the guideline, check his pressure gauge, communicate with his buddy and deal with any problems while at all times maintaining perfect buoyancy control. This level of skill is simply not required by the vast majority of recreational divers which means that they are unprepared for wreck penetration.

In recent years rebreathers have become popular tools for wreck penetration. On each breath a diver on open circuit sends a stream of bubbles to the ceiling. These bubbles disturb the silt and rust on the ceiling which slowly rain down on the divers below. Even with perfect buoyancy control the open circuit diver cannot avoid disturbing the visibility because of these bubbles. The lack of bubbles from a rebreather removes the disturbance to the ceiling and stops the reduction in visibility. However, the biggest advantage of a rebreather for penetration dives is that they can provide a much longer supply of gas. If a diver loses the line or becomes lost in a wreck for any reason then on open circuit they have a very limited supply of breathing gas. As their apprehension rises, so will their breathing rate and their breathing supply drops even faster. A rebreather diver, on the other hand, has a much greater supply of breathing gas and therefore has longer to solve the problem. If nothing else this can reduce the level of apprehension felt by the diver and allow them to think more rationally about getting out of the situation. Nevertheless there is a tendency for some rebreather divers to take more chances as they know they have longer to solve a problem whereas an open circuit diver would have avoided the risks because they know they don't have the luxury of an extended gas supply.

It is clear that wreck penetration at depth has a much higher level of risk than normal recreational wreck diving. The overhead environment coupled with the virtual overhead of the decompression ceiling, reduced visibility, sharp edges, trailing wires and lines all increase the risk. For this reason recreational divers should not venture into wrecks without the knowledge, skills and training to safely conduct these dives.

Advanced wreck courses focus on the skills and knowledge required to overcome these dangers and to safely explore wrecks in deeper water. The competent advanced wreck diver has amongst the highest level of skill of any diver.

Cave Diving 40

*"In Xanadu did Kubla Khan
A stately pleasure-dome decree:
Where Alph, the sacred river, ran
Through caverns measureless to man
Down to a sunless sea."*
Samuel Taylor Coleridge[57]

Cave diving is considered by many to be the ultimate in technical diving. The challenges of diving when deep underground and miles from the nearest exit, combined with the fact that many of the developments in technical diving have come from the world of cave diving, means that you cannot understand technical diving without having at least a basic understanding of cave diving. The appeal of cave diving for many is that it is one of the only areas where true exploration is possible. Almost the entire surface of the land has been explored, mapped or photographed. Yet there are still many miles of unexplored caves. This means that it is one of the few areas of exploration where you can truly explore somewhere knowing that you are the first person to see that particular passage or feature. It is this desire to be the first to discover what is beyond that next corner that motivates many cave divers.

Cave diving, along with wreck penetration is a form of overhead environment diving. This means that the diver is unable to ascend directly to the surface at the end of a dive or in an emergency. They may have to swim a significant distance horizontally before they reach the exit. In addition the complicated nature of many caves makes navigating back to the entrance a significant challenge. Visibility within a cave can also vary considerably. It might be crystal clear when you swim into a cave but silt on the bottom may be kicked up by the actions of the divers and cause visibility to drop to zero. In some caves visibility may be zero even before the diver enters the cave and the whole dive must be carried out using touch. Caves are often carved out by underground rivers or springs and thus may involve significant water flow.

As a result of these risks cave diving was known during the 1960s and 70s as the most dangerous sport in the world. Many divers died because they did not appreciate the risks involved. Over 400 divers have died in the North Florida caves alone. Open water divers, often instructors, started to dive into cave systems without the appropriate training and equipment. The pioneers of cave diving, people like Sheck Exley and others used a process known as Accident Analysis to identify the reasons for these accidents. Exley carried out a detailed analysis of cave diving accidents and from this introduced key

---

57 This quote is also at the start of, and inspired the title of Caverns Measureless to Man by Sheck Exley. For more information about the origins and philosophy of cave diving you cannot find a better introduction.

rules that succeeded in reducing the accident rate. These were summarized in his 1977 book *Basic Cave Diving: A Blueprint for Survival*[58]. This is still considered to be one of the best books on cave diving. Exley realised that in all the fatalities he looked at, the cause of death could be attributed to one or more of three causes. Later analysis by Wesley Skiles added another two causes to create the five key rules of cave diving.

1. BE TRAINED FOR CAVE DIVING, AND REMAIN WITHIN THE LIMITS OF YOUR TRAINING

Many cave diving accidents involve people who have no specific cave diving training. It is common to find that even accidents that involve divers who have some level of training are caused because they have exceeded their training. These divers often make fundamental mistakes without even realising that they are making a mistake. The problems, equipment and techniques that are involved in cave diving, are different to open water diving and it should be no surprise that they require additional training and yet divers still venture into caves without adequate training or go beyond their level of training and experience.

2. MAINTAIN A CONTINUOUS GUIDELINE TO THE CAVE EXIT

A cave can have many passages with numerous twists and turns. When the complex structure of a cave is combined with decreased visibility due to silt-outs, it should be no surprise that it is often much easier to get into a cave than to get out of it. A guideline gives a route back to the exit and is essential in any cave. Not having a guideline is the number one cause of fatalities in caves but getting caught up in your own guideline is also a significant risk therefore the ability to safely lay and follow a line is one of the most fundamental skills in cave diving.

3. KEEP TWO THIRDS OF YOUR STARTING GAS VOLUME IN RESERVE TO EXIT THE CAVE

Many cave diving accidents have occurred because the divers simply ran out of gas before they could get to the exit. The 'rule of thirds' which involves keeping one third of your gas volume as a reserve in case of emergencies is the minimum that should be kept as a safety margin. In some cases, such as swimming out against a current then even two thirds may not be enough.

4. REMAIN WITHIN THE SAFEST POSSIBLE OPERATING LIMITS FOR YOUR BREATHING GAS

The risks of narcosis and oxygen toxicity can significantly increase the danger of cave diving. In a cave the diver must keep their wits about them and for this reason narcosis can be even more of an issue. In an overhead environment it is typical to aim for a narcotic depth significantly less than would be used for an open water dive. Cylinder markings are also critical to ensure that the right cylinder is breathed at depth to reduce the risk of oxygen toxicity.

5. USE THREE SOURCES OF LIGHT

Once beyond the daylight zone the loss of a torch will mean the loss of any vision. While not fatal in itself this can be very disconcerting and has been identified as a contributory factor in many accidents. Even if the diver has contact with a guideline the exit will still take considerably longer in the dark than if they had a source of light. Dive lights are still amongst the least reliable parts of our diving equipment and for this reason it is essential that any cave diver has three sources of light; this means one primary and two backup lights.

By using these five rules the risks of cave diving can be reduced to an acceptable level. It is now much more unusual for trained divers, using the rules above to be involved in fatal accidents and many cave divers now argue that properly trained, experienced and equipped cave divers are in fact safer than the majority of recreational divers.

---

58 *Basic Cave Diving: A Blueprint for Survival* published by Cave Books, (ISBN 0-939748-25-8) and also available to download for free from the NSS-CDS website

Figure 42: Cave Diving

In order to overcome the challenges of cave diving the pioneers in this area had to develop a whole new range of equipment and techniques. As a result cave diving has been the source of many of the innovations we commonly use in all areas of technical diving. Modern technical diving equipment is largely based on cave diving innovations with wings, backplate and harness, long hoses, umbilical torches and spools all developing from cave diving. The Hogarthian equipment configuration that has become so popular amongst technical divers in the UK, US and many other parts of the world was originally developed to deal with the problems encountered in the North Florida cave systems.

Similarly a number of techniques have also come from cave diving. All aspects of technical diving teach the use of rule of thirds, hand signals, team protocols and line laying techniques that were originally developed by cave divers. Wreck divers originally used a whole range of navigation techniques for wreck penetration but have now adopted the same line laying techniques that are used by cave divers.

Despite the advanced nature of cave diving the basics of technical diving are still critical. Buoyancy control in a cave is even more important than in open water. Being able to maintain buoyancy is critical as hitting the bottom can create 'silt-outs' that can destroy the visibility, while hitting the ceiling can also dislodge silt but may also destroy cave formations that may have taken millions of years to develop. Trim is also important in order to fit through limited passages and to keep your fins up and out of the silt. Good finning technique is also critical in order to avoid disturbing the silt or damaging the cave.

Training for cave diving has traditionally been split into a number of levels. The first level, known as *Cavern Diving* involves dives that still remain within the daylight zone. That is the diver can enter an overhead environment but stays within sight of daylight. At this level the basics of line laying, dive planning and teamwork are covered. The next level is *Cave Diver* or *Intro to Cave* where the diver can travel further into a cave system beyond the daylight zone. At this level divers are limited to simple navigation involving following a pre-laid line known as a mainline. Gas planning may be limited to using the rule of 1/6 rather than 1/3, in other words the diver only uses one sixth of their available gas before turning the dive and starting their exit. The final level of cave diving training is *Full Cave Diver*. This allows the diver to progress to more complex navigation such as jumps from one part of a pre-laid line to another to explore side passages. It also covers exploratory diving where the diver is laying new line and surveying previously unexplored areas of a cave. Of course, like any other area of technical diving, courses are only part of the story. Cave divers also need to practice and build up their experience. In particular it is common to serve an apprenticeship between completing *Intro to Cave* and *Full Cave* to build up experience under a mentor of the basic cave diving techniques before progressing further.

Cave diving started in the UK with the first cave dive taking place in 1936 into the caves of the Mendip Hills in Somerset. The exploration of Wookey Hole led to many of the innovations in UK cave diving[59]. In the UK cave diving has been driven by cavers who needed to progress through relatively short flooded passages or sumps between lengths of dry cave passages. For this reason the caving aspect is considered more important than the diving aspects and there is comparatively little overlap between cave diving and other forms of diving. On the other hand the Karst systems in northern Florida have produced much larger cave passages that are entirely flooded and as a result cave diving in the area has placed more importance to the diving techniques rather than pure caving techniques. It is the north Florida style of cave diving that has had the greatest impact on other areas of technical diving and generated all of the innovations previously described. Many of these caves have been formed by underground springs, many of which are used as the water supply for the local area. The large outflow of these springs can make for challenging levels of flow within the caves. Mexico has a very different type of cave systems. These caves, known as cenotes, are relatively shallow caves, sometimes only a few metres deep. These cenotes can however be extremely long and complicated cave systems and for many years Mexican caves held the record for the longest cave network. Although generally shallow there are some deep sinkholes that can descend to over 100m/330ft deep. The Dordogne/Lot area of France contains a number of cave diving locations. These are larger and clearer than UK caves and are more like the caves in Florida, although they do not have the same high flow levels. They are popular with UK cave divers due to the large size, clear visibility and relative ease of access. There are also cave systems in other areas of the world including Thailand, Greece, Sardinia, Russia, South Africa, Australia and many others[60].

Although many technical divers have little interest or intention to venture into cave diving this doesn't mean that they cannot learn from the techniques and equipment used in this area. Many of our current technical diving techniques have come from cave diving and it is likely that future development may also come from this area.

A lot of the techniques and equipment used in modern wreck penetration have been adapted from Florida cave diving. These include line laying, use of reels and spools, team diving, light signals, etc. In fact it is easy to assume that wreck penetration and cave diving are interchangeable. Even though a lot of the equipment and techniques may be similar, the environment has a number of key differences.

Caves often involve a much longer penetration than wrecks. It is possible to find caves that are hundreds or even thousands of meters long but it is rare to find a wreck that allows more than 100m/300ft of penetration. When diving a wreck for the first time we can usually find a photograph or a blueprint and even if this is not available, the overall shape of wrecks follow a standard layout but when diving a cave for the first time everything about it is unknown. The maximum depth of a wreck is determined by the seabed but the depth of a cave can be unlimited. The limited penetration in wrecks means that scooter management is not an issue whereas in caves, managing the use of scooters is a key skill. It's easy to get a long way into a cave with a scooter, if the scooter then has problems you need to be able to get back out. Caves can have multiple, complex branches and therefore navigation in a cave and the associated navigation skills and procedures, is more complicated than a wreck.

Before you start to think that caves offer more of a risk than wrecks you should remember that wrecks also have unique challenges. Caves are more stable than wrecks, having been in place for thousands of years. Caves do change but on a geological timescale, whereas wrecks can deteriorate in a

---

59 Wookey Hole: 75 Years of Cave Diving and Exploration. Jim Hanwell, Duncan Price, Richard Witcome. CDG ISBM 978-0-901031-07-5

60 The Darkness Beckons by Martyn Farr gives a history of the development of cave diving. Published by Diadem Books; ISBN 0-906371-87-2

much shorter timescale. Wrecks have sharp edges, cables and other hazards that are not present in caves

Decompression in a cave may be constrained by the contour of the cave but has the advantage of having a hard ceiling and floor whereas decompression on a wreck is usually mid-water with much more challenging buoyancy problems. It's impossible to use a habitat for decompression on a wreck whereas cave divers can do their decompression while siting in a (relatively) comfortable habitat. Long decompression on a cave dive can be facilitated by set-up dives to leave gas at staged points in the cave. Set-up dives are not normally feasible for wreck diving. Caves usually have just one exit which means that cylinders can be staged knowing that you will be coming back the same way or not coming back at all. On a wreck there are usually multiple exits and in an emergency, you may chose to exit through a different hole than the one you came in, for this reason staging cylinders are not such a good idea and therefore wreck divers tend to carry all their cylinders with them rather than staging them.

Caves often have a permanent line, other than in a virgin cave, whereas wrecks very rarely have fixed lines and consequently you will need to lay line on every wreck penetration. Entry to a cave, especially in Florida and Mexico, can be as easy as parking, kitting up and jumping in. Although this is not always true and some caves require extensive travel above and even below ground to reach the water. Wreck diving involves getting to, and finding, the wreck location before you can even think about diving it. Wrecks involve boats with all the limitations involved including rough condition and seasickness. Wrecks often have a limited tidal window and can only be dived at specific times of the day whereas caves usually don't have tides although they do have flow and for this reason can often be dived at any time of the day or night.

Cave dives don't get blown out due to rough sea but may be cancelled due to excessive flow or limited visibility. You can get sea caves and you can get wrecks in lakes but in general wreck diving involves sea water and cave diving involves freshwater and sea water is harder on gear than freshwater. You can kit up in the water when cave diving which makes stages easier, but on a wreck dive you must jump in fully kitted up. The quality of wreck diving in a location is primarily due to historical considerations combined with the depth of the sea bed whereas the quality of cave diving is primarily down to geology

LINE ARROW **COOKIE** **REFERENCE MARKER**

Figure 43: Cave Markers

As we can see each environment has unique challenges and just because you have experience in one environment this does not mean you are an expert in another environment. When switching between wrecks and caves always seek expert advice. If you want to dive in caves seek out an experienced cave instructor while if you want to dive in wrecks seek out an experience wreck penetration instructor.

Figure 49: Equipment logistics may be a significant factor

Expeditions

41

"Going into the unknown is invariably frightening, but we learn what is significantly new only through adventures." **M. Scott Peck**

One of the reasons that divers get involved in technical diving is their interest in exploration, whether it is finding a previously unknown wreck or being the first to explore a passageway of a cave. Not all technical divers will be able to achieve this goal and for many the exploration of wrecks that only a few people have seen before is their goal. In the same way that only one team can be the first to climb Everest only one team can be the first to find a new wreck but that doesn't mean that climbing Everest is not a challenge for others.

Our first challenge is to define what we mean by a technical diving expedition. It is a term that is often misused with any technical dive being referred to as an expedition. There are a number of things that all go into the definition of an expedition. The goal, the location, the logistics, the distance and the problems involved, all factor into whether we can call something an expedition. This means that in technical diving, like in climbing, a distinction has developed between expedition technical diving and 'regular' technical diving. At one extreme we have technical divers booking on to a regular charter boat to dive a wreck that has been dived thousands of times before. They may be using trimix, decompression gasses, rebreathers, decompression trapezes, etc. and are definitely carrying out a technical dive but to most technical divers this is far from an expedition. At the other extreme we have a trip to a foreign country to attempt to find a wreck that has never been dived before and indeed the location and depth of which is not even certain. Arrangements will need to be made to ship or hire suitable equipment, transport and gasses. A suitable dive boat will need to be identified and last but not least the wreck must be found and dived. This second example would definitely fit into most people's definition of an expedition. From these two examples we can see some of the characteristics of an expedition. Any trip needs to have at least one or two of these characteristics to be considered an expedition.

The first consideration is the dive itself. An unknown wreck or a wreck significantly deeper than the normal technical diving range is a common characteristic of an expedition. When finding an unknown wreck a wide range of historical research is required to narrow down the search area. Charts and reports may need to be acquired and numerous discussions with the Hydrographic Office, Navy and other agencies may be involved. For a wreck in another country this may add a whole new range of bureaucratic complication. The location may be known or suspected but may be significantly deeper than is normally dived. In the past a wreck lying in 80m/230ft would have been a significant challenge and would have been considered at the pinnacle of technical diving exploration. These days however, technical divers are routinely diving 80m/260ft wrecks as a regular charter. As I write this, 100m/330ft is still considered a significant boundary for many people but 120m/400ft seems to be the point where the logistical challenge of diving to these depths puts these dives in a different category. Wreck dives in the 150m/500ft range are at the very leading edge of technical diving expeditions. In only a few years time it is possible that 120m will be considered commonplace depth with 200m/650ft being considered at the leading edge.

The next consideration as to whether we would call something an expedition is the location and specifically the distance to be travelled. Of course a location which is thousands of miles from where we live will be local to someone who lives in that area. So the key point is not just distance but the difficulties that the distance imposes upon us. The further the distance the more challenges are likely to be encountered and therefore the real question is not distance but the logistical problems being faced as a result of the distance.

Logistics have always been a key factor in expeditions. In the great days of exploration it was often the logistical preparation that determined the success or failure of an expedition rather than the heroic nature of it's members. The same challenges are faced today by technical divers. By its very nature technical diving requires huge amounts of equipment, supplies, spare parts and consumables. When diving locally technical divers will have their own supply of equipment and spares, they can get gas fills from one of a number of dive centres and can often get spare parts locally or shipped to them within a day or so. However, when planning a trip to a remote location this becomes much more complicated. It may be possible to ship equipment to the remote location. This has the advantage of ensuring that the team has familiar equipment and knows exactly what they will be using. The disadvantages are that it can be very expensive and can be very slow. In addition, there is always the risk of equipment being held up in customs or damaged or even lost in transit. To try and reduce the cost and time problems it is common to take some equipment but source cylinders, regulators, gasses and rebreather consumables at the remote location. This can also introduce all sorts of complications. Even if they are available the size, configuration and quality of them may not be what we are used to. Certain things may simply be not available. Also sourcing these things locally can be almost as expensive as shipping them.

In the UK we are incredibly lucky to have a strong support system in case of a technical diving incident. The Royal Navy and Coastguard helicopters mean that transport from a boat to a suitable hyperbaric chamber can be very fast. Furthermore there is a strong network of hyperbaric chambers throughout the country. Finally the NHS means that all of our treatment is available free of charge. We are incredibly fortunate to have such a system in place but it sometimes means we take it for granted and don't appreciate that in other areas we may not have the same level of support. In many areas there are no suitable hyperbaric chambers and even in areas that do have hyperbaric chambers there is no coordinated way of evacuating a DCI casualty to a one. In this case expedition planning will include looking at how to transport a DCI casualty to the nearest chamber and in the absence of a chamber how the expedition can be self sufficient. This can include bringing your own hyperbaric chamber or where this is not possible, planning for in-water-recompression (IWR).

There are a number of locations in the UK where there are one or more boats that specialise in technical diving. At the very least there is a good selection of boats that have hydraulic lifts, GPS and echo sounders, oxygen kits and knowledgeable and experienced skippers. These obviously tend to attract technical divers. There are many UK technical divers who have never had to kit up on the deck of a boat with no benches or climb back up a ladder wearing full kit bevause there is no lift. When travelling to some of the less frequently dived areas, in the UK or abroad, it is much more common to find boats whose primary purpose is not technical diving but fishing, tourist trips or maybe recreational diving. This means that when planning an expedition one of the biggest challenges is to find the best boats available. This may have to be a RIB, fishing boat or a tourist boat.

Figure 44 The UK has a number of excellent dive boats

The boat and crew is only one part of the overall team. Unlike a day boat approach where everyone dives independently and the skipper is largely there to shuttle the divers out to the dive site and back, an expedition needs much more coordinated teamwork. This starts with picking the team. An expedition leader will want people that they know and are capable of carrying out the dives to be attempted. Depending on the expedition there may be specific roles required. In addition to the divers who will dive to the planned wrecks there may be support divers as well as surface support. In some expeditions these may be separate roles but in others the members of the expedition may take turns carrying out each of these roles. Support divers can be split into deep and shallow support divers. Deep support may involve the diver being ready and equipped to dive to the maximum depth in case of emergency or they may be in the water at one of the deeper decompression stops, often the first gas switch stop. They are there in case the diver on the bottom needs assistance or has a problem with their first decompression gas. Shallow support divers will wait for the divers at a much more shallow depth, often at 21m/70ft or less. They are there in case the deep divers need additional decompression gas and are on hand to take used decompression cylinders. They may also have set up a decompression trapeze ready for the divers when they get to their last few deco stops. Support divers are often newer technical divers who have offered to help in order to gain further experience themselves and to see how an expedition is run. Surface support can range from having someone on hand to help you clip on additional stage cylinders through to having on-site medical staff. On one occasion when diving from a Navy vessel we had a full medical team and two decompression chambers on stand by on the boat, just in case of an emergency as well as a RIB in the water as a chase boat in case anyone didn't make it back to the decompression trapeze.

Other tasks that may be required can be split amongst the dive team. One person may be in charge of dive planning, another in charge of filling while another is in charge of logistics. The key to successful expeditions is to ensure that all the tasks are being carried out in the most effective way.

Not all technical diving involves expeditions and many technical divers will never be involved in a true expedition. It has certainly become a much overused term. Despite that for those that are looking at exploring sites and locations that have never been dived before or are looking to dive to depths beyond even the normal technical diving range, the skills to plan and carry out an expedition are vital.

Figure 45: Good support divers are essential for expedition diving

Missed Decompression

42

"Accept failure as a normal part of living. View it as part of the process of exploring your world; make a note of its lessons and move on." **Tom Greening**

Technical diving inevitably involves mandatory decompression and many aspects of technical diving are focused on maintaining buoyancy and dealing with issues in the water to avoid missing any mandatory decompression. If a diver does miss any of their decompression then there is a significantly increased risk of decompression illness and it is definitely going to spoil your day. For recreational divers the standard response to a rapid ascent or loss of buoyancy is to get back on to the dive boat, go on to oxygen and monitor for symptoms. For technical divers this is still an option but there are other potential options. This chapter describes the differences between these options as well as discussing when, if ever, they are applicable.

OMITTED DECOMPRESSION

The first option if a diver has missed any of their mandatory decompression is to employ an omitted or missed decompression protocol which involves going back down and making up for the decompression that was missed. This is often confused with In Water Recompression (IWR) but in fact, they are very different. The key difference is that In Water Recompression involves recompression at depth to treat signs or symptoms of decompression illness that have already been observed, in other words treating an already bent diver. Missed decompression protocols are used for divers who have missed one or more decompression stops but show no signs or symptoms of decompression illness. Some hyperbaric experts consider the distinction to be irrelevant and maintain that if decompression stops are missed the safest place to be is on the boat breathing pure oxygen and if signs or symptoms of decompression illness do present themselves, awaiting evacuation to a recompression chamber. In this case the argument is that the danger of re-descending outweighs any potential benefit from going back down to carry out missed decompression stops.

The other side of this argument is that decompression illness does not occur immediately on surfacing, the signs and symptoms may take several hours to appear. If a diver has missed decompression stops and surfaces without any signs or symptoms they may be able to re-descend quickly enough to prevent decompression illness from occurring. To many technical divers it seems preferable to try and prevent decompression illness rather than sitting on the boat waiting for it to hit.

There are some conditions that need to be considered before using an omitted decompression protocol. First of all the diver must be symptom free, if they have already developed symptoms then we are talking about In Water Recompression which is covered below and in the majority of cases should be avoided. The diver must also be able to descend within five minutes of hitting the surface. Beyond this time the chances of symptoms starting to appear increase significantly. The diver should also have enough gas available to complete the missed decompression protocol. There is no point in going back down only to have to cut the procedure short due to a lack of gas. The diver should also have someone with them, either a support diver in the water, a support diver on the boat or alternatively by descending back down to join their buddy or other diver. Finally, it is important to communicate with the surface cover or boat skipper. Boat skippers hate it when a diver breaks the surface well before their planned time only to disappear back down. They don't know if the diver has deliberately gone back down to complete their decompression or is unconscious and is sinking into the depths. For this reason it is important to signal your intentions to the boat or at the very least, send up an additional DSMB once you get back down to your decompression stop.

It has been argued that even if no signs or symptoms of DCI are detectable, bubbles may already have started to form. This can be taken as an argument for or against re-descending to complete missed decompression. It can be argued that as bubbles are already forming it is likely that symptoms of DCI will occur during the decompression. However, it is also possible to argue that bubbles continue to grow for hours after their initial formation and therefore by recompressing them it is possible to stop the bubbles reaching a point where they start to cause DCI.

A study by Farm, Hayashi, and Beckman[61] on diving and decompression illness treatment practices among Hawaii's diving fishermen, suggests that immediate recompression within less than five minutes is effective in reducing bubble size. If bubble size can be immediately reduced through recompression, blood circulation may be restored and permanent tissue damage may be avoided. Rapid reduction in the size of the bubble can prevent permanent damage because irreversible injury to nerve tissue can occur within just ten minutes of the nerve tissues being starved of oxygen.

The US Navy's procedure for omitted decompression is shown in Figure 46:

Another procedure which has gained popularity is to descend to the stop before the one that was missed and redo this stop. Then do double the missed stops.

> If the diver has missed stops 6m or shallower; is showing no signs or symptoms of decompression illness and can return to the water in less than a minute – descend to the required stop depth and continue with the planned decompression.
>
> If the diver has missed stops 6m or shallower and is not able to return to the water in less than a minute but is showing no signs or symptoms of decompression illness then the diver can return to the missed stop and multiply all remaining stop times by 1.5.
>
> If the diver has missed stops at 6m or deeper; is showing no signs or symptoms of decompression illness; a standby diver is available and the water conditions allow then the diver can return to the depth of the first stop and repeat the decompression schedule for any stops greater than 12m. Stops at 9, 6 and 3m should be multiplied by 1.5.
>
> On completion of omitted decompression the diver should be placed on oxygen for at least 30 minutes and if any signs or symptoms of decompression illness are detected should be evacuated to a recompression chamber for treatment.

---

61 Farm, Hayashi, and Beckman. (1986). "Diving and decompression sickness treatment practices among Hawaii's diving fishermen". Sea Grant Technical Report UNIHI-TP-86-01

Figure 46: US Navy Omitted Decompression Protocol

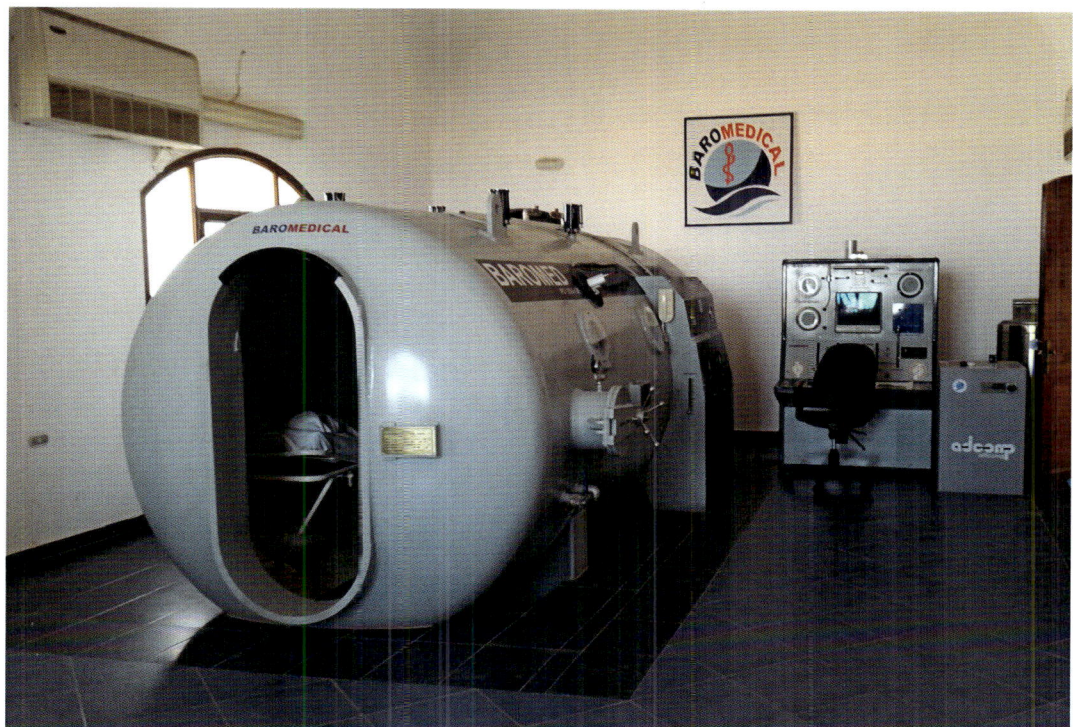

Figure 47: A recompression chamber may not always be readily available

IN WATER RECOMPRESSION

In water recompression (IWR) is a highly controversial subject. IWR involves treating a diver who is already showing signs or symptoms of suffering from the bends by re-descending and following a treatment profile in the water rather than in a recompression chamber. In most areas of the world the practice is completely counterproductive and has serious safety consequences.

The time involved in recompression treatment is generally several hours. This introduces a number of logistical problems into the process. For all but the most tropical regions several hours of recompression in water can result in the casualty becoming extremely cold and even hypothermic. As well as the normal dangers from hypothermia the cold will also reduce the effectiveness of the treatment because the cold will slow the rate of off-gassing from the peripheral areas of the body.

Supplying enough gas for the casualty and support diver to spend an hour or more in the water is also a challenge. The procedure will need a large number of support divers and attendants to ensure that enough gas is available. Of course if the support divers were also involved in the dives then these repeat dives may potentially put them at risk from subsequent decompression illness.

For IWR treatment to be effective, the casualty needs to be breathing pure oxygen. This is in order to ensure the maximum inert gas gradient which will give the fastest rate of off-gassing. Pure oxygen will also help by saturating the blood and tissues with dissolved oxygen, which will help to oxygenate the hypoxic areas caused by the bubbles in the capillary beds or tissues. Unless significant pre-planning for IWR has been carried out, there may not be sufficient supplies of oxygen to complete the treatment. Even if enough oxygen is available the risk of central nervous system toxicity is extremely high. In a recompression chamber a patient may breathe oxygen at a partial pressure of 2.8 bar for extended periods of time. Even so it has been shown that the body can tolerate higher partial pressures of oxygen while in a warm, dry, comfortable recompression chamber than it can while immersed in water. For this reason the depth to which the casualty can be returned and hence the effectiveness of the recompression is reduced. If the casualty suffers a CNS toxicity hit while in a chamber then the treatment is simply suspended until the casualty recovers. A CNS hit underwater is much more serious and may result in drowning or other injuries unless suitable precautions have been taken.

Communication between the casualty and their support diver(s) as well as between the support divers and surface crew is very limited. Also the facilities for additional treatment such as intravenous (IV) re-hydration are simply not possible underwater. If the casualty deteriorates while underwater then further treatment may be difficult. Identifying the extent and progression of symptoms while underwater is also difficult. Many of the tests used to detect decompression illness, such as the five minute neurological exam, are difficult if not impossible to perform underwater. Balance cannot be tested, touch and sensation cannot be established and it will not be possible to estimate limb strength.

The location of the dive site is also a major variable. If a convenient sandy sea bed at 9m/30ft with no current is easily available then this is ideal. On the other hand if an incident occurs on a live-aboard, anchored over a deep wreck while the current is starting to turn. Then the conditions in the water; no convenient bottom and strong tides, introduce a number of problems into the treatment procedure.[62]

In the UK, US and many other popular diving locations the presence of excellent emergency services and easy access to recompression chambers, combined with the logistical problems associated with IWR, make this procedure completely unnecessary. For these reasons almost all diving physicians, chamber operators and training agencies maintain that IWR recompression should not be attempted. DAN's advice is clear: "In-water recompression should never be attempted".

While this is the standard advice there are times when IWR may need to be considered. If you are diving in very remote areas where the nearest recompression chamber is 24 or 48 hours away then IWR may be the only option. In situations such as these, experienced divers will greatly extend their safety margin to try and ensure that they do not get into this position but despite the most cautious planning there is always the chance that an unearned decompression illness hit will occur.

To deal with these extreme cases a number of IWR protocols have been developed. One such method has become known as the Australian method. This involves the diver re-descending to 9m/30ft while breathing pure oxygen. They stay at this depth for 30 minutes in the case of a mild bend or 60 minutes for a severe bend. If symptoms persist then these times can be extended to 60 and 90 minutes respectively. The patient then ascends at the rate of 1 metre every 12 minutes. This results in a total treatment time of 126 to 156 minutes for a mild case and 156 to 186 minutes for a serious case.[63]

Depth (Metres)	Elapsed Time (minutes) Mild	Elapsed Time (minutes) Serious
9	30-60	60-90
8	42-72	72-102
7	54-84	84-114
6	66-96	96-126
5	78-108	108-138
4	90-120	120-150
3	102-132	132-162
2	114-144	144-174
1	126-156	156-186

Table 22: Australian In-Water Recompression Table

It is recommended that, to carry out this treatment, a shotline with at least 10m/30ft of line is rigged and if possible a seat or harness is used to attach the casualty to the shotline. Furthermore, the casualty should be wearing a full face mask in case of oxygen toxicity. If the casualty suffers an oxygen toxicity hit while wearing a standard scuba regulator they may lose the regulator and be at risk of drowning. With a full face mask they will still be able to breathe safely.

---

62 Pyle, R. L.; D. A. Youngblood. (1995). "In-water Recompression as an emergency field treatment of decompression illness". AquaCorp 11

63 Edmonds, C. Lowry, C, Pennefather, J. and Walker R "Diving and Subaquatic Medicine" ISBN 0-340-80630-3

If insufficient oxygen is available to complete the treatment then the casualty should be returned to the surface rather than continue the treatment on air. After surfacing, this procedure specifies that the casualty should breathe pure oxygen on a one hour on, one hour off basis, for a further 12 hours. The support divers accompanying the casualty should be replaced on a regular basis.

The US Navy Diving Manual[64] also includes a procedure for conducting IWR. Although designed for use with an oxygen rebreather it can also be used with an open circuit or surface supply source of pure oxygen. This procedure involves the casualty descending to 9m/30ft while breathing pure oxygen. The casualty then remains at 9m/30ft for 60 minutes for mild symptoms and 90 minutes for serious symptoms. The casualty then ascends to 6m/20ft and spends a further 60 minutes at this depth followed by another 60 minutes at 3m/10ft. This results in a treatment time of 180 minutes for a mild bend and 210 minutes for a serious bend

Depth (Feet)	Elapsed Time (minutes) Mild	Elapsed Time (minutes) Serious
30	60	90
20	120	150
10	180	210

Table 23: US Navy In-Water Recompression Table

After surfacing the US Navy treatment specifies that the casualty should breathe oxygen on the surface for an additional three hours.

It is clear that IWR recompression is a process that can only be carried out after considerable pre-planning and preparation. The provision of sufficient supplies of oxygen together with a full face mask delivery system is not something that will be available for an ad-hoc treatment. As such IWR can only be considered as a last resort treatment in situations where evacuation to a recompression chamber is not an option.

> The latest advice from DAN on IWR is that In-water recompression may be an alternative to chamber recompression in remote locations, if there is neither a nearby chamber nor the means to quickly transport the patient to a chamber elsewhere. The technique involves bringing the diver underwater again, to drive gas bubbles back into solution to reduce symptoms and then slowly decompress in a way that maintains an orderly elimination of the excess gas.
>
> While in-water recompression is simple in concept, it is practical only with a substantial amount of planning, support, equipment and personnel; appropriate water conditions; and suitable patient status. Critical challenges can arise due to changes in the patient's consciousness, oxygen toxicity, gas supply, and even thermal stress. An unsuccessful in-water recompression may leave the patient in worse shape than had the attempt not been made. The medical and research communities are divided on the utility of in-water recompression. It is beyond the scope of this publication to consider all of the relevant factors, but it is fair to say that there are probably more situations when in-water recompression should not be undertaken than situations when it would be a reasonable choice.
>
> Source: https://www.diversalertnetwork.org/health/decompression/In-water-recompression

Figure 48: IWR guidelines from DAN

---

[64] US Navy Diving Manual, 7th Revision Change A. United States: US Naval Sea Systems Command. 2018.

Photo Credits

Pete Bullen 13, 130, 176, 184

Derek Covington 224

Audrey Cudel 75

Aldo Ferruci 23, 29, 224, 237

Jesper Kjøller 24, 30, 40, 48, 52, 58, 66, 72, 76, 82, 94, 104, 110, 116, 124, 140, 154, 164, 180, 188, 192, 208, 216, 218, 238

Alasdair Pooley 88, 228, 231

Adam Royce 87

List of Illustrations, Tables and Diagrams

Figure

1	My main interest is in wrecks	13
2	aquaCorps Magazine	17
3	The continuum from recreational diver to technical diver	18
4	A technical diver kits up for a 100m dive	19
5	aquaCorps magazine did much to popularise technical diving	22
6	Technical diving allows you to explore some incredible shipwrecks	23
7	Using a rebreather to explore a wreck in Sardinia at 110m	29
8	Technical diving is as much about planning and preparation as it is about death defying escapes from tricky situations	33
9	Quotes – Why I got into technical diving	35
10	Top ten contentious issues in technical diving	43
11	The Good Divers Are Living	54
12	An inverted twinset	70
13	One piece harness	79
14	A correctly fitted one piece harness	80
15	One piece harness with a break	80
16	One piece harness with a break and a safety loop	80
16A	The author in single cylinder hogarthian configuration	87
17	DSMB with low pressure inflator	90
18	A selection of reels and spools	91
19	A reel as a primary and spool as a backup is a common choice	92
20	Emergency DSMB in use	93
21	Decompression cylinders	100
22	Bailout stages being used with a rebreather on a deep wall dive in Grand Cayman	100
23	Picture of a gas analysis tape	101
23A	A selection of technical diving computers	109
24	Suit inflation system mounted on the backplate	113
25	A suit regulator with inflation hose and OPV	113
26	The buoyancy swingometer	120
27	Lung volumes	121
28	If you can reach this far you can reach your valves	136
29	A well fitting drysuit will not restrict your movement	136
30	An example of poor technique	137
31	An example of good technique	137
32	It's easy to reach your valves when you have the right technique	137
33	It can be very difficult to tell where a leak is coming from	141
34	Even your buddy might find it difficult to tell where the leak is coming from	142
35	Closing the right hand post	144
36	When technical diving goes wrong the consequences are often more severe	161
37	An APD inspiration with the over the shoulder mounted counter lungs	183

38	CCR Diver carrying a separate open circuit bailout cylinder	184
39	Hard copy diving tables	217
40	Using a PC planning tool to generate a dive plan	220
41	Using slates and wetnotes for dive plans	221
42	Cave Diving	231
43	Cave Markers	233
44	The UK has a number of excellent dive boats	236
45	Good support divers are essential for expedition diving	237
46	US Navy Omitted Decompression Protocol	240
47	A recompression chamber may not always be readily available	241
48	IWR guidelines from DAN	243
49	Equipment logistics may be a significant factor	234

Table

1	Advantages and disadvantages of a variety of twinset sizes	68
2	Advantages and disadvantages of independent and manifolded twinsets	70
3	Advantages and disadvantages of upright and inverted twinsets	71
4	Advantages and disadvantages bungied versus unbungied wings	78
5	Advantages and disadvantages of one piece harness versus harness with a break	81
6	Hogarthian vs. Traditional Equipment Configuration	87
7	Guidelines for technical diving using a computer	108
8	Advantages of various finning techniques	133
9	Key steps in reaching your valves	138
10	The steps in a shutdown drill	143
11	The GUE valve drill	146
12	START can be used to ensure all areas of the pre-dive preparation are covered	160
13	Situational Awareness Considerations	163
14	Advantages and disadvantages of rebreather and open circuit diving	175
15	Rebreather terms	179
16	Pyle Deep Stops Process	196
17	An example of Pyle stops	197
18	Deep Stop Table	201
19	Various classifications of potential breathing gasses	210
20	NOAA CNS Oxygen Limits	215
21	Sample dive planning table showing min gas and TTS for a range of depths	222
22	Australian In-Water Recompression Table	242
23	US Navy in-Water Recompression Table	243

Diagram

1	TDI Flowchart	28
2	The Incident Pit	56
3	Swiss Cheese Model	57
4	Omitted	
5	Buoyancy control	123
6	Trim position	128
7	Situational Awareness	163
8	The OK Plateau	167
9	Borelli's rebreather	171
10	CCR Schematic	172
11	Gradient factors shown graphically	198
12	Gradient factors applied to a Bühlmann model	199
13	A gradient factor based ascent	199
14	Impact of deep stops on bubble formation	200
15	The advantages of using a rich nitrox mix for decompression	203
16	Different depth ranges require different gases	211
17	Gas requirements rule of thirds	219
18	Minimum Gas and Time to Surface	223

Index

A
Accident analysis 53, 56, 57, 59, 229
Ansel Adams 31
AquaCorps 11, 17, 22, 41, 55

B
Backplate 22, 65, 77, 79, 81, 84, 112, 113, 136, 210, 231
Benjamin Franklin 53
Bill Stone 41
Billy Deans 41
Break and safety loop 80
BSAC 12, 18, 50, 155, 159
Buoyancy Control 12, 19, 23, 25, 50, 73, 86, 117, 118, 119, 121, 123, 125, 126, 133, 144, 147, 152, 166, 167, 178, 191, 194, 202, 219, 227, 231
Buoyancy Control Device (BCD) 18, 25, 65, 69, 71, 73, 77, 79, 81, 84, 118, 119, 122, 126, 127

D
Decompression Illness 12, 14, 19, 38, 39, 50, 53, 59, 95, 96, 111, 159, 193, 194, 202, 239, 240, 241, 242
Delayed surface marker buoy 89, 92
Delayed Surface Marker Buoy (DSMB) 65, 79, 81, 86, 89, 90, 91, 92, 93, 117, 126, 162, 165, 166, 206, 240
Diver Propulsion Vehicle (DPV) 78
Dr Ed Lanphier 41
D-rings 79, 83, 86
Dr Richard Vann 41
Dr R. W. "Bill" Hamilton 41

E
English system 73
Equipment maintenance 47, 55, 60

F
Fitness 37, 38, 39, 45, 47, 60, 86, 219
Florida cave divers 73

G
Gas switch procedures 74

H
Harness 43, 65, 77, 79, 80, 81, 84, 86, 136, 160, 231, 242
Henry Rollins 73
Hogarthian equipment 83, 231

I
IANTD 21, 32, 155, 207
Independent cylinders 68, 69
Internet 22, 32, 41, 42, 43, 49, 56, 67, 84, 199
Inverting 70, 71

J
Jacques-Yves Cousteau 11, 21, 205

K
Kelly Johnson 83

M
Michael Menduno 17, 41
Muhammad Ali 77

N
Navy divers 70, 71
Neale Donald Walsch 45
Nitrox 11, 12, 13, 17, 18, 19, 21, 26, 27, 49, 100, 107, 111, 112, 119, 157, 166, 172, 181, 190, 191, 194, 202, 207, 210, 211, 213, 214, 215

O
Obesity 39
Out of gas 69, 160, 161, 166, 167, 173, 222, 230
Oxygen toxicity 13, 14, 19, 27, 39, 56, 59, 60, 85, 100, 105, 106, 173, 177, 183, 190, 191, 207, 210, 211, 213, 214, 215, 217, 230, 242

P
PADI 17, 18, 32, 59
Personality Types 32, 33
Pony cylinder 26, 65, 67, 99, 118

R
Rebreather 65, 68, 79, 89, 90, 99, 100, 103, 105, 107, 111, 112, 113, 135, 153, 160, 171, 172, 173, 174, 175, 177, 178, 179, 181, 182, 183
Richard Pyle 33, 41, 195
Rigid Inflatable Boat (RIB) 236, 237
Rob Palmer 25, 193

S
SDI 17, 18, 105, 132
Shutdown 26, 51, 69, 70, 71, 74, 79, 84, 135, 137, 138, 141, 142, 143, 144, 145, 149, 162
Side mount 73, 74
Size of cylinders 69, 70
Smoking 39
Stephen Coleman 49, 159
Stress 45, 46, 47, 49, 50, 51, 56, 85, 90, 91, 121, 126, 143, 144, 148, 161, 166, 167, 219, 221
Swildon's Hole 73

T
Tao Te Ching 65
TDI 21, 32, 49, 59, 102, 155, 210
Techdiver 42
Trimix 13, 18, 19, 23, 27, 28
Twinset 26, 27, 28, 43, 60, 65, 67, 68, 69, 70, 71, 73, 74, 77, 79, 81, 84, 85, 99, 100, 111, 112, 113, 118, 127, 135, 136, 137, 166, 167, 171, 173, 174, 202, 210, 219

W
Wing 65, 67, 71, 77, 78, 81, 84, 85, 90, 95, 112, 118, 119, 120, 126, 127, 142, 162, 183, 231
Wookey Hole 73, 232